The
Leper
Messiah

RML

The Leper Messiah
Copyright © 2018 by R.M.L.

Black Leper Books
rmlwriter.com

ISBN
978-1-77302-278-9 (Hardcover)
978-1-77302-279-6 (Paperback)
978-1-77302-277-2 (eBook)

In Memory of my mother,
Suzanne Josephson
and
the Levinson Family

Table of Contents

Glossary of Names

In the East

Bethlehem

The House of David

Obed – Grandfather of David

Jesse – Father of David

Nitzevet – Mother of David

<u>Sons</u>

First born – Eliab

Abinadab

Shimma

Nathanel

Raddai

Ozem

David

The Scorpion: The warrior priest who becomes David's protector, the former thief who sold David to the slave trader, and the baby in the cave.

In the West

The Isle of Burton

House of Greythorn

Grandfather – Champendeau

King – Moormund

Queen Fram, died in childbirth

<u>Sons</u>

Firstborn – Dramoor

Bru

Grail – Father of Princess Rose

The twins – Roma and Riga

Arlemay (the traveler, the blue-eyed one, the Leper Messiah)

At Greythorn Court

The Princess Rose

Lady Beth – mother of Rose

Chapter 1
The Seven Scorpions

"I am bread and milk," said the stranger who used the sound of his voice as a guide through the heavy mist and rain.

"No," a woman replied. "You are darkness."

Before dawn, outside of Bethlehem, the first few rays of light appeared against the great caves that dotted the mountain looming upwards.

"Can this be?"

He wiped his brow and peered into the darkness. He fell down on his knees but moved quickly away and watched as a black scorpion stung a desert viper.

"Aye, my little friends, go on." He watched intently.

A sliver of light played upon the scorpion as it scurried between rocks while the viper with its tongue out inched closer.

The two fought a lonely, timeless battle: the scorpion, tail raised high, fought with evil intent but was pushed back by the blinding rain while the viper slithered through the mud with ease.

The creatures faced each other but were washed away in the storm to continue their old battle far from human eyes.

A baby cried from the caves.

The robed stranger stood up. "I have bread and milk."

A woman wrapped in a sackcloth peeked through the cave's entrance with a sly smile on her face.

"And with me came the seven scorpions," she whispered. "And then did I speak magical spells to the poison of the scorpion saying, 'Oh poison, come out.'"

"Is this the cave of the hungry?" the stranger asked.

"We have nothing for you here," she said as she moved away from the entrance.

"I heard the baby cry," he said.

"Who are you?" she yelled into the wind.

"I am bread and milk."

The dawn crept slowly upon the desert and its light shone through the *wadis* and great valleys while the darkness held fast among the caves and the cold desert air swept around the mountains.

"Bread and milk?" the woman asked.

"Bread and milk," he said.

The robed man appeared at the cave's entrance and pulled off his hood to reveal a wet and scarred face.

Without a word he sat on the earthen floor and brought out a bag of bread and cakes. He placed a small knife on the ground.

The woman's cheap necklace and rings jingled as she sat and watched the cakes being spread before her. She grabbed at the food.

The man grabbed her wrist and looked her in the eyes.

"No, first you must curse Jacob and the Hebrews."

She laughed.

He held her wrist. "Say it."

"Curse Jacob and the Hebrews."

The man released her wrist and watched as she ate greedily.

"Are you a priest?" she asked through mouthfuls.

"Yes, from Moab."

"The Moab priest," she whispered.

"What?"

"Nothing."

She finished the food and picked up her baby. Her eyes were brilliant, her face stern yet beautiful and her long black hair was tied back with twine.

"The boy will need all his strength," the priest said. "He will run and play from Bethlehem to Damascus."

The Moab took his knife and cut his thumb and the blood flowed onto the cold, stone floor of the cave.

"I know exactly what he will do," said the woman whose eyes pierced the dark of the cave walls.

The priest turned toward the baby and touched the child's face with his thumb, leaving a bloody mark.

"It's all about blood," he said.

The dawn light crept into the cave.

"Whose blood?" the woman asked as she wiped the baby's face.

The priest's eyes grew wide. He looked around, frightened by spirits that no one else could fathom.

"Davooowd is his name."

The woman brought her child to her breast and watched as he suckled.

"You will leave my al-Arab alone." She touched the child's cheek.

"No harm will befall him," the Moab said.

She glared at him.

"Jemb al-la tiqrab, jemb al-haiyyi fru nam. By the side of the scorpion do not come; by the side of the viper spread your bed and sleep."

A scorpion emerged from the back of the cave.

"Nish-e aqrab naas rah ast tabiyyat-ash hai," the priest muttered.

He bent close to the earth, watching the insect crawl on the rocks.

"Little evil one," he said.

He placed his hand over the creature. "Will you sting or will you be my instrument?"

The priest struck at the scorpion and held it tightly until its blood ran onto the cave floor.

"Blood, blood, blood," he said. He squashed the remains and drove them deep into the hard, cold earth.

He drew angry breaths and closed his eyes while trying to let the Bethlehem morning breeze clear his troubled mind.

The priest looked at the baby.

"Now, my little one, I had a dream about a blazing light and its resting place. Davooowd must die; he must not give the burning light a resting place."

The Moab did a little dance.

"I must take his blood, the one they call Davooowd."

The baby giggled.

"Yes, I will take his blood." He looked at the child and then picked him up and rubbed his fat cheeks.

"Yes, you will help. You will be my instrument if I fail."

A ray of light pierced the cave depths and a rattling noise was heard far from the entrance.

The mother's eyes went dark. She spread her hands over the cave floor and hissed a curse. As she spoke, her head bent low to the ground.

"Lady of the Burning Sands, Sekhmet, Mistress of Terror, May no enemy find me, May no harm approach me, Your sacred fire surrounds me and No evil can withstand your eyes."

The sad mother became a fiery vision. Her hair fell around her shoulders, her face glowed and precious jewels shimmered on her neck.

The rattling noise grew until it filled the cave and on the wall appeared the shadow of a viper rising to its full striking height.

The woman let out a shrill yell, "Lalalalalalalalal!"

The viper swayed from side to side as the rattling continued.

The woman cradled seven scorpions in her hands.

"False priest," she whispered at him. She bit off the head of one scorpion then another. "False words."

She wiped her mouth as the arachnids fell to the ground.

"You, priest, do not know whether these creatures are evil or ward off evil."

The viper's shadow grew larger on the cave wall as the rattling continued.

The woman, the fiery vision, began to stroke the viper's head while the snake calmed itself as it began winding its long tail around the woman's feet.

The priest huddled in a corner with eyes downcast.

"False priest," she said again.

The fiery vision, the goddess, raised her arms as the morning flooded in to beat back the darkness. The viper slowly coiled around her waist and then crawled onto her head where it perched glorious in the sun's rays.

"I am The Mystical Rose, mother of Nitzevet and the light of the burning bush, who sees all and will not let spirits nor demons harm thee, little one."

She glared at the priest.

"My sweet child, the light of The Rose will guide thee and the path of The Rose will lead you from east to west and beyond. Fear not, my little one, for you are the one true scorpion."

A halo of light illuminated the fat baby as he lay quiet.

Then the Mistress of Magic called her seven scorpions by name and they came to her: Tefen and Befen came to her side, while also came Metet and his brother Mesetef and in front Petet, Theter and his brother. And with them she went fearlessly into the light.

Chapter 2
The Lion and the Lamb

An early fall breeze blew over the Bethlehem hillside ruffling the orchards and whispering of the cold, damp weather that was approaching. The wind picked up and row upon row of olive trees bowed in the presence of the Autumn King.

Rain began to fall above the hills and mist crept over Mount Gilboa, which brooded over the valley below.

On the way home from the fields, Obed, grandfather of David and Shimea, walked between his grandsons.

"Well, my two farmers," Obed began.

The two turned to each other, smirked and knew what was coming.

"Which harvest is the biggest, grain or fruit?"

"Spring grain harvest," David said.

"It's forty, no, fifty, percent of our food," Shimea put in.

Obed bent over and picked up a handful of dark soil. He rubbed the dirt with his thumb and forefingers before it fell from his hands.

"Barley and wheat in the autumn and barley harvest first in the spring," Obed smiled at the rich soil.

"Barley is strong." The elder statesman punched his fist against his deep chest. "It can take the harsh rain."

Obed had lost his wife Adel 15 years before and so he busied himself as one of the heads of the village, dispensing advice, upholding what few laws they had and helping his daughter Nitzevet look after her rough-hewn boys.

He continued, his hands holding the reins loosely as the donkey walked slowly behind.

"But we don't eat until the Feast of Harvest," he cautioned the boys as he walked.

"Now in Galilee, the air is cool and damp and so the crops come a little bit later then Feast of Harvest, but we still celebrate all the crops."

"And in the Jordan Valley it is warmer and they come earlier," Shimea said.

Obed let out a chuckle. "Good, my farmer boy."

"And after Feast of Harvest we bring in grapes, olives, dates and figs," David said.

Obed smiled and continued through the quiet droveways.

"Barley and wheat in the spring with chickpeas, lentils, sesame and millet later, and figs and olives deep in the season."

"What about the Egyptians?" David asked.

"They have irrigated gardens not the hilly, terraced crops we have," he yawned. "Now when does the wine festival come?"

"Fifty days after the Feast of Harvest," Shimea said.

David kicked at the ground as his slightly older brother walked on triumphantly.

"Fifty days... blah blah," David whispered under his breath.

"Now, my boys, which is heavier in weight or bulk: fruit or grain harvest?"

The old man's eyes twinkled.

"Fruit," Shimea said. "It has more water so it's heavier."

Obed hugged David and shook him playfully.

"Good, my farmer," he said to Shimea.

The tired boys finally came to the small, quiet village and made for their house just as dusk was falling.

Obed unhitched the donkey and slapped his rear.

"Celebrate the Feast of Tabernacles for seven days after you have gathered from the threshing floor and winepress," he said tiredly.

The next day the hot autumn winds brought the workers out to Obed's lands for harvest; Shimea and David looked out over the valley as men and women stood in the deep fields wielding plowshares and sickles. They bent low and moved the sharp edges against the wheat and barley that fell time and time again. At the end of the field the large piles of crops were stacked for threshing.

"We live and die by rainfall, my boys," Obed said. He picked up a stone and placed it on the retaining wall made of larger stones on the hilly terrace.

"See the two streams; one is for the orchards the other for drinking now."

Obed wiped his hands on his worn wool pants and looked out over the sun-drenched valley. The mountain water trickled slowly down as far below the villagers worked the fields.

Iram stopped in the middle of the fields and wiped his brow. "We have half the field to cut."

Hannah, his wife, passed him a water bag.

"Strange things happened in that house last night," she whispered to her husband. Her apron and yellow blouse were wet with noonday sweat.

"Woman," he breathed heavily. "Strange things happen ever since Nitzy was born."

He touched his sun-beaten and tattered head cloth. "She's been blessed by the Lord."

"It's not right." She took a drink herself and held the sickle by her plump body. "Something is not right and the boy David wanders the hillsides alone. No friends. No company. What does he do all day?"

Iram started swinging his sickle and watched as the barley tumbled down. He lowered his 60-year-old body and began to get into a rhythm, the sun beating down while his hand held the sickle; *shush, shush, shush* went the blade against the strong barley husk. He loved to work the fields and even as a poor, young boy he worshiped the sound of the sickle and felt his power over the land.

His father, Reuben, who had traveled from Damascus, was a poor tradesman but Iram dug his hands into the soil and never forgot the feeling. He felt renewed each autumn when Obed would knock on his door and ask if he would help work the fields. It made him feel young again.

Shush, shush, shush, shush went his blade clean and true.

His wife had moved onto another woman, Haga, and she handed the water bag to the slight, white-haired woman.

"It's not right," Hannah whispered.

Haga wiped her smock and smiled at Hannah. "Yes," she said.

She looked away from Hannah, for she had lain with Iram not two years ago and thought her words would give her away. She remembered how lustful and responsive he was to her needs. A thin smile appeared on her face.

She turned away and began to swing at the barley with renewed vigor.

Abe, Iram's oldest son who had become the village blacksmith, rode out on the donkey to tell the workers that the midday meal was served.

"Father," he called. "Come."

The workers slowly came to a stop and brought their tools to the end of the field where the barley lay in neat, freshly cut piles.

Iram continued while the others began to make their way through the high fields.

"Would Haga be sitting close?" he thought. He laid low the barley as his mind raced but then he heard Abe calling.

"Father."

13

He slowed his sickle and stood for a long time in the tall fields with the soil between his toes and sweat pouring down his smock.

He looked up at the brilliant sky and dropped his farming tools. He led a simple, hard farming life with only a few years of famine when the rains did not fall. But he was proud of his boy Abe and his family was respected for hard work. He had his health and the love of his wife. He tried to believe in Yahweh but still prayed to Baal, the rain god.

Two young men picked up a long wooden bench and brought it from the side of the barns and worksheds to a grassy opening.

The crowd of workers walked over as women emerged from the barn with a tray of food.

The young men went back into the barn and reappeared with four jugs of beer that were set down on the long table.

"Come, drink!" one man yelled as he opened a jug and tasted it, the cool barley beer running down his farmer's tunic.

Abe laughed and took it from the man.

"Careful, it's as precious as rain." He took a long draught.

The women put out the food and giggled as the two young men begged to sit between them.

Iram emerged from the deep fields and washed his face and hands in a barrel of water. He let the water flow onto his face and looked for Hannah.

Haga smiled quickly at Iram and then turned away toward the far end of the long table.

The noonday sun beat down on the hardy men and women who slaved over the rocky fields and stony hillsides as they beat back the wilderness and planted their hopes and dreams deep in the soil.

"Come," said Iram when he found Hannah and sat down on the bench as she walked over.

A large woman with a bright red face handed Iram a hot piece of fresh bread. Plates of cheese and figs were set before them as well as a large bowl of chickpeas and flatbread.

The young men continued drinking from the jugs until Obed appeared, his face wet with sweat.

"Come, boys," he said. "Bring that over here."

He took it quickly and gave them a dark look. "You know better than that."

He hoisted the jug to his shoulder and drank from it.

"The old man gets his drink first," he laughed as the beer rolled down his smock.

The older workers quieted their voices as he wiped the beer from his chest.

He stood at the head of the long table and smiled at all the workers whom he had known since he was a young boy.

"Iram," he called as he spied his old friend. "Please do us this honor."

Iram stood up, his legs tired from bending.

A gentle, hot wind blew up over the rocky hillside and through the deep valley while it whispered through the freshly cut barley.

Iram covered his head and slightly bowed as he recited:

"Blessed are You Hashem our God, King of the Universe, who creates a variety of sustenance."

The other workers responded in unison, "Hallelujah."

Hungry hands passed the bowls quickly around the large tables.

Obed sat at the head with his grandsons on either side.

"Is there going to be war?" David asked as he ate a slice of bread and cheese.

"There is always war," Obed said. "In the highlands, along the shepherd paths, there is always a battle."

Shimea ate in silence and drank beer.

"Is Saul a good king?" David continued.

Obed drank his beer. "He is the first king because we need to have a united front against the Philistines."

"I mean is he a good fighter?" David asked.

"Yes, he was strong at Jabesh-Gilead."

Obed dribbled some beer on his smock and wiped it away.

"But we don't like kings. The tribes would rather fight the Moab or the Amalekites or the Philistines, and if not them, then we fight ourselves."

"I fought alongside Saul against the Ammonites at Jabesh," one farmer said. He ate his bread and drank beer. "He was strong."

"Do you like kings?" David said as he looked at his barrel-chested, white-haired grandfather.

Obed nodded his head in response.

"Yes, my boy."

He watched as Shimea rose and walked over to the others who were walking to the threshing floor.

"A king unites the tribes and protects us from our enemies."

David stood up. "I will do that."

"You?" Obed looked down at the redheaded runt of his family. "Well, you just might."

He laughed and the other workers listened intently. War with the Philistines was ongoing and becoming worse. The Hebrews were not allowed to hold iron tools or weapons and the calls for battle were growing louder and louder from the tribal chieftains. Obed saw no other way.

"We fight to survive; we have to fight for soil," one broken-toothed man said.

"Yes," Obed said.

"All we do is fight," said the worker as he drank more beer.

"And now the Philistines have taken the Ark from Shiloah to Ashdod," another farmer said.

"We have no spears, not one sword," the broken-toothed farmer said. "Give me one iron tool and I'll take back our Tent-Shrine."

"I will go with you, brother, and we will meet in the Tent of Meetings," Obed said.

"Ah, if it were only so."

The wind blew the great fields of barley and wheat back and forth under a menacing sun.

"When can we start the threshing?" Obed called to Iram down the long table.

The brown-skinned man put down his beer.

"We have enough to start late today or tomorrow," said Iram as he wiped his mouth with his hands.

"Can we take some of the workers up to the threshing floor today?"

"Yes," Iram said.

"We need to finish before the rains come."

Obed ate a piece of bread and cheese.

"I'll come up," Shimea said.

Obed nodded his head.

David looked down at the floor and mimicked Shimea.

"I'll come up," he said.

"Boys," Obed said.

Iram stood up. "Abe, take the women up to the threshing place."

He pointed to the young men still drinking beer. "We will do the rest of the harvesting while they start."

The men quickly put down their beer and sat up straight.

"Yes, Iram," one of the boys managed.

"Good," said Iram as he left the table.

The threshing floor was high above the rocky, stony paths that encircled Bethlehem. It was level and clear of stones, grass and brambles and was where the chaff was separated from the grain. The high plains wind blew off the lighter chaff and the remaining grain fell to the floor.

Haga's cheeks became red as she walked along the path that led up to the hilltop, for it was there on the threshing floor where Iram had made love to her in the darkness. She stayed behind Hannah and the others as her mind wandered back to that night. Her fingers gently touched the bushes and wild plants that dotted the rocky pastures. She walked along the inhospitable land and saw everything in a sweet light of beauty and romance. How she longed for him to whisper to her "Tonight," and all her hardship and sorrow would vanish. Her rough skin would become dew-like again, her hair soft as the night breeze.

She could not know that many couples including Iram and Hannah had had their first kiss in this high plains chapel. Jesse had asked Obed for Nitzevet's hand in the privacy of the hill. Boys came here with their first jar of beer and threw stones off the hillside, raging at the night.

"Let David and Shimea take the threshing board up to the floor," Obed called to Iram.

The threshing board was a wide, heavy piece of wood with sharp pieces of stone and rock attached to cut the grain.

The two boys raced up the hill while workers gathered the stalks of barley. One man brought a donkey to the fields and the others started packing the long stalks on the beast's back for the trip through the stony terrain.

The tall fields were dotted with stacks of freshly cut barley; the wind was warm and the entire village had come out for one of the most important harvests of the year. The rains had come and washed away the fears of the community and now they could be joyful and perhaps even have enough grain to save in the storehouses.

It would take the rest of the afternoon to move all the barley up the hill and two more days of cutting before all the fields were harvested.

Obed climbed the hills to the threshing floor; he worried about the rains setting in and ruining the crop, but the workers were experienced and he could see that a comfortable winter with food in everyone's belly was upon them.

He also understood that King Saul and his men would pass by and take provisions that would deplete the storehouses. Jesse and Obed's seven grandsons would join Saul against the Philistines as a fighting unit and the soil would turn red with blood. War was coming.

After the barley was brought to the threshing floor the turner began his work. He arranged the stalks in the center of the floor and the donkey pulled the threshing board over them.

"Good," Iram smiled. He was pleased to see the grain neatly stacked and waiting to be stored.

"Ha," cried the turner as he forced the donkey over the floor. He would stop the beast and then turn over the barley so that both sides were cut.

The turner took off his hat and wiped his brow with his farmer's wool tunic.

"A goodly crop this one." He pointed to the heavy grain that lay in the hot sun, the flies buzzing about in the heat.

Iram looked watchfully over the crop.

"Enough to feed us for the winter."

"And more."

The turner began again to push the donkey across the floor, slashing and cutting the barley stalks.

"*Heehaw, Heehaw,*" the donkey brayed as the threshing board scraped the floor.

Iram sneezed as the thick air flew into his nostrils.

The cut stalks were set in the sun to dry before the winnowing and the villagers took pitchforks and picked up the barley husks to point them upward.

Hannah and the other women raised the cut stalks high into the air and walked so the wind would loosen the chaff and the heavy grain would fall to the stone floor. The grain would then be placed in great wicker baskets and taken to the storehouses.

Obed brought David and Shimea and they all picked up the grain and let the chaff blow in the wind. He looked fondly at his grandsons, lifted his pitchfork high and felt his soul fly free. He saw his past behavior good and bad tossed to the wind, the bad or impatient side of him swept away and what was left dropped on the stone floor.

"You see how far we can fly," Obed whispered to David as the chaff disappeared on the wind.

David watched the chaff from the barley blow over the stone fields and valleys and wondered how far he might travel from this stone threshing floor. The threshing floor was nothing more than a huge gulch dug out of the hillside by the wind and laid flat by the villagers but in that instant he saw more.

He saw beyond the heat of the day and the harsh world his family lived in for it was here on this Bethlehem threshing floor that he witnessed his past and his future. With his pitchfork high his view was far and wide and he felt a great depth of passion. He ran wildly and continued raising his pitchfork while the others looked on. He had been in the sun too long.

"I see!" he yelled out. "I see!"

Obed caught him by the sleeve.

"David, David," he said gently. "Calm yourself." Obed had seen that far-off look in his daughter's eyes.

"Come." He cradled the nine-year-old in his arm. "Down to your mother."

The Lion

A few days later Nitzevet cradled David in the late afternoon shadow of an olive tree. She gently anointed his forehead with rose oil and whispered of her mother's love through the rolling hill country of Hebron.

"I am The Mystical Rose, the light of the burning bush that burns brighter than the sun. The light of The Rose will guide thee and the path of The Rose will lead you from east to west and beyond."

The boy squirmed out of his mother's grasp while rubbing at the oil and ran toward the hunting party emerging from the dark orchards.

David's father, Jesse, approached first, drinking from his wineskin with a wolf carcass hanging over his broad shoulders.

"You did well today, Shimea." He slapped the boy on the back. "You are a hunter now."

Nathaniel and Abeem, trailing their brother closely, laughed as he tripped over a branch.

"Yes, he can hunt but he can't walk," Abeem smirked, his head high and his brown eyes glistening with pride.

"We need to hunt the lion before the rains set in," Jesse said as he looked out over the hillside where the last sliver of light was beating back the shadows.

David ran to the hunting party and gazed up at the tall boys. He took a slingshot from the pocket of his gray tunic and aimed it menacingly at the brothers.

"I can hunt too," he cried.

The brothers walked on.

"I can hunt too!" David said loudly. He kicked an older brother in the shins.

Abinadab pushed the boy away and continued down the orchard trail while Jesse and Shimea walked the path in tandem, drinking from the flask and laughing to themselves.

"The lion," Jesse said. "We should go back tomorrow and kill it."

He rubbed his hands in the November rain.

"Be back by sundown," Nitzevet reminded him a little later.

She placed a jug of wine upon the family table, a rough-hewn, wooden gathering place that sat outside their home.

"I thought I heard a growl from the hillside," Abinadab commented.

"I'll kill it with my sling," David yelled. He aimed at a tree branch and let fly his stone. With perfect aim the branch fell to the ground.

"We need to harvest before the rains come," Nitzavet said to Jesse.

"Yes, yes, we will," he said hurriedly. "But we need to catch that lion first. He will attack the sheep and then run for the hills."

"It's dangerous," she said.

"I have Shimea the great hunter to protect me now," Jesse laughed as his son gulped his food ravenously and glanced up.

The brothers laughed at this and slapped the boy on his back.

"We go tomorrow then?" Ellab asked. "We should take the dogs too."

"Yes, up around the hillside near the limestone ridge." Jesse's eyes glowed in the growing dark. "I saw his eyes watching us."

"I will kill it," David whispered.

Jesse looked down at the scrawny boy and saw an eerie determination etched in his angelic features.

"I don't know what you will do." He turned away toward his wine.

"Kill lions."

Shimea gave a short, brazen laugh before biting on his chicken bone.

Nitzevet gazed at her husband imploringly.

"I will," David continued. "I'll kill it."

"We should have the boy look after the sheep," Ellab thought out loud. "He should do something useful."

Jesse looked up at his son. "He could help rather than sit at home."

"He is only a boy of nine," Nitzevet intervened.

Jesse took a softer approach.

"All he needs to do is watch and tell us if there is danger."

David looked up at his mother.

"I can do that."

He gave her a knowing smile. She grew calm and held David tighter. Somehow she understood that her littlest boy would be safe among the lions and bears that stalked the hills of Judah.

"I will be on guard and my slingshot will protect the sheep."

He rubbed again at his forehead where the rose oil was placed that afternoon.

"Take the boy out tomorrow into the hills," Jesse said. "Show him the valleys but don't go beyond Sharon."

"Yes, Father," Shimea said proudly.

Later that night, despite his exhaustion, David hid behind two saddlebags and underneath a bench, his ears straining to hear the urgent voices of his father and brothers who were in deep discussion.

They huddled around the fireplace and the din of oxen sounded in the background.

A goat bleated, *"Bahhhhhh,"* from below the mud floor of the small shelter.

"Light and darkness," Jesse explained. "For what is light without dark? And he is all of these things."

"Let there be light!" Shimea exclaimed.

"Yes, from the beginning," Jesse muttered.

"The light?" Abinadab asked.

"The holy one is all," the father whispered. "He is the light. He makes the colors that we see before our eyes and the darkness that falls on us."

"And darkness?"

"Anger and judgment, that is darkness."

Jesse let out a chuckle as he saw that Shimea had fallen asleep on the chair. The father scratched his beard and turned his attention back to his other sons.

David was heartbroken. The words were not so important as the way they were chosen in order to guide his brothers on the right path. He did not know his path and had no guide to lead him so tenderly along. He was alone.

The next morning David picked the largest stones from a clay jar and put them in his leather pouch. He tugged at his leather sling and buried his fear far down in his tunic pockets.

He looked out into the tiny, stone courtyard of the squat wood-beam house to see only the family goat rummaging for food.

"Shimea," he called out. David ran up the outside stairs that led to the flat roof of beams, straw mats and clay top. The large family spent a great deal of time up on the roof with the gentle breeze and view of the Boa Valley.

"David, come." His mother looked up as he approached.

She passed him a wooden platter of figs and dates. He ate a few and then looked at Shimea who was wolfing down his breakfast.

Dawn crept over the sleepy town of Bethlehem and the valley shimmered in the morning heat.

"Come," Shimea said as he picked up his spear and threw his bow and quiver over his fox cloak.

Nitzevet put thick, fresh bread and figs into a pouch and bent to kiss David on the head.

"Mother," he said as he pushed her away gently. "I am going to kill lions."

Shimea ran down the rooftop steps, left the family dwelling and walked out into the cool morning breeze while the mist was gently disappearing from the vineyards and horse paths that surrounded the stony village.

"Bahhhhhhh, bahhhhhhhhhhhhh, bahhhhh," broke through the still morning air.

The goat herder waved his stick and guided the animals through the village to the grazing fields above.

The dust rose and the bleating continued.

"Bahhhhhhhhhhhhh, bahhhhhhhhh, bahhhhhhhhh."

Soon the village path was filled with animals and the air was thick with the foul smell of dirty fur and goat droppings.

"Bahhhhhhhhhhhh, bahhhhhhhh, bahhhhhhh."

"Haw!" yelled the herdsmen as he guided the goats through the narrow pathways.

He slapped one animal on the rump with his stick. The dust continued and the bleating grew almost frantic as the herd pushed its way through the thick air of the tiny village.

"Haw!"

"We will cut across the Boa," Shimea pronounced.

Without another word the boys walked quickly along the narrow pathways of the town. The morning breeze swept them past the rectangular stone houses and from the north-west they looked out over the valley and hills terraced with orchards of figs and almonds.

Shimea stopped at the town's stone well and pulled up the water bucket to fill his water bag. He splashed his face and the back of his neck before playfully dousing his younger brother.

A weather-beaten farmer looked on disapprovingly as his ox cart, clapping on the stone path, pushed toward the fields.

"Haw!" he yelled to the oxen as he pulled away out of sight.

The two ran towards the stone fence and past the last house as the dew clung to their worn leather sandals. Shimea ran through the open gates so their sheep would follow them past the olive orchards and upward to the pastures above the limestone ridge. David ran into the corral and went to the back of the fence.

"Haw! Haw!" he yelled to the sheep as they moved nimbly out of the gates and across the fields.

Shimea took his stick and kept the flock together with a few swings in the air and well-placed hits on the herd leaders. The animals obeyed as they traveled down the rolling fields past rocky pastures and through woodland trees and deep valleys.

The sun rose in the sky. A dusty trail followed them upward toward the high ridges that overlooked Bethlehem.

David came to the spot where he usually stopped. He took out his slingshot and quickly set up the targets he used to hone his skill. The rocky ledge was where the piece of wood went then the olive branch, battered and notched with previous hits, and all along the hillside evidence of another target. He counted to ten and then started to run quickly, his slingshot cocked and ready.

He somersaulted over a small hill and came up firing at the olive branch that took multiple hits dead-on and then he turned quickly, letting out a volley of shots that hit the wood and shattered it to small bits.

Next he dove into a thicket of brush and laid still on his stomach, taking deep breaths to slow his heart. He took aim and fired at a lofty branch 75 feet away and hit it straight and true. David then pocketed his slingshot and dropped to the ground. Balancing on his toes and using only the power of his arms, he raised his body up and down. He could now do this 100 times before a short rest. He wiped his brow and repeated the motions twice more.

Afterward he stopped and looked up at the sheep that stood in judgment.

"I will take aim at you and your mother!" he barked at a young lamb standing by her mother and chewing its cud. "Then we will see who is laughing."

The lean, young boy sat down and drank water from his animal skin pouch before returning to darker thoughts.

"King of the goats!" he cried out into the hillside. "I am king of the sheep and goats!"

The cry of a lamb caught David's attention and he looked up to see the frightened animal caught in a thicket. Its shrill bleating had caused the other sheep to move away en masse. David took out his knife and cut the thick branches away while the lamb kicked and screamed. He firmly grasped the shaking animal and carried it to safety.

"Nursemaid to goats," he yelled into the wind.

The boys stopped under a large tree, breathing deeply. As their eyes met they laughed in unison at their dusty clothes and their life in the wild.

Shimea took some bread out of the pouch and split it with his younger brother.

"The Sachne Pools are not far off," David said innocently.

"Just beyond the next hill," Shimea agreed.

David stuffed his bread in his mouth and disappeared over the ridge.

"Father will kill us," said Shimea as he quickly finished his bread and followed his little brother. David ran down the hill tearing at his tunic and holding his pouch as it flew by his side. Ripping off his sandals he headed straight for the artesian well, which fed into the pools.

The glistening water soothed the rough countryside, each pool flowing into a larger one. Blocks of limestone surrounded the pools. A thicket of brambles and brush grew behind Sachne while Mount Gilboa brooded over the craggy landscape far above. Clouds hung over the hilltops and a battle raged between light and dark on the mountainside.

Underneath Mount Gilboa the two boys played as only youth can in the sunlight of childhood. They sat on the edge of the Sachne Pools while small fish nibbled their toes.

"Why do the brothers shun me?" David asked.

"I don't know," Shimea answered. "I do what Father wants me to. That is all I know." He picked up his tunic and put on his sandals. "We must get back to the sheep."

David dressed, not wishing to break the morning's spell. His life had been hard without the love of his father or brothers but today he would wash away his sorrows in the water of Sachne. Maybe after today his father would be proud of him and finally see him as a working member of the clan. He raced up the hill and onward to the sheep grazing peacefully along the grassy plains of Sharon.

"They are busy eating their fill," David called to Shimea.

He held fast to his leather pouch and his slingshot. Shimea was not behind him so he made his way back to the pools.

"Shimea," David called out across the rocky plains.

He hurried back to the rock quarry.

Shimea was standing in place, his body shaking. The beast sat there in the rough brush behind the pools waiting and watching. His eyes were yellow and deadly. His muscles bulged with every movement. Grace and death licked its lips and yawned in the noonday sun, almost too lazy to strike.

When Shimea moved an inch so did the lion. He looked frantically at his younger brother who now had dropped to the ground to avoid detection. The lion licked its tongue in the air and stood up from his sun-bleached perch. He roared once and took a few slow steps toward Shimea who was now frozen with fear. The boy closed his eyes and began to whimper.

"My brother, I must protect my brother," said David as his heart beat heavily.

He quickly took out his stones, found the largest one and slipped his slingshot out of his tunic.

"Steady," he controlled himself.

He slowed his breathing and laid flat on his stomach while maneuvering to get a better view of the beast. The heat of the day, the feel of his tunic, the ground he lay on, even the earth and sky had disappeared. He held his breath and with perfect aim hit the lion on the forehead. A loud, angry roar rang out against the quarry rocks.

"Forward, move forward," he repeated wordlessly.

David stood up without fear and fired shot after shot into the large head. Stone after stone landed. The beast, still focused on his prey, began to retreat. It roared and snapped at the air. It pulled up on its hind legs and let out another great roar, shaking its shaggy mane in anger. Stones kept flying and hitting the great yellow head. The animal began to snap at the hot wind. It twisted its body back and forth against the assault.

David was relentless. The lion squatted on all four legs and bellowed at its attacker. David shook violently as he ran toward the pool. His breath came in gasps, his pouch almost empty.

He targeted the lion's forehead and let fly. With a loud thump, it staggered and went limp. A gasp escaped its lungs, echoed off the rocks and disappeared in the wind.

For a moment silence filled the rock quarry.

Then David hunched over his kill and using his last stones fired shot after shot into the great mane, watching as the blood flowed freely into the pools. Back and forth and back and forth again, his hands worked skillfully though shaking with emotion and exhaustion.

Shimea stood in amazement. He approached the young hunter slowly and gently pried the slingshot from his bleeding fingers.

"Oh, my brother," said Shimea as he hugged David and they collapsed together on the rocks crying and holding each other.

"Brother," David cried as he held tightly.

"You came at him with such anger," said Shimea as he looked him in the eye. "I've never seen anything like it."

"I remember running," David gasped. "Nothing more."

"Lion to Lion," Shimea cried.

Abinadab came running down from the hills with his bow and arrows locked and ready. He moved gracefully and swiftly over the plains.

"Brothers," he called as he ran toward the pools.

He stopped as he reached the two boys still arm in arm on the sun-bleached rocks. He spared one glance at the massive mane and bloody head of the lion before shooting an arrow into its heart. The body jumped as the arrow pierced the tough hide.

"Always be sure."

From his satchel he took a ram's horn and with one mighty blow the rolling hill country resounded with the deep, mellow call that brought the hunting clan together and the Hebrews to worship.

But David's heroics were not the end of his lonely days. Jesse continued to avoid the boy but showed him a grudging respect while David's brothers followed their father without question.

The sullen David wandered the hills alone and his frown spread over all of Judea. The Israelites had been humiliated by the Philistines at Shiloah, and even worse, the Ark of the Covenant had been taken from them on the field of battle.

This loss played hard on the proud, warring tribes and so they crowned their first king, Saul, also a shepherd boy from Gish and the tribe of Benjamin.

* * *

Obed looked around the barn with its hay bales running up to the high roof and harnesses hung on the walls. The horses whinnied in their stalls. A strong winter wind blew open the barn door and torches flickered in the night air as the townsmen waited.

"So," Obed said as he stood before the men of the village. "How many men do we send to Saul for his campaign?"

"How many steel swords do we have?" one man yelled.

Obed cast a glance toward the man while Jesse stood up. He wore a bear cloak around his slender shoulders.

"My sons and I make seven."

"Good," Obed nodded. "During the time of Joshua we did not have a choice; we had a general levy. And now...."

"We need steel weapons!" the man shouted again.

"Aye," another said.

"We turn our farming tools into death," Obed said. "Come, how many do we send from our village?"

"Twenty?" one man asked.

"A goodly number," another said.

Obed played with a piece of parchment in his hands.

"Listen!" Obed yelled at the men. "Listen."

He raised his hands.

"Jesse is to lead the tribe of Benjamin into battle. Our men leave for the war town of Gibeah. Each tribe and each clan will send their warrior sons to battle and then return to their fields and farms."

Chapter 3
The Leper Bridge

Nitzevet played with a piece of bitumen that she held between her manicured nails and put the mortar firmly between two cracked, unbaked mud bricks in the small courtyard. She looked around her squat, two-floored home, swept the earth with her sandals and smiled.

David squirmed on the wooden stool as he watched his mother cook in a pot placed on a small clay top fed by a char-coal fire beneath.

"When?" the boy asked.

A goat *"baaahed"* in the back room of the first floor that was separated into three sections.

"Soon."

She motioned him closer, and as she did her golden earrings glistened in the sliver of light that penetrated the darkness. Her bronze ram's head bracelet moved gently.

"First you chop onions and garlic."

She laughed as he turned away from the onions. "Then add okra, potatoes and tomatoes."

David moved closer to the pot.

Nitzevet threw back her long, black hair and put it behind her ear. She watched him closely.

The sliver of light disappeared as the sun went down over the rolling hills and highlands that rose over the small village of Bethlehem.

"Come," she said slowly. "Look and see."

She whispered, "I am The Mystical Rose, the light of the burning bush that burns brighter than the sun. The light of The Rose will guide thee and the path of The Rose will lead you from east to west and beyond."

David peered into the pot.

An early evening wind blew through the first floor of the house and lifted the corners of the reed mat that covered the earth floor.

"The Desert Rose," David heard as he watched the pot spill over like the great sands over the desert.

Nitzevet took David gently by his head and peered into his eyes.

"I see all and will not let spirits or demons harm thee."

David squirmed from his mother's grasp and ran away.

Nitzevet removed the small piece of bitumen from the court-yard wall and played with it again before preparing the rest of the *hulba*. She broke up the vegetables, added just enough water to make a broth, then added salt and pepper.

Darkness crept upon her. The fire burned and the pot bubbled. She gently inhaled the steam that rose and felt it hot on her face and breasts. The heat took her back to her visions that at a young age drove her from her father's tent and out to the great sands. She had taken the family's goat and sold it to pay for passage along the eastbound trade routes that led to the city of Palms, home of Queen Zenobia. With the wind in her eyes, she pulled her headband against the breeze that blew her hopes and dreams across the sands.

She remembered the words, "Outcast to his family, a traitor to his king, divine to his people."

Nitzevet shuddered as she stirred the pot and looked around the dark, quiet courtyard. She hesitantly glanced at the outer plaster walls made of lime.

As a young girl she did not fear the lions and bears that roamed the high plains and stalked men and sheep. She knew this and yet felt safe on her long walks in the lonely valleys, deep woods and high mountain passes.

"Nitzy," said her father Obed as he rubbed her back. "Be careful."

He smiled at her. He knew. The other village girls were relegated to sewing, cooking or whatever their mothers and fathers desired them to do. Their lives were hard and simple.

Nitzevet was untouched. She looked down at the stone and earth floor then sat thinking about her youth.

The Rose came full of mercy and dark judgment to Nitzevet and the caravan. The young girl ran between the slender pillars followed by the wind and sand that whispered, "You are mine." She looked back, her long, raven hair blowing wild as she tried to escape.

"Nothing will harm thee for you are mine," The Rose whispered. "You are mine and from you will come the one."

Her spirit rose and she seemed to fly above the coming dark. She looked around, breathed as if never before and gulped in the sweet air that lifted her far above the world of men. Then quietly the sacred ibis perched on the stone courtyard wall and peered into the darkness. Her lips trembled as she pushed her hair behind her ears.

"Outcast, Traitor, Divine," was scrawled on the wall. Nitzevet bowed her head and trembled.

Her cooking pot boiled over and the hot flames brought her back to the night's duties. A goat *"bahhhed"* from within the house and a calf cried for its mother's milk. Nitzevet walked quickly into her front room where David slept on a bearskin. She kneeled next to him.

"How will I protect you?" she said as she stroked his thick, red hair. "What hardships yet what wonders you will have?"

The boy moved slowly toward his mother.

"You shall have the earth and sky." She combed back her long hair. "The desert will turn to rain and fruit for you. The very sands will become honey for your sweet mouth."

Late the next day Nitzevet stood high up on the limestone ridge that overlooked the valley; wind and rain swept along the mountain ridge and blew down along the terraced foothills that overflowed with dates, figs and olives.

David walked silently beside her clutching his slingshot as the rain slashed at his wool tunic. They climbed higher to where the shepherds' paths and droveways disappeared.

"Will you see it?" David asked.

"Yes." She placed her hands on his shoulders as they walked further into a thick afternoon fog.

"There is no light, no dark." He moved up the mountain pass.

"There is always a battle," she smiled and moved on.

Mount Gilboa was lost in the fog. The mists played like dark angels upon the mountain paths.

"Between who?"

"The sons of darkness and the sons of light," she said as she pushed upward.

David hurried after his mother.

"Always never forget." She looked back at her son.

Nitzevet stopped on the mountain path where a small rope bridge covered a deep gorge. She stood close to the bridge and started to push brambles up and away from the posts; as she did so a deep-rooted bush hidden by the underbrush came into relief. The bush unfolded and there in the deep fog and mist, high above Bethlehem and beyond the valleys and rolling hills, was a blood-red rose.

She motioned David towards the rose bush and took his hand.

"Here," she said as she took his finger.

"Ouch," he said as the thorn pricked him.

"We worship here in the high places."

She walked over to a rough altar carved out of the mountain that was simply a dug-out place for a person to stand and look out. Her hair blew madly as she stood in the *Bamah* of the high places.

Nitzevet whispered to her son, "Two spirits of man."

"This is the man who would bring others to the inner vision so that he may understand and teach to all the children of light the real nature of men, touching The Rose of knowledge."

Down in the valley they saw lanterns heaving in the blowing wind. The procession of light moved slowly from the pastures up to the foothills, through the thickets and brambles of the high country and slowly upward.

The light disappeared in the dusk around mountain turns then became bright once again.

The rope bridge whispered in the wind of the coming struggles. It twisted and turned as one of the wooden steps broke free and fell into the gorge below. David looked across the tiny, threadbare bridge and then down at the sharp rocks.

"*Tzaraath*," Nitzevet said.

"Where do they travel to?" David asked.

"Egypt," his mother replied. "They take the mountain passes to avoid towns and villages."

Soon a chant was heard as the lepers approached.

"Unclean, unclean, unclean," was heard and swallowed by the wind. "Unclean."

The lepers appeared on the mountain path, each holding a lantern with heads bowed low. Ten robed men stood in a single file, all of them stricken: they had stumps for hands, no ears and little flesh remained on their faces.

The leader held up his lantern and approached Nitzevet only to bow low in respect.

"I beg you to let us pass," he asked.

Nitzevet looked at the leper.

"Are you for Egypt?" she asked. Nitzevet brought David in front of her and put her hands on his shoulders.

The leader stood back.

"I beg you, let us pass." He bowed his head lower as he was not used to speaking to others.

"You have nothing to fear and we do not fear you," she began.

The nine other lepers stood waiting silently. They pulled their dark, camel hair robes around them and huddled together against the mountain air.

"Where have you come from?" Nitzevet continued.

The leper took his hood from his face.

Nitzevet's hands remained gently on David's shoulders.

The man's face was eaten away; his ears and nose were ragged flesh. He brought out his bloody, rotten stump of a hand and motioned towards the others.

"We are from the Kush."

"Soba?" she asked.

"Yes."

Nitzevet moved close to the leader and reached out to touch his wet and dirty robe. He shrank into the shadows. The rain beat the men and the bridge swayed wildly in the mountain winds.

"Go in peace," she said as she moved to the side of the pass and allowed the small troop to move on across the gorge.

The lepers moved slowly up the pass towards the narrow, broken bridge.

Chapter 4
The Moab Priest

Later that night the large Moab dressed in a black robe stood at the door of Jesse's home, the rain and wind in his dark face, which was hidden by his hood.

David heard the knock and was quickly at the wooden door.

"Rough night for man and beast," said the Moab as he wiped his forehead and peered behind David into the home. "Who is here?"

"Nobody."

"Hmmm."

The Moab smiled a rough, toothless smile as he pushed past the boy into the front room of the house. "No father or mother."

He looked around at the spartan room full of work and hunting tools. Goats *"baaahed"* in the back room.

"I am here."

"Yes you are, child." The Moab shook his wet robe and stroked his rough face. "Yes you are."

Outside the wind picked up and the rain splattered onto the dirty roads that led through the village and up to the high country where lions and bears roamed.

Inside the dimly lit front room silence took hold, the Moab looking around but not making eye contact.

The Moab priest did not feel the cold nor see the rain that soaked his robe; rather his passion burned brighter than the diamond sun.

The priest saw only the cave dwellers writing late into the afternoon where the rocky, barren cliffs surrounding the city of Kir lay bare to the winds.

"*Out of the house of Jacob will come the one to unite them,*" *the high priest said.*

"*What must we do?*" *the Moab asked.*

The high priest's eyes were open wide as he saw his visions.

"*In Bethlehem, he is born.*"

"*And so?*"

"*Kill him.*"

The rain beat against the house. Suddenly a loud, guttural scream rang out. The Moab priest grabbed a knife from his robe and turned.

Nitzevet charged the Moab, her face etched with grim determination, her eyes wild. With the quickness of a cat she leapt at him.

The sheep and goats in the back room rustled in their pen and cried out in alarm. David slipped into the corner and hid under a work bench, his eyes wide with fright.

Nitzevet raised her hand and cut the Moab's arm with her knife. He pushed her as they fell and she was flung against the lime plaster wall. She growled as she hit the earth floor but stood up quickly. The Moab priest turned toward her and let his wet robe fall to the ground.

Her saliva fell to the floor as she bared her teeth.

"A wild dog protected him," said the Moab as his knife glistened in the dark.

She lunged at him again screaming. He caught her and hit her arm but she kept her feet.

The wind blew up outside and screeched wildly along the droveways and paddocks of the village. Nitzevet's breath came in gasps as she stood her ground. The Moab felt his cut and saw the blood flowing from it.

"Give him to me," the Moab breathed. "I'll spare you."

Nitzevet combed back her hair. She crouched low and charged again with her knife raised.

The Moab leaned away from the charge and pushed her as she tripped going past him and hit the work bench. The tools spilled over and fell loudly to the floor. The Moab breathed deep and hard as he picked his way around the farming tools. He tripped on an ax handle and fell backwards.

Nitzevet fell upon him slashing with her knife. She growled loudly as her knife sliced his stomach and arms. He put up his elbows but she kept cutting at his flesh. Blood spilled onto the floor until a large pool covered the tools and reed matting.

The Moab lay still and Nitzevet remained on her knees breathing loudly. She looked over at David still crouched under the wooden bench. Her eyes burned through the darkness. David ran to his mother and they collapsed together on the bloody floor.

Nitzevet grabbed his hand and took him into the moonlit courtyard. The breeze blew the orchards and terraced landscapes that hugged the high country surrounding the village. The trees bent low as moonlight shone on the black pot, which Nitzevet had brought here so many years ago.

She took the fire stick and turned over the dying embers until they became spirits in the night. From beneath her robe a pouch appeared and she poured the contents into the pot.

Nitzevet kneeled over the pot and breathed in the hissing steam that rose into the night air. She pulled David close and he also took in the water and steam.

Nitzevet fell into a trance and began to spread her arms wide and to reach for the stars:

"Oh blood of Noah, sister Sybil of the Hebrews, show me, show me."

She fell to the ground her arms still stretched high.

"Rose, tell me your divine code…. show me the way."

David knelt, holding his mother in the moonlight.

Nitzevet rose up and then fell back to the earth twice more. Out of the pot came a long, thin line of steam that rose up over the two as they lay close to the earth. Nitzevet murmured as she lay bare to the world.

"Who, who?" she whispered over and over.

Chapter 5
The Scorpion and the Poppy Seed Cakes

The little Scorpion's legs gave out in the marketplace as the three boys chased him mercilessly through the narrow streets and alleyways. He fell in front of the lamp trader's stall and sent the bronze lamps flying into the air while the poppy seed cakes fresh from the baker's oven fell onto the hot sand.

"Akhraj min huna!" the trader cried.

The little Scorpion was just one of hundreds of urchins who roamed the streets hungry and desperate.

The three boys followed quickly behind and fell on the sand grabbing at the hot poppy seed cakes.

The fat Scorpion picked himself up before running down a narrow, dark alley at the end of the marketplace. The last of the sun's rays dipped below the minarets that rose above the city and the calls to evening prayer were heard echoing off the narrow street walls. The Scorpion hurried down one alley and then another as he looked up at the unfamiliar balconies and heard voices in the dark.

The nine-year-old boy was alone; his mother had died in the caves outside Damascus and the strange priest who had taught him words and symbols that now haunted his sleep as well as his waking hours had disappeared.

He remembered what his mother had said:

"Jemb al-aqrab la tiqrab, jemb al-haiyyi fru u nam."

"By the side of the scorpion do not come, by the side of the snake spread your bed and sleep."

All that remained from his younger years was a scorpion bite on his inner thigh. He could still see the scar and often felt a stabbing pain but then he would recall his mother and he never wanted the scar to disappear for it was a symbol of love.

He looked around the dark, dusty neighborhood, unsure of his way and felt the stabbing pain in his leg. Suddenly his mother's voice came to him:

"Lady of the Burning Sands,
Sekhmet, Mistress of Terror!
May no enemy find me,
May no harm approach me,
Your sacred fire surrounds me,
No evil can withstand Your Eye."

He stumbled in a doorway and grabbed his leg as the burning pain shot through his body. The streets were silent but then he heard voices.

"Where is he?" one boy said.

"We must kill him," another said as they turned down the alley.

"The others think he is cursed," said the third boy as he wiped his wet and sticky poppy seed hands on his worn tunic. "He reads certain things."

"The dead don't read." The first boy looked down the alley in the darkness and clenched his fists.

"Did you bring the knife?"

The gleam of the finest Damascus steel was brilliant in the dark alley.

The Scorpion shoved himself into an alcove hidden from the street as he convulsed. His shoulders and head fell hard against the door and foam appeared in his mouth. His eyes grew large as he watched his scorpion scar open slowly. He felt pain as the wound became a deep hole. He slumped and passed out from the searing heat that he felt in his head.

A single black scorpion emerged from the open scar and fell lightly to the ground before scurrying into the Damascus night. A loud, rattling noise was heard in the dark street and on the narrow wall a shadow emerged, its tail high with evil intent as it struck three times.

The little Scorpion did not hear the screams of the boys or watch as their throats closed from paralysis. He was unaware of the night's activities and lay for a long while in the shadows unable to move.

The black scorpion that appeared from his long-ago sting returned to where it had come as if nothing had happened. The Damascus night was still.

The next day a pauper's funeral was held for the three street beggars and the rotund baker of poppy seed cakes stood over the bodies in the heat of the noonday sun.

He read from the *Book of Going Forth*:

"May you be given bread and beer,

Beef and fowl,

Clothes and ointment,

Everything good and pure,

Such as the soul of the dead live upon."

A group of children dressed in rags watched as a wagon pulled up and the three bodies were placed on its straw floor.

"Haw," said the driver as he whipped the donkey and it pulled forward down the long lane that led away from the marketplace and the city.

The little Scorpion stood watching in the shadows, shaking and holding onto a leather pouch his mother had given him long ago.

Chapter 6
The Leper Messiah

"I dream of the garden," David whispered.

He was half-drunk with adventure and love as he staggered forward in a long line of camels and horses and dust.

Men had only their hopes and dreams to protect them as the sands called along the great eastern trade routes that led from Rome to Persia, India and China.

The dust rose far across the Persian desert as Bedouins disappeared into the distance, lost in water holes, sparse vegetation and a burnt orange knot that tied sand and sky together.

David and Shimea's world was earth and sun. The days were filled with the heat and the long camel line that went up and down the great valleys. The sand hills rose and fell and the sun followed behind like a hammer that fell at each crossing and each path they followed.

David dared to look out over the valleys and hills in the brutal sun, if only to glimpse her for a moment, but she was not there. He saw visions of the girl he had met — a young princess — and her voice and her smell. He would see her in each camel footprint or the jagged and sharp edge of a dune that they crossed and then left behind. Then her voice became a cool oasis that calmed his mind and allowed him to move on slowly throughout the lonely caravan. He was so far away from the rocky and hard farmland of his family that often he would wonder if he could ever return. She took hold of his soul.

A lone rider stood high above on a jagged clifftop and watched the small caravan that seemed lost among the desert sands. He turned back and surveyed the white sand plains and the cloud of dust that rose into the angry morning sun.

"We shall sit and talk with them," Arlemay said.

The slight man, his *keffiyeh* blown by the wind and concealing his face, guided his horse and two camels back toward the town of Aleppo to begin the grueling 12-day ride from there to Damascus.

He decided not to wait for the large caravans that traveled into the Euphrates Valley but rather take the long trip himself as he had done before.

Omar and Ali, his servants, packed two camels with a half load of supplies: 250 pounds.

"Count it out." He handed his purse to Omar.

Omar counted out the 300 dinars that would be needed for safe passage from the Bedouins and tucked it in a purse under his long robe.

"*Ta-aal,*" he motioned to his companions as they started down to meet the caravan.

The slight man scratched his face and hands before wiping his nose.

David and Shimea came out to greet the strangers.

Omar tore a piece of pita bread and devoured it as he whipped the camel.

"Haga will make *Mulahwajah* for us when we are home," he smiled longingly. "She will put in onion, leeks, fresh roux, lamb and ground coriander."

"Brother, don't forget cinnamon," Ali licked his lips.

"Yes, yes, cinnamon."

"And pepper."

"You like *Hasty*?" Omar pushed a piece of flatbread in David's face.

Arlemay laughed as he moved on towards the great sands spread before them.

"Stir in some honey and then sit in the courtyard and watch the Barada River flow by and be humbled that you live in Damascus, the greatest city on earth."

The three men sat cross-legged under a tent where David and Shimea sat.

The three had come by this ritual on their travels, always long and difficult but made bearable by the thought of Haga's cooking in Hussein al-Rashid's house, where enigmatic, young, westerner Arlemay was a long-term boarder and treated like a son.

Hussein al-Rashid was a high-ranking education *visar* in the Caliph's civil service, who looked after all matters of translation of ancient works throughout the region.

"But, Master, we have a problem."

Blue eyes flashed as Arlemay turned to Omar.

"What?"

"There are five of us and we made *Hasty* only for two." Omar shrugged his shoulders and raised his hands.

Shimea poured some mint tea and David served the three strange men.

The men laughed in the face of the Badiyat Ash Sham, which stretched between the fertile banks of the Mediterranean in the west and the Euphrates River in the east.

"We will ride to Palmyra where the water is sweet," said the quiet blue-eyed man as he spread his arms wide.

"Where do you travel?" he asked David and Shimea.

"We are searching," David said.

"Ah, women?" Omar laughed.

Shimea began to laugh and could not stop. "They know you already," he said looking at David.

"Stop," the blue-eyed traveler said.

"Yes, Master," the servants cried as they arranged themselves out of the sun.

The dust rose far across the Syrian desert as Bedouins disappeared into the distance. The travelers seemed lost between the water holes, sparse vegetation and the knot that tied sand and sky together.

"Where are you from?" David asked.

"The west, across the seas," said the blue-eyed traveler.

The two looked at each other and smiled.

"What are you doing here?" David asked.

"That, my friend, is a very long story."

Arlemay laughed and looked out over the sands.

"What do you see, Omar?" he said.

Omar covered his face from the sun with his hand and peeked through his *keffiyeh*.

"Nothing," came the desolate reply.

"Out here there are no laws, no codes that men can live by."

"We must make them," David said.

"Yes, yes, my son," he laughed. "My name is Arlemay."

"I am David and this is Shimea. We are sons of Jesse," David said.

A scorpion crawled quickly over the rocky landscape and moved closer to a viper in the sand.

The small group of men watched the little battle in the heat of the day until Arlemay took his riding glove and swatted the scorpion out of the way. The viper slithered along the sand until it was within striking distance of the men.

David quickly reached for the snake's head and grabbed it, holding the mouth away and flinging the creature far away from them.

Arlemay looked at David cautiously and then smiled. "If a leper comes give him an audience."

He laughed and took another bite of his *Hasty*.

"*Ta-aal*," he said. "Come, we go now."

Omar whipped the camels again and soon the three were over the last hill.

That night as the desert sand swept around him, Arlemay recalled his times in the west at Greythorn:

He discovered a mountain cave that was not inhabited and his shelter quickly became a living diary as the boy wrestled with his hopes and fears.

"How many days since home?"

He wrote down the numbers.

"Alone," he wrote. "Tired and hungry."

He spread his work over the cave walls. Each word was a badge of courage scrawled in nervous energy and slanted forward in grim determination.

"But I am still here," he thought. "Still tired and hungry."

He drew strength from the words and felt emboldened by the cool air that swept in and around him.

He stood with a lit torch and walked further back into his den of loss until it was fully illuminated, a sea of words that rolled up and down the stone wall.

"Bathe in the stream and comb hair. The mother may be in the forest," he recited.

"Protect women so they don't die; protect the young!"

"Why did she die?"

"Who am I?"

"Father, Father, kill, become King, kill, Father, Father!"

"Brothers, where are you, brothers?"

"They will come back for you."

"Why?"

"Mother, protect me, what should I do?"

Pride rose in his throat at some words and laughter at others as the boy passed by the rough words and drawings that made up his lonely world.

One day as Arlemay dipped his water bag into a cool mountain stream, a worn and haggard face surrounded by long, dirty hair and etched with sorrow appeared in the water. He shrank from the sight as a wild animal would from civilization.

He drank greedily, gathered his bow and arrows and fox pelts and left the mountain stream with the image burned into his mind.

The man-child dashed through the forest bed up the winding mountain trails and looked out over a stone ledge for the last time: the forest stood still, and far down below the treacherous coast was empty and the rough seas heaved. He heard the wind sweep through the trees while watching the great snowy owl take flight, swirling and swirling above.

Days later the young cave dweller continued his diary. Far back in his den, the sea of words rolled up and down the stone wall.

As he wrote each letter, they quivered in pools of water that were beyond his fathom. He touched each letter as they appeared before him. They stretched out into a timeline that he entered unknowingly. As the wind blew deep into the cave, the letters changed from what he wrote into shapes and symbols that Arlemay did not understand.

The 22 letters of the Hebrew alphabet appeared shiny and brilliant before the stone writer.

Tav (A) seal of your ring, Shin (B) because your own name is Shaddai, Kuf (C) sign of the Truth, Tzadi (D) Righteousness, Ayin (E) redemption, Samech (F) support the fallen, Nun (G) Fearful in praise, Mem and Lamed (H) King, Kaf (I) Destruction, Yud (J) first letter of the holy name, Chet (K) Goodness, Zayin (L) War, Hein and Vav (M) name of God , Dalet and Gimel (N) The Benefactors, Bet (O) Blessing, Alef (P) Head of letter.

The letters on the cave wall began to dance. They hung in the air each with its individual energy and tonality. The cave was alive. The letters were children, children calling out to Arlemay.

"Me first, me first!"

Energy resounded off the walls in a sing-song lyrical chant.

The little lord of the forest giggled and approached the string of characters that hung above his head and swirled around him. He turned and laughed, spun around in pure joy then stopped as something caught his eye.

"NINE," was scrawled on the cave wall.

He trembled like the leaves on the branches that protected his mountain world.

The stone writer heard heavy voices deep within his sanctuary. He crept inch by inch toward the noise while hugging the cave wall.

"Father is not coming with horses to find me," he said in a calm voice. All childish ideas were buried as one youthful tear fell from his piercing blue eyes.

"I must join the cave letters."

He removed the bone bracelets from each bicep and gently placed them on the earth. At the back of his cave, he uncovered a leather pouch that held a white tunic and a long hunting knife.

"I must join my friends on the wall."

The knife was lovingly taken out of its sheath and placed on the soft dirt floor. He flexed hard muscles, beat his breasts and then yelled from the entrance of the cave.

"Oooooooh, Ouuuuugh!"

Animals scattered into the underbrush as the signal of change woke the sleepy mountain world.

With great reverence the lost boy put on the clean, rough tunic and brought the hunting knife to his throat. He slowly touched the blade to his skin, feeling its sharpness. He yelled again into the emptiness of his world. The blade felt sharp and close.

"No one is coming." He pushed harder against his throat.

"I must join my friends."

The Rose came to him then, rising high over the cold stone floor as he bent low.

"Do not shed your blood, for it is my blood."

She bent over the young cave dweller.

"You shall go to the east and be my mouth and tongue. And my leper."

* * *

"Allah is great," Ali yelled as they approached Palmyra.

"Ahh," Omar let out a sigh of relief, "A hot cup of mint tea."

Soon the desert gave way to the splendor of the City of Palms.

Palm trees lined the busy paths and a great pool of water stood in the center of the town, holding the promise of life and love.

As the three men stood at the gates of the town a parade of light and music followed. A slight rain fell as elephants and tigers walked through the town on great iron leashes held by bare-chested men. Young boys and girls laughed and giggled in the market square waiting for a glimpse of the Desert Rose.

Queen Zenobia with her beauty and strength had conquered all of Syria and Egypt and her armies had reached as far as Asia Minor.

Nine veiled women carried baskets of roses and scattered them along the path.

"Allah is with us, my friends," Ali spoke in awe.

"Allah is always with us," Arlemay mentored.

"But in many ways today," Omar whispered.

When the village children turned their eager faces upward, the colorful silk drape slowly parted and a smile emerged from the recess of the throne. A single rose was gently handed to a dark-haired girl.

Arlemay in that instant gazed upon the Queen as she looked out. Her eyes darted to him then disappeared.

The procession made its way slowly to the Temple of Bel with its majestic arches, past the agora and toward the amphitheater on its way to the palace. The smitten lover raced past the children down to the baths and past the Tetrapillion in the hope of one more glimpse of the Desert Rose.

"Master, Master," Omar cried as he followed him.

"Master," said Ali following him quickly through the alleyways and warrens.

Ali grabbed his tunic. He flipped a coin and shoved it into his master's face.

"There, you see, there is her face; you saw her again. Now come."

"I must see her again," Arlemay said.

"They will cut you open and leave you to the desert," Ali whispered into his ears.

"I must see her again," he repeated to himself.

Dusk fell over the village. A diamond sun sank behind the distant mountains while from the minarets came the last call for prayer. The carriage was gone and the crowd moved slowly away from the palace gates leaving the three men standing alone.

"*Allah Akbar,*" echoed through the quiet streets and rang off the pillars of the temple only to disappear out over the desert.

"Master, please," Omar whispered.

Arlemay saw six large olive baskets outside the gates and jumped into one of them. All was black as he waited for the supplies to be carried into the palace.

When he was inside and the basket was still, he pulled back the beautifully colored silk drape and beheld her.

"My desert lover, you know not what you do, for I am The Mystical Rose, the light of the burning bush that burns brighter than the sun. I am life and beauty while also withering death. I grew first in the garden only to burn disease from your body and be placed around your neck in the victory.

Fear not my blinding light for it nourishes the world. When he left the garden, it was I who remained to watch on high, guarded by the angel Zagzagel.

From the Tree of Life, I see all and will not let spirits or demons harm thee."

* * *

"Wake up, my boy, wake up."

Hussein al-Rashid tugged at Arlemay's white tunic as he lay in his bed. The plump civil servant turned to Omar and Ali in frustration.

"All he does is sleep."

The two stood in the doorway of the room in quiet concern. Ali picked at a piece of bitumen between two bricks of the wealthy house.

"He mumbles about a rose," Omar offered.

"I know, the Desert Rose, Queen Zenobia," Hussein said in frustration. "She lived 100 years ago."

"But, Master, we saw her."

Hussein al-Rashid raised his hands for quiet.

"Enough. Enough of such foolishness."

The two men fell silent and studied the dust on their sandals.

"Have him ready for this evening," said the fat man lovingly tucking the light bed sheet around Arlemay. "We have many special guests for our dinner party tonight but we must have a story of adventure from our boy."

He looked at the devoted pair.

"Haga will make you *Mulahwajah.*"

He smiled and waddled out of the second floor room toward the courtyard and gardens.

Hussein al-Rashid looked around his beautiful home with pride and anticipation of the dinner party tonight. The upper walls were smooth lime plaster and below were beautiful carpets from Syria and Egypt. The earthen ground floor was covered with animal skins and reed matting, which highlighted the baked red brick and stone lintels of the shutters and doors.

The landscaped courtyard with its high stone wall, rose garden and pistachio trees was his favorite place in the house.

"Haga," he called as he walked toward the kitchen.

"No," came her response.

"But what are we going to have?"

"Nothing." The old woman appeared with a wooden spoon in her hand. "Dried camel breath and brackish water from an old well."

"Please."

She smiled and poked Hussein's belly.

"My master needs no food."

"But for the others."

"Come."

She turned and walked back into the brick kitchen with Hussein waddling behind her, smelling the aroma of another wondrous meal.

On a wooden table arranged on a tray were small wedges of pita bread, feta cheese, broken walnut pieces and fresh herbs — sprigs of mint, basil and parsley.

The main dish of chicken and eggplant *khoresht* sat on top of a stone oven. A large pot of basmati rice simmered beside a tray of rice cakes. Lamb stuffed with fruit, nuts and onions made up the rest of the feast. A huge bowl of fresh fruit — apples, pears, oranges and clementines — was placed on a wooden table.

The mild-mannered civil servant nodded approvingly and stepped outside into his courtyard but then returned.

"Haga," he questioned. "Weren't your people part of the royal house of Queen Zenobia?"

"My people," came the reply. Haga quietly touched the dried rose petal that she kept in her apron.

"Your ancestors, yes?"

"My great grandmother was the handmaid," she said hesitantly.

"Yes, yes, I remember something like that." He thought for a moment. "And you had a sister, Roxanne."

"Yes," Haga stirred the rice.

"What happened to her?"

"She traveled far away to the west."

"To the west, to the west."

Haga touched the rose petal and thought of the distant past.

When the village children turned their eager faces upwards, the colorful silk drape moved slowly backward and a smile emerged from the recess of the throne. A single rose was gently handed to a dark-haired girl.

"Haga, Haga," Roxanne called to her sister, "Look what the queen gave me." She proudly showed the beautiful white rose in her hand.

"Oh Roxanne," Haga cried while trying to wipe her tears away. She looked down at her younger sister with sadness. "You will be leaving me soon. I can feel it. You have been chosen!"

Little Roxanne looked up at her sister in bewilderment.

The civil servant grew tired of the conversation and walked past the kitchen into the courtyard.

A red-necked grebe chirped in a cypress tree entwined with almond blossoms.

The paradise garden was based on the *Chahar Bagh* design with the garden divided into four water channels symbolizing the four rivers of Paradise.

He breathed in the sweet air, stood facing the great Barada River and smiled as the water swept his hopes and dreams toward the evening sun. More than life itself, he wished that his son's stories would come to light for they were great adventures.

"Omar," he said as he turned toward the house. "Omar, I must have a story from our little traveler tonight."

"Yes, Master," Omar shouted from the second-story window. "He is writing now."

"I will pay him handsomely for it."

"Yes, yes," Omar turned back to the room.

"Master wants to know how much you will pay for the story."

Hussein al-Rashid felt his purse tucked underneath his tunic.

"Forty dinars," he called out.

The reply floated quickly down on the jasmine-scented air:

"The Forty Thieves!"

* * *

Days later Arlemay disappeared from the busy streets of Damascus and journeyed into the Persian desert once again. Before he left he kissed Haga the cook and his beloved Uncle Hussein al-Rashid good-bye and bestowed all his fine clothing and belongings to his loyal servants, Ali and Omar.

"But, Master," Ali said as he pulled the bright-colored tunic over his head. "We come with you."

Omar stood proudly as he tried on a long coat. "Yes, like we always do."

"I must go alone now."

The traveler smiled at the two servants.

"My friends, my brothers," he said.

They stopped looking at the beautiful clothes and surrounded the man with tears and hugs.

"But why?" Omar said through his tears.

Arlemay hugged his brothers. He brought both of them close.

"All will be revealed," he said softly. "All will be shown."

"When?" Ali cried gently.

"Soon."

He closed his eyes and remembered visions from many years ago and saw letters dancing in front of him. He could not see deep into the meaning of the string of characters that brought him such joy years ago but knew he must follow them wherever they led.

He remembered that the one who brought the scorpion and viper together would be king. The vision took hold of his soul and danced all along the great desert sands.

At night he would not sleep but stared at the stars in the sky, hoping and praying for a sign. During the days he would wander past watering holes, searching in vain for a glimpse of her, a whisper of her voice. He looked into pools of water, hoping not to see his reflection but hers…. The Desert Rose.

The desert sands were not as hot as his desire to reach her again. With feverish energy he moved deeper and deeper into the wasteland. But on his lonely travels he heard faint whispers on the desert wind:

"My desert lover, you know not what you do for I am The Mystical Rose, the light of the burning bush that burns brighter than the sun.

The light of The Rose will guide thee and the path of The Rose will lead you from east to west and beyond.

Fear not, my desert lover; I am the soul of the world!"

As he passed the caravans that dotted the barren landscape the traders would yell and wave but he did not answer. His world was no longer the world of men. He had left behind the cares of the world and was searching for something greater, something deeper within himself.

Day after day, he pushed on relentlessly until he stumbled over a dune and into a dry gully. His mouth was caked with dust and his clothes were torn as he held his hands up in prayer and called out in the lonely dusk.

"Please, show me the way, show me the path," he said gasping for life.

He fell backward and lay still throughout the cold desert night.

At dawn she came to him, a shimmering image of white who hovered over the ragged scarecrow of a man. Her wings protected him as she looked down but not directly at him. She swirled in the wind and dust around the threadbare man.

Her voice was cool water that he drank in hungrily.

"Go to the land of Canaan; there will I speak to you again."

"The land of Canaan," Arlemay muttered as he sat up to behold an oasis full of spring water. The blue water glistened in the sunlight and was surrounded by fruit trees with branches of low-hanging oranges and grapes in abundance. The traveler drank from the spring and ate the fruit.

Arlemay traveled with renewed spirit and purpose as he pushed along the trade routes and over the great expanse to the whispered destination:

"The land of Canaan."

He stood high on a valley peak and surveyed the ridges and sand spread before him. The sun was a thousand daggers that pierced his very soul.

The dust of a caravan led him to an area where the sand swirled. He tucked his tunic around his ears and fell into the sand. The wind beat at him with a vengeance. The storm raged and the desert shook. Then just as it had come the storm subsided.

Arlemay looked up and in the distance saw a fire burning. As he came closer he saw a bush that burned continually with flames rising higher and higher into the orange sky.

Around the bush roses grew in abundance, and as the fire grew, so did the beauty of each single rose until there were 876 varieties in a garden untouchable by man.

He fell prostrate in front of the burning bush, his head buried in his hands, not daring to move or look up:

"And go down to Jebus and there meet the one they call David and heed his call."

The desert sands swirled around the burning bush.

"But before you do this, go forward and bring my laws and codes to the east and the west so that people shall know how to live with each other."

The fire subsided as the rose garden was in full bloom.

"I will give you the path so that you may bring these codes to those who know. To those who don't know my eyes are blind."

A great crack burst out of the subsiding fire.

"Go to the cool waters of Galilee to find these scrolls."

Arlemay wandered for weeks, dazed by the sun and blinded by the light of The Rose.

"Where am I?" he said when he woke up in a small fishing hut. His fingers and toes were numb.

"You are at Galilee," the old fisherman answered as he fed the dirty man soup.

"Have you seen her?" He sat up in the hut and reached out in the darkness. "Have you seen her? It is too hot; the fire is too hot."

He shielded his eyes and then scratched his arm and leg. He wiped his runny nose with the sleeve of his robe.

"Who?" the old man replied.

"The Rose." He stood up but then fainted and remained on the dirt floor close to death.

The villagers brought him back to the living. Days later the old man lifted his head and forced him to drink fish soup.

"You are weak still."

"No, The Rose gives me strength." The ragged man sat up and looked around.

Other fishermen came to the old man's hut to see this stranger.

"He is not from here?" one man asked.

"No family," another whispered.

A woman began to weep as she looked upon the troubled, withered frame.

She took hold of her husband and cried into his sleeve.

"Abandoned," she cried.

Arlemay grabbed a torn fishing net and began to mend it. His hands worked expertly along the net as if he were a craftsman who had worked his trade for years.

"'I have never done this before," he giggled madly to himself.

The villagers watched the bearded man-child mend the line.

He was giddy with delight. "It's her sign," he called as he ventured outside into daylight for the first time.

He kneeled in pain against the brilliant light.

He spread his arms upward and called to the heavens, "I will gather men from this village for you! Follow me, as I know the path."

For days and nights he fixed the fishing nets and would cook for the men as they came back with their catch.

"Abe, come and listen," he said one night. "We could fish for days and still go hungry for what we need. We are not feeding our souls."

Abe was a great blond giant, strong and steady. You looked at his shoulders and knew that he would carry your burden for miles without rest.

"What would we do?" Abe said.

"The Rose would be our guide."

The light of The Rose will guide thee, and the path of The Rose will lead you from east to west and beyond.

"But my family, my wife and children."

"Come with us and we would all celebrate The Rose."

One day Mira, the wife of Abe, came to visit the net mender.

Mira put down a heavy leather bag.

"You have brought something special to these poor men," she said.

He looked up at her and smiled.

"I try," he said as he continued to work over a gnarled fishing net.

"What have you brought?" she asked gently.

"A better day, a better understanding of how to live."

"How is it better?"

"You are a wise woman and Abe is blessed to have you for a wife."

"I don't need your blessing." She placed the heavy leather bag at his feet. "But I need to know what these are."

Mira opened the bag and took out a small clay jar. "I found these and have kept them hidden until now."

Arlemay took the long, narrow jar and reverently caressed it.

"It's what I have been looking for," he muttered.

"They were buried in a cave near the water. I saw one sticking up." She looked at the bag. "There are nine jars."

He held the earth-colored container as a woman holds her newborn.

Mira looked at the bearded man with burning eyes.

"Will it show us how to provide a better life for our families, how to bring more peace into our lives and teach our children?"

"Oh, yes."

He shook with joy.

"Yes, Mira. It will show us a better life, a better path without empty nets and hungry mouths. It will show you an ocean where you can feed your family's soul."

"Take them; they are yours." She picked up the leather bag. "I will talk with Abe about this."

That night the men returned to the shores with little or no fish.

Abe came to the net mender, sweating and tired from work.

"What will I tell Mira?" Abe said with head in his hands. "I can't go home."

Arlemay took Abe by the shoulders and brought him to where the fishing nets were kept. He motioned to the other men to follow him.

"Let me feed your families tonight." He said. "Let me show you the path." He went to a basket and showed them jumping fish.

The men shouted with joy and picked up the fish in their hands, hugging them and dancing around the nets.

"But how did you?" Abe stood in amazement. "Did you go out on the water today? We saw no other boats."

"No, my friend, it was a brighter light and a better path."

The men sat down and listened.

"This is a gift, not an easy one and one that I cannot promise in the future," he started hurriedly. "But I give this willingly to show you the love of The Rose. She wants a better life for all of us, a life where our children do not go hungry." He picked up the fishing net.

"Where we can mend our sorrows and find a better way."

"How will we live if we follow you?" Abe questioned.

"How do you live now?" came the reply. "How long can you continue this way?"

The men looked down in agreement as they took their portion of fish and went home to their families.

Arlemay and Abe were alone as the dusk fell and the waves beat along the coast.

The large leather bag that Mira had brought was taken out from under the nets.

"I can't read any of this," Arlemay laughed as he took out a portion of the scroll from its clay jar.

"What is it?" Abe looked at the delicate work and fine print on the scroll.

"Your Mira brought it to me today."

"My wife Mira had this?

"Yes, but it is in…. I don't know what language," he shook his head. "I read only Farsi."

Arlemay wiped his nose and scratched his arm and leg.

Abe looked at the scrolls. "Hebrew and Aramaic."

He gave the scroll back to his friend. "I know Hebrew."

"That's why I came. So you could read the scrolls."

Abe studied the writing for a long time before he spoke again.

"It's hard to understand but it is a secret society that has written down 'laws and codes.'"

He studied the scroll. "It is from a splinter group of priests who wrote down these codes."

"Moreover, all who would join the ranks of the community must enter into a Covenant in the presence of The Rose to do according to all that she has commanded and not to turn away from Her through any fear or terror or through any trial to which they may be subjected through the domination of Belial. When they enter into that Covenant, the Kohen and the Levites are to pronounce a blessing upon The Rose of Yeshua and upon all that she does to make known Her truth; and all

*that enter the Covenant are to say after them, 'So be it, Amen.'
Then the Kohen are to rehearse the bounteous acts of The Rose as
revealed in all Her deeds of power, and they are to recite all Her
tender mercies towards Yisrael; while the Levites are to rehearse
the iniquities of the children of Yisrael and all the guilty transgressions and sins that they have committed through the domination
of Belial. And all who enter the Covenant are to make confession
after them saying, 'We have acted perversely, we have transgressed,
we have sinned, we have done wickedly, ourselves and our fathers
before us, in that we have gone....'"*

Arlemay enlisted Abe and they preached near the shores of
Galilee. The men gave up what little life they had and left
their fishing nets for the towns and villages of the area to
spread the word of The Rose.

"Have you seen my Rose?" the stranger asked a woman on
the outskirts of Hebron.

"Your little girl?" the woman questioned.

"Yes, she is only four years old," the woman answered. "We
are just passing through and I can't find her."

"No, but come with me." The woman would serve her something to eat and drink in the dusty village.

The town square was small and had a marketplace where
a person could buy fruits and vegetables. Men stood in
doorways or sat drinking strong coffee. A few children ran
through the square but were shooed away by an old man.
The women hurriedly bought a few items and rushed home
to small huts made of clay and brick, their doors left open to
the sun and heat of the day.

"She is young but very powerful, her eyes," Mira continued.

"Her eyes?" the woman asked.

"She is your daughter also and your sister. She is your soul," Mira laughed.

Abe wandered into the taverns and workshops asking the same question to gain the attention they needed to talk about The Rose.

"Brother, she is your daughter and your sister, too," he would begin as they sat down on a stool in a horse stable.

Arlemay stood outside a small stable, his long, tattered cloak flowing in the late afternoon breeze, his walking stick at his side. The people gathered after their workday.

"Brothers and sisters," he said as he stroked his long beard. "The Rose is the fingerprint of God. Let her light touch you. Let her path be yours, for she is the way."

He read from the scrolls:

"The Rose's Light or Darkness, two spirits of man," he called out.

"This is for the man who would bring others to the inner vision, so that he may understand and teach to all the children of light the real nature of men, touching the different varieties of their temperaments with the distinguishing traits thereof, touching their actions throughout their generations, and touching the reason why they are now visited with afflictions and now enjoy periods of well-being. All that is and ever was comes from The Rose of knowledge."

"What about punishment?" one man yelled.

"Aye, what laws?" another said.

"Yes, yes," Arlemay said. "We shall set up tribunals and have judges who give us the law, men who are like shepherds guiding us."

He put up his hands. "They will be elected for a term and drawn from the Levi tribe, four men and six laymen."

"What about our property?" another man called out.

"It is yours," Arlemay said. "All you need to give is two days' pay toward charity, orphans and those less fortunate than yourselves."

He drank from a water bag. "We are the brothers of the towns not the brothers of the desert."

The men nodded in approval.

"But," Arlemay said. "For lying about the property and lying about anything else to benefit over another, you will have to atone for six months."

The Rosarians traveled from desert town to desert town preaching about the codes and laws that had changed their lives.

One day they stopped at the blacksmith in the town of Bethlehem as one of the horses had a problem with its leg. The blacksmith stroked the horse and picked up its leg to look at the foot.

"Easy boy," he said. "Forty shekels."

He put down the horse's leg.

"Mira," Abe called. "We better be on foot and let the man do his work now."

Ten families were moving slowly along the Euphrates Valley in two wagons during the heat of the late afternoon desert sun.

"We must travel to Damascus," Abe said.

"Why?" asked Arlemay, who was nervous of returning to his beloved city.

The donkeys brayed as they walked while tied to the back of the wagon.

Abe looked at their leader.

"We have no funds, little food and the children are crying."

The traveler was silent as they walked along the trade routes he had once traveled with Ali and Omar. The dust rose up while the wind beat about the wagons and the desperate souls within.

He knew what was in Damascus but hid his selfishness and decided to return from his five-year sojourn.

"Yes," Arlemay said. "We are for Damascus."

Abe ran ahead and told the group their destination.

"Mira, we are going to drink from the mighty Barada River. We are going to Damascus." He jumped up and kissed his wife.

"I will find work as a teacher and Omar will go to school. You can shop all day long in the marketplace."

They kissed and began the long journey to the jewel of the east, the crescent city.

Arlemay saw his dream dying and knew that once in the city it would be hard to keep his company together. He disappeared under the cover of a wagon.

"Why?" he cried as he scratched at his legs and ankles.

His thumbs and fingers were stubs now from the leprosy and he hid his hands underneath his robe.

He remembered the first time he saw The Desert Rose and the passion that overtook him. Was it all for nothing? He remembered his torn youth:

Arlemay dipped his water bag into a cool mountain stream, a worn and haggard face surrounded by long, dirty hair and etched with sorrow appeared in the still water. He shrank from the sight as a wild animal would from civilization.

He drank greedily, gathered his bow and arrows and his fox pelts and left the mountain stream with the image burned into his mind.

The man-child dashed through the forest bed up the winding mountain trails and looked out over a stone ledge for the last time: the forest stood still, and far down below the treacherous coast was empty. The rough seas heaved dangerously. He heard the wind sweep through the trees while watching the great snowy owl take flight, swirling and swirling above.

"Will I always be the unwanted?" he thought. "And now the unclean."

The wagon shook slightly and the wind blew through as figs, dates, nuts and loaves of bread began to fill up the hot, dry wagon.

"Replenish yourself and journey to the city of Jebus," the voice said.

The wagon continued to sway in the noonday sun as the food poured in. Arlemay continued to cry as he looked at his disfigured hands and feet.

"Will nuts and dates help my fingers now?" he sobbed. "How will bread help me walk?"

He threw a loaf of bread into the air.

"Who will listen to me, who will listen to a leper?" he said. He pulled back his sleeves to show his ravaged hands. "Who will look at me and smile?"

"Go to Jebus."

Arlemay's sunburned face was lined and caked with the Persian desert. He rode slowly toward the watering hole and cautiously dismounted away from the band of men that surrounded the well. The men wore brightly colored, rough tunics and large leather belts.

The morning sun rose like a diamond and all one could see in any direction were hills of sand and beyond them great drifts of sand.

He drew near and quickly filled his animal hide bag with water.

From behind the men he could see boys playing with a small ball. They kicked at it and he heard their voices ringing far out into the desert. One child kicked the ball and it landed at Arlemay's feet. He smiled and kicked the dried piece of leather back to the children. The men smiled and looked on.

"Come, my friend," one man called out. "Take some mint tea with us."

Arlemay drank from his water bag and tied it to his camel.

"You want tea?" another called.

"Yes, yes," Arlemay said. "I want tea."

He walked over to the colorfully dressed men.

"Where are you going?" he asked.

"Just to the market," a large man said. "For bread and cheese."

He spread his arms wide and motioned to the desert sands.

"Just to market."

He started a small pantomime: looking from a doorway he put out his hand then brought a rug to cover his head as if it were pouring rain. His friends laughed and they all started to run and hide from the rain.

One man handed Arlemay a hot bowl of mint tea.

"We are for Damascus," he said. "Join us; we are only five days ride away."

"Where are you from?" Arlemay asked.

"We are Roma from the Hindu Kush."

The man who had given him tea now did a soft shoe sort of dance among the sands.

"We entertain in Damascus in the open markets."

The boys yelled as one kicked the ball through the great legs of a camel. The camel spat and tried to bite one of the boys.

Arlemay sat down in the sand near the water hole.

"Hindu Kush," he said to himself. He was glad to think of something new rather than Greythorn and his pain.

"Great mountains and all manner of danger," the man smiled.

"I could entertain," Arlemay said to himself. He drank his tea.

"You are for Damascus?" he asked again.

"Damascus," the man said as he continued his dance among the sands. "We go."

Chapter 7
Arlemay in Damascus

Little Nuri, as the Roma called Arlemay, walked off the northwest corner of the Citadel and headed toward the marketplace for Bab Sharqi Street in the hot noonday sun. He stopped at the coppersmith *souq* where the smiths were beating pots and pitchers of copper into all shapes and sizes. The noise was too great so he covered his ears and carried on toward the shops.

He found himself in a rug *souq* where handwoven rugs in all shapes and colors with the local motifs were magnificently displayed. The market spread before him with its labyrinth of arcades and shops. He looked across at the Shoraj market but then disappeared into an aromatic wave of coffee, tea, spices and soaps.

The great bazaar that stood along the Barada River was overflowing with people escaping the heat of midday. The ceiling was high with thatched work around it and open wood beams. On each side of the bazaar were walkways and paths that started from eight rectangular open doorways supported with two white Ionic pillars.

Wooden tables and chairs littered the open tile floor before the market entrance. Inside was bedlam: barkers stood at each stall yelling and pointing to their wares that ran row after row.

"Come," yelled the shopkeepers, each trying to outdo the other.

Little Nuri walked by himself along the winding, narrow paths, happy to escape his past and find pleasure in his new life in the east. He no longer dreamt of the mountain ranges or the cold streams that used to plague his nightmares. He was free. The long, lightweight tunics he wore and his fez made him disappear into a totally new world far from Greythorn.

He walked on quickly and decided to have a strong coffee at the open café next to the marketplace. Two men came from another alleyway and followed Nuri to the café.

One man hid a knife in his tunic while the other tried to push past the crowds that stood in their way. The taller man looked up and beyond the crowd and pointed.

"There." He looked back at the other man. "It is him."

The two pushed past men and women who protested but soon went back to what they were doing.

"Come."

They hurried down tile steps that glistened in the sun and turned the corner in order to follow the slight man with a light step.

The man they followed now seemed to be going off course. He turned back and smiled briefly but continued past the open-air café and disappeared down warrens and alleyways at much greater speed. The two men now had to jog to keep up with him.

They turned to each other in puzzlement as Nuri kept walking. Suddenly he was gone but they turned around to see him following them. They froze as he disappeared once more.

"There he is," one man cried out.

The two men slowed as dusk took hold of the alleyways. The stores were closed and even the wild dogs that usually roamed the streets were nowhere to be seen. In the distance they saw him running down another alley. They followed him into a cul de sac and were trapped. The man with a knife held onto it tightly as they looked around.

Nuri stood with his back to them, his slight figure bent in anticipation. A figure rose above them and looked down upon the two helpless men:

"You know not what you do."

The Rose's eyes burned as she spoke, glaring at the two assailants.

The two looked up and were immediately blinded by the sight of her. They stumbled around in pain and fear while clutching each other.

Later that evening when the marketplace was empty and the merchants had all gone home, another crowd waited in the dark for the open-air theater to begin.

The group of gypsies standing in their bright Roma tunics of blue and red raced through the empty bazaar looking for their comrade, the man-child who had brought them so much money in their few days in the city.

Two horse-drawn wagons waited while women and children waited for their men to return.

The gypsies ducked behind a large curtain draped over a doorway only to see him sitting at a table applying makeup and dressed in a pure white tunic with long sandals laced to his knees. A dagger was placed in his belt and a wig was on the table before him.

"You are late, my friends," he said calmly.

"Little Nuri," one man exclaimed. "We looked everywhere for you."

"Here I am," the beautiful man-child replied.

The men looked at each other in disbelief but carried on in silence. They prepared for the next show, each man changing clothes or preparing his lines with the other.

'Regret' first?" one man asked.

Men and women with loud voices called for the actors to begin and threw loaves of bread and tomatoes at the empty stage.

"Where is Little Nuri?" one woman cried out. The crowd clapped at this and began to chant. "Nuri, Nuri, we want Little Nuri. The gypsy boy."

One actor in a long, black robe and dark wig walked onto center stage and began.

"Ladies and gentlemen of Damascus!" he yelled while holding a tablet. "We bring you 'Regret,' 'Alexander the Great' and 'Roxanne, the Daughter of Darius, a Comedy of Love.'"

The chant continued while the tomatoes flew across the stage, hitting the actor.

"We want Nuri, we want Nuri, the gypsy king." The crowd pushed forward against the makeshift stage and continued their wild behavior.

The open-air market was lit. A wooden table and one large flask of wine with two goblets were on the makeshift stage. Three entertainers sat in the corner and began quiet, drunken discussions.

One player bowed while the others began to walk the stage.

"My lords and ladies," he began. "Here is a simple tale of loss twice told."

The player took off his cap and gestured toward the crowd in a humble fashion.

Two men faced each other and one poured the ale while the other waited in silence.

"She only comes out at this time of night, the trees creaking, the wind blowing with the rain upon our faces."

"Oh no, she haunts the waking hours also."

He took the drink and poured it into the two glasses.

The voice of an innkeeper sounded throughout the hall as a man wearing an apron appeared.

"Last call, gents, we're closing."

The drunken couple threw their arms around each other and headed to stage left while a single drunk lay on a couch dead to the world.

"She is always with us, waiting and watching...."

"Why does she watch?"

"She preys on weakness; she waits for the right time to strike," said the player who stood up and drunkenly grabbed an invisible dagger. "And when you least expect it."

He drove the knife into the other man. "Right into the heart."

The other man agreed in drunken laughter while turning to face his friend and wrapped his hands around the invisible dagger. "Bad, that is."

He shook his head and poured more wine.

"Not bad," the other player drew close to his friend. "Evil, I say, evil."

"No, I need a pint of courage to keep her away but she comes free-flowing with the drink," the player admitted.

"But she is always there just below your waking senses, watching you as you bring in the harvest or pull the old mule out of the ditch."

"But I don't think of her then."

The other man stood up again and shook his drunken friend.

"But she is thinking of you."

He got down on his knees and looked into the man's face.

"She is thinking of ways, weaving more stories that you have yet to be part of."

He grabbed the man's lapels. "Don't you see it?"

He looked up and pointed to one ray of light. "There, look, look at the beautiful web how it shines in the light and how intricate it is with all of its tentacles perfectly aligned, all there to entrap you."

The drunken player stared up at the light as did the audience rapt with the player's words.

"See how she attracts the eye, see her terrible beauty." He waited as the man continued to look up. "See how she transforms when you look at her from different sides, new colors, new shapes and new poisons to slip into your consciousness."

"Come," he said as he stood up and walked to center stage and called to the audience. "Come, come and make ready to hear a story, come and feel the pain of loss. Come and see how your action sets all in motion, a pebble into a raging stream of loss."

Suddenly a bell tolled slowly three times, forcing the two men to look up from their drunken stupor and realize how alone they were. They huddled together, pure humanity in front of an eternal fire as the bell stopped.

One man slowly returned to center stage and began again.

"Three years of trouble and torment: the loved ones that are broken and left behind while you push on without thought or care. At first you are jubilant, free and without a care to hold you."

He turned to the audience and looked up again at the imagined spider web.

"Look," he cries, "look at how she turns slowly weaving a tale of loss." He took his hands and wrapped them around himself.

"The web is new and you can still move through it without worry but she is imperceptibly wrapping herself around you."

The other man took a drink and gulped it down, worrying about what would happen next.

The audience was deathly quiet as they all felt their own short-comings and lost chances that had rolled away, dice in a dreadful game of chance.

"But you continue through the years not thinking of your actions long ago but worrying about new situations, not realizing that the ones you made long ago are catching up to you. The spider is wrapping you up now."

He stopped and looked at his friend.

"See yourself, what you have become and done in those three years. You haven't accomplished what you wanted. You still have the same worries, still the same fears to face."

The other man drank deeply from his ale. He cupped his face with both hands and ran them slowly down the sides of his cup while straining to see himself in the light. He stood and faced the crowd.

"What have I done, what can I do now?"

He covered his face and sobbed loudly.

The stage was dark but a single flame of a torch was lit and slowly a body appeared from stage left.

A tall, thin waif of a girl wearing nothing but rags and heavy makeup, white on the face and red lipstick, appeared holding a torch.

The two men at first were afraid of this being that appeared before them at this sad time of night. They quickly realized that it was only a poor child perhaps lost and in need of help.

"Child, it is too late to be up now," one man offered quietly.

"Yes," the other agreed. "You should be sleeping."

The men approached the waif and tried to help her.

"I fear it is much too late," she whispered. The entire audience was transfixed by this child and strained to hear her. "The road is pitch black and very late at night."

"Yes, yes," the one player sympathized. "Better to go back to sleep."

He motioned to the upstairs rooms above.

"It is much too late for that now," she laughed.

"Not too late, a good night's sleep is what you need." He guided her to stage left.

She laughed at the player in a wild-mannered way, which made him upset.

"Well enough child, go to bed," he retorted. "I am not your parent."

"Look," she cried while pointing out and up across the audience.

The two men followed her gaze and stopped in fear at what they saw.

"The web," the one man shuddered. "See it in all its menacing glory."

The other man covered his face in fear. "Enough," he cried.

The waif continued to laugh at the two men and finally looked at both of them.

"Poor souls, do not worry about me." She turned on the drunks who were still staring out into the distance. "It is too late for you!"

The candle was extinguished and the players left the stage quickly.

The stage was quiet and then suddenly Little Nuri appeared. He looked angelic in a long, white tunic, with a laurel of thorns in his blond hair and piercing blue eyes.

He walked cat-like onto the stage and eyed the crowd with evil intent. His manner was haughty and with an air of condescension that drove the women crazy. The men laughed but felt inferior to his blatant sexuality. His lips were ripe, his shoulders bare.

He turned his back on the crowd.

They loved his stage presence and shouted for more as he danced quickly from left to right in a dazzling display of athleticism and pure sensuality.

He came at the crowd again from center stage.

"Oh, you rubes," he cried. "You do not understand love but want to feast on it like a banquet."

"Yes, please," one woman near the stage pleaded.

He came close to her, bent down and reached out as if to touch her and then abruptly threw up his hands in disgust.

"I'll have you later, whore," he laughed and disappeared to stage left.

The audience was silent as it waited. Moments later, King Darius stood with a white shirt open and a sword at his side. He wore a crown on his head and had a beard and long sideburns pasted on his face.

The two men met in the middle and drew swords.

"You want to marry Roxanne and then I want my kingdom," Darius cried while striking a blow with his sword.

The other man avoided the sword and replied, "You want to sit on your throne as much as I want her sitting on mine."

He lunged lustfully forward and thrust his hips forward twice. The crowd roared at the lewd gesture and clapped widely.

Darius grew large in rage and went for Little Nuri but time and time again was too slow for the man-child who danced like a boxer and taunted the heavier actor at every turn.

"You shall not have her ever."

"I have conquered all the known world but it is she who has stolen my heart."

"You have no heart," the angry Darius cried as he lunged again.

"It's not a heart that satisfies a woman," said Nuri as he turned to the crowd and lustfully thrust his hips out again. His lips were red with sensuality and his hair blown back by a breeze that came ripping off the river and settled over the marketplace.

Roxanne, the princess, a man in a long dress with large melons stuffed in his chest, appeared on stage in mock terror at her father and Alexander fighting over her.

"What," she cried. "Why are you fighting like this?"

Darius set foot toward center stage, his chest brimming with fatherly pride.

"I am fighting for your honor and virginity."

"And I am as well," countered Nuri.

The princess turned to the crowd and talked directly to them in a deep-throated, bawdy voice.

"Two men fighting for things that were lost years ago."

The princess turned to the two men on stage, wiggling her behind to the crowd and leaving them hooting at her vulgar walk.

"My honor," she began, putting herself in between the two men.

"Yes," Darius yelled. "He may have my lands but should he not ask for my daughter's hand in marriage."

"I wager it's not my hand that he so desperately seeks, my good father."

The princess turned to the crowd waving her behind in the air.

"And when he is done with you?" Darius asked as he sheathed his sword. "What then, my sweet daughter?"

"I'll suspect that he will," she said as she turned to the crowd and winks, "come again."

"Will you give me her hand in marriage, great Darius?"

Nuri comes to meet the two at center stage and takes the bawdy princess by the hand while turning to the crowd and holding his nose in disgust.

The crowd loves this and claps loudly while yelling wildly at the scene before them.

After the crowd leaves, Nuri is by himself and cries. He takes off his gloves and looks at his ravaged fingers.

"I cannot continue," he says as he scratches at his legs and feet. "I am unclean."

Nuri pulls up his sleeves and pinches his dark-patched skin. "Who will look at me and smile now?"

He buries his head in his hand. "At the leper."

Chapter 8
The Desert Thief

Even in the hottest part of the day he still saw the evening fire and heard her voice.

The fire illuminated three faces from the darkness of the great Badiyat Ash Sham. The beautiful young woman wore long triangular earrings that shaped her face while her black hair was cut short. Her headdress sparkled with jewels and she wore a long, purple robe with a hood that covered her neck. Her wrists were adorned with colorful bracelets that shone like a diamond mine.

David's shoulder-length red hair blew in the wind. Shimea sat beside him carving a piece of wood with a knife.

"*Il-ah*, our moon, became *Al-lah*, the supreme god," the beautiful girl said. Her bracelets jingled as she moved.

"*Il-ah* is your moon?" David asked.

"Yes," she smiled at David. "But I prefer *Al-lat* or *Al-Manat*, goddess of the temple."

"They sound better," Shimea said.

The beautiful girl bent close to the boys. "My *visor* says that Allah is the supreme god now."

She turned away from the caravan as if she had just told a gorgeous secret that would change the world.

"Yes," said David who was in love.

The two farmers from Bethlehem had never seen a girl such as this. She was on what their mother called "pilgrimage" to the City of Palms.

She looked at the two and laughed gently. She was excited to meet strangers on her caravan, boys who were not like the ones at court but rather naturally charming and innocent.

"Tell us more," David said. Her every breath was magic and her words flowed like a sweet river.

"Yes," said Shimea as he stopped his carving.

The firelight brought out the beauty of her dark skin against the purple silk robes she wore.

Behind the beautiful girl stood six large men, bare-chested and each with a scimitar at his waist. They wore purple headdresses and had their arms crossed, watching intently as the night fires burned brightly.

The girl looked behind her at the guards.

"Caravan raids," she whispered to David. "So we travel under cover of darkness."

She took her ivory fan and hid her face from sight.

"We would protect you," David said.

"Of course we would," Shimea agreed.

All three looked up at the sliver of moon that hung high over the Arabian Peninsula, each wondering what the world held for their young lives. They would not trade this night for any market in the world for they felt alive and believed that at this very moment the secrets of the universe would unfold as gifts for the future.

"We are for Mecca," the girl whispered. "Once we reach Haram we are safe."

"Haram?" David asked.

"Twenty miles outside of Ka'bah there is no violence, no one will attack you."

"We should have Haram," David laughed.

"Mecca is very important to us spiritually and financially," she continued. "There are 7,000 prophets buried in the sanctuary in Ka'bah."

"We should have 7,000 fighting men," Shimea said.

David nodded.

"You are under our protection now," she said as she smiled.

The fire crackled and filled the night sky. David's donkey brayed and spat on the desert sand. The group looked at the beast and laughed. The three would travel together to Mecca over a six-day period.

"Come, eat and drink with us each night," Sheba said. "But you must learn our lessons as well."

Sheba smiled her beautiful smile and held her head high, her eyes gleaming in the night. "And who we are descendants of."

"Quartan," David replied.

Shimea looked down at the fire. He was a farmer and had no head for this history.

"Good." She smiled at him.

And so the boys were schooled in the ways of the Arab world by the light of the desert fires.

"A descendant of Noah's first son, Shem," David added.

He hoped to never leave this beautiful girl.

"What is a *Mukkarib*?"

"An officer," Shimea said.

"No," Sheba said. "More, please."

Her bracelets gleamed in the night like a comforting light on a brooding sea.

"A chief," he tried.

"Priestly kings," she corrected him. "They ruled South Arabia and Eastern Africa."

The three sipped sugary sweet tea and continued their desert home school as the fires lit up the vast emptiness that lay behind and before them.

"Now, gentlemen, you both know this."

Sheba turned and faced them her smile lighting up their small, rough lives.

"What is a full camel load?"

"Close to 500 pounds," David said. He wanted to remember everything that came from her sweet mouth.

"And how many shekels of silver to pay for safe passage to Mecca?"

"Seven hundred," David said.

Her eyes smiled at him and he felt the rush of a new beginning throughout his body. His heart soared and his mind raced as he tried to anticipate what question she might ask next. Each answer was his way of saying, "I love you and will die for you. I will protect you for all time and be your servant."

"So, my little scholars," Sheba said. "What changed us, what allowed us to prosper and grow?"

"Rain," Shimea, the farmer, felt sure he knew this answer.

"That allowed us to sustain ourselves, correct," Sheba said. "But…."

David answered slowly, "The saddle."

Sheba squeezed David's hand in the firelight. Her eyes were like saucers of milk and honey that he could drown in and be lost forever. They listened to a pack of wild dogs yelping in the distance as they ran after an oryx, an antelope with twisted horns. The moon was high in the night sky and cast a brilliant light over the great hills and sands that stretched wide and far in all directions.

The night air was cold. David placed a blanket over Sheba's lovely, flowing silk robes.

"We have plenty more to go over."

She pulled the blanket close to her.

Shimea had fallen asleep by this time, curled up in his threadbare blanket. The guards had changed and only three stood watch as the fire burned low.

"Tomorrow." David kissed Sheba on the cheek.

She rose, took off the blanket and headed for her tent. The guards followed as the dying embers of the fire faded to a smoldering mist.

In his dreams, David saw a long line of dust covering the caravan as the sun beat down on the two brothers.

"David, David," said Shimea as he pushed David's shoulder to wake him. "What are we doing?"

David shook his brother off and continued in his dream world.

"David," Shimea yelled at him again.

The two sat on a cart, their donkey long ago left at the edge of the desert.

"We will go to Mecca," David said slowly.

"With her. She will show us the way."

"You are becoming an Arab," Shimea said.

"We live beside them; we are farmers and shepherds together," David said. "We must know all we can about them."

"I am a farmer," Shimea said. "What do I know of history and names of long-dead prophets."

"Learn," David said. He wrapped his *keffiyeh* tightly around his hair and wiped his smock along his dry mouth and sunburned face.

Sheba told David and Shimea the Arabian traditions about Adam and Eve: they were both cast out of Paradise and wandered alone, Adam far off and Eve in Arabia. They were lost for over 200 years. God finally allowed them to come together again in Mecca and Adam prayed that he could build a shrine similar to the one in paradise. And so the Ka'bah, cuboid building, was built.

"We are close," Sheba said one night. She wore a simple, white seamless robe and she held two more in her hands. "You must wear these now."

The boys quickly ducked behind the cart and took off the desert clothes that carried so many layers of dust and sand.

The long caravan trail of camels and donkeys and tired travelers stopped at the great Ka'bah.

"We are in a holy and pure state, Ihram," she motioned them forward. "Stay with me now and follow my direction."

It seemed that the entire world was taking the *Hajj*, the pilgrimage to Mecca.

In all directions and from sand dune to hill, camels, tents and men filled the desert landscape. The long train of caravans reached into the distance. There was little room to move for risk of being spat at by a camel.

Animal skin tents of all types and length were erected so that the very sands disappeared beneath a carpet of dust and boots.

A sea of white robes rolled over the hot desert sands. Men yelled and pushed forward in a great rush, each whipping his camel or donkey forward at a mad pace.

"I've never seen anything like this before," said David looking at Shimea.

Shimea carefully led David through the great mass of white robes. He began to chant as others did around him until hundreds of men were chanting:

Here I am, Oh God, at Your command!

Here I am at Your command!

You are without associate!

Here I am at Your command!

To You are all praise, grace and dominion!

You are without associate!

David looked at Shimea. "You have learned well."

He grabbed Shimea's white robe as they walked in the narrow paths between tents.

"Why did we not see Sheba yesterday?"

"She spent the day reading and preparing for today."

"So many people."

They both stopped and looked at the many white robes that dotted the brilliant, hot landscape.

Shimea coughed and sneezed as the dust rose in the noonday sun.

"Just after dawn she left for the Valley of Arafat," Shimea said. "They will stand or sit all day at Mount Mercy. They collect stones for the next day."

Shimea looked back at David as they made their way through the crowds. They stopped and drank from a water bag.

"On the third day, they throw rocks at pillars that represent the fight against Satan and Abraham's trials," Shimea continued.

"How do you know all this?" David asked

"You were not the only one listening to Sheba," said Shimea as he was pushed forward by two men.

"Nor the only one who has fallen under her spell."

Shimea laughed and pushed on through the hot, dusty crowd.

He grabbed David's robe and continued, "Then they perform seven *Tawaf* or turns around the Ka'bah."

David stopped as they approached the wall of men and women, the camels and the donkeys and looked out over the great, hot cloud moving toward the Ka'bah.

The Ka'bah stood in silence, the black cube made of granite 15 cubits high and 12 cubits across. The interior was hollow, empty and covered with a *Kiswah*, a black cloth embroidered with golden words.

"David," Shimea looked back.

David stumbled slightly and his brother gathered him up. Shimea saw a tent with the flap open. A woman beckoned him in.

"*Ta'ala*," she smiled and motioned him onto the rough, wool rug that lay on the sand.

David rested on the floor and drank water. The woman, dressed in her white robe, smiled and clasped her hands in prayer to comfort the weary traveler. Shimea thanked her and kneeled.

"Take me to the desert," David pleaded to Shimea.

"Rest."

He stroked David's forehead and stayed kneeling while his brother laid back and closed his eyes.

"To the desert," said David, who was in and out of consciousness over the next few hours.

The woman brought figs, dates and water to the tent. Inside the tent was a simple wooden chest and dusty boots. The folds of fabric were hot to the touch and the dust blew in from the caravans but the old lady's smile was calming.

"You are brothers?"

"Yes," Shimea said.

"You have traveled far?" the old woman asked.

"Yes."

"You don't know each other," she said. "You are like strangers to each other."

She smiled.

Shimea looked down at his sleeping brother with the long, wild, red hair, the upturned nose and fair features so unlike any of the other brothers.

"No," Shimea said, "I don't know who he is."

"Do not worry but protect him. He is your flesh and blood," she said. "You have seen all that has happened to him, his pain, his anger and how he has helped you."

She glanced down at the sleeping David. "Love him."

The next day the two brothers attached themselves to a caravan leaving for Medina and then the City of Palms. They paid the caravan leader the last of their dinars and made ready for the long trip home. The entire trek would be 700 miles. Camels carrying 300 to 500 pounds would walk 70 miles a day and sometimes four days until the next watering hole. The caravan stretched six miles in a snaking line of dust.

The boys were relegated to the supply wagon pulled by a nasty dromedary. The animal turned on them and spat bile onto the sand.

"We'd better hurry."

Shimea threw his satchel onto the already-moving wagon and jumped up onto the wooden platform in between bags and tools. He reached out his hand as David did the same and both found an area to sit amongst the supplies.

"Home," said David as he sat back against a bag of grain.

"We have to cross the desert first, brother," Shimea smiled.

The wagon sped up as the six-mile caravan lurched forward in an endless stream of dust and wind.

David punched Shimea in the arm and yelled, "Into the desert."

Shimea shook his head and laughed at his baby brother with the wild eyes and an angelic smile plastered on his ruddy cheeks.

The line of camels raced far ahead of the supply wagons and the dust rose up into the great sky so that nothing was seen for miles.

The two boys coughed in the dust and covered their mouths and noses with their head scarves.

The old woman's words resounded in Shimea's head, "Love him."

"I will love him," Shimea whispered to himself as the camels broke off and disappeared into the distance.

The wagon struggled up a hill and then fell downward, throwing the boys headlong into the front. They laughed loudly as they both landed headfirst in the bags of grain.

"Secure the wagon," said a leader of the caravan who galloped up from behind.

He was a small, squat individual mounted on his beautiful, white Arabian stallion. The man's eyes gleamed as Shimea had counted out the 700 dinars and placed them in the leader's hands. His smile grew wide and his gold tooth glowed brightly as the money was safely placed in a pouch tied to the wide, black belt that hung under his robes.

"We are 300 camels and 500 men."

"Yes," Shimea said as he moved the supplies.

David put the bag of grain behind his back and settled in for the long journey.

"Nobody would attack us." His horse moved as the leader handled the reins. "But be careful and tell me if you see anything."

The boys nodded in agreement.

"David," Shimea said as the wagon jerked forward on its way over the desert. "I know why they put vinegar in your meal and dislike you."

David sat up and watched his brother.

"Father doesn't think you are his."

"What?" David's face turned red.

"It's a long story but I think I understand." Shimea scratched his face. "It's simple."

He dropped his hands as the wagon hit a bump.

"What do you mean?"

"I mean that father thinks you are not of his blood."

"What?" David looked around the great open sands and tried to comprehend. "Not of his blood?"

"This is what the brothers said." Shimea tried again. "Grandmother was a Moab and she was a convert."

"So?" David turned on Shimea.

"Hear what I have to say," Shimea continued. "Moabs weren't allowed to become part of our tribe but Moab women were accepted."

"Okay, Moab women," David said.

"Father recently felt that he was not a part of the tribe and somehow wanted to feel more like he was."

Shimea looked around for words.

"There's nothing out there but sand," David said. "Look at me."

Shimea turned toward his brother.

"David." He reached out and took his brother's hands. "I love you and will stay with you always."

David believed his brother and grasped his hands as well. The entire desert had awakened his soul.

"Yes," he said. "I, too."

The two boys hugged and felt their bond growing stronger.

"And so what about Father?" David sat back.

"He wanted to have another son, a pure one from a pure woman, so he left our house."

Shimea was not proud of this and so looked out over the great expanse as the wagon pulled forward on the rough trail.

"He asked the maid servant who he knew was a pure woman to lay with him."

David shook his head.

"David," Shimea continued. "It never happened. The maid servant told Mother and it was she that laid with father in the dark."

David took a moment; his eyes focused on the hills that rose and fell on a never-ending carpet of sand. Above them were high plateaus that jutted out angrily over the vast expanse.

"We are never going back," David said.

Shimea looked at his younger brother and saw a determination that had never been there before in his ruddy, young features.

"Where do we go?" Shimea asked.

"We have close to 100 days to make a plan," David said.

"Agreed," Shimea said as the wagon bumped along the desert trails.

"I know these camels," Yazan, the youngest camel puller, said to David, "but they pay me nothing, not enough to pay for new sandals after I wear these poor ones out."

He lifted up his ragged and broken leather sandals. "See?"

One camel turned and spat on his feet.

The two boys became friends with the camel pullers and the men working the files. Each file consisted of 18 camels and each puller had to understand his camels to ensure their health, because a sick camel would mean cargo would be lost.

The most experienced camel puller became the "Sir," the boss of the camel pullers while the man in charge of the cargo, the "super cargo," was simply the owner's eyes and ears. Each camel puller was in charge of his file and the lead camels. The front camel was attached to a rope that a camel puller would hold, while the rest of the camels were also held together in a string line.

"No, Baby," Yazan said.

Baby was an Arabian camel weighing 2,000 pounds and standing 7.5 feet high.

Yazan lifted up a date so that Baby could reach down and take it in her mouth. She looked at him and shook her large head.

"The loaders put too much weight on her so she is not happy today," Yazan said. "But I will change for tomorrow."

The great beast snorted and put her head down toward Yazan.

"They don't store water; they store fat," Yazan said. "This I know and I know all about them. Someday I will have enough camels to run a file and I will pay money out," he laughed. "But now I will clean my poor sandals."

The boys laughed and walked on foot up and down the great sand dunes that flowed one into the other along the caravan line.

The next morning the caravan awoke to howling winds and a sandstorm from the south with sand that rose more than 30 feet high.

"Hurry," shouted Yazan into the wind.

The two boys hid underneath the wagon. Shimea dragged a bag of grain and placed it in front of them as they hid from the storm.

Yazan was hunkered down with Baby not far away as the wind picked up and beat about the caravan.

All the camels had dropped to their feet and were lying in the sand, heads down against the storm.

"It can last for days or minutes," Yazan called to the boys. He held onto his head scarf and bent down again.

David clung to the spoke of the wooden wheel. His eyes were stinging from the wind and sand but there under the supply wagon and in the storm he saw a clear path. He would write to his mother who had a friend at Saul's court.

"I'll never see Bethlehem again," he thought. He held tight to the wagon wheel. He did not yet know what he would be but he knew he wasn't a farmer like Shimea or a hunter like his brothers.

As the sand swirled about the caravan his thoughts became clear. He returned to the lion he had killed and how everything had seemed to slow down, the heat of the day, his own breathing and the grave threat all came in segments like an orange that had to be picked in a certain way so that all would be safe from danger. There in the darkness of the storm he saw a great light box and its light covered the world. It blinded him but when he opened his eyes it was gone.

The sandstorm continued blowing through the caravan, the wind howling as a young animal might if left out in the cold for too long.

Shimea yelled into the storm. "What do we do?"

"We wait."

David spat out sand and brushed his eyes.

Yazan and Baby were buried in the spot they had chosen.

David slowly let go of the wagon and felt calm. He breathed deeply and saw a new life for himself and his brother.

Suddenly large, rough hands grabbed David's feet and pulled him from under the wagon. Two large men dressed in camel pullers' clothes, their faces hidden by *keffiyehs*, grabbed him; they tied his arms behind his back and quickly forced him towards a camel that was standing head down in the wind.

"Shimea," he yelled to no avail. The wind and sand drowned out his cries.

Shimea quickly got up from the wagon and looked around but did not see his brother. A camel brayed in the distance and he saw the shadows of two beasts moving against the winds.

"David," he called out. "David!"

He ran to the front of the wagon and desperately scanned the desert for his brother. He heard the camels braying again and saw the faint outline of Yazan and Baby still buried in the sand.

He pushed his way toward Yazan.

"Yazan," he called into the wind. "Yazan."

The sand pushed him back and he held his head scarf over his mouth and nose.

"Yazan," he said as he tried once more to make his way against the wind. He then knelt and in a slow, crouching movement made his way toward the young camel puller.

"Yazan," Shimea gasped as he collapsed next to the boy.

Yazan looked up in confusion.

"What?" He pulled his scarf tightly around his face and neck.

"They have taken David," Shimea yelled into his friend's ear.

"What, who?"

"I don't know," Shimea pointed to the wagon. "Men by camel."

He suddenly thought back to the night David was attacked by the Moab.

"The Moab priest," he said to himself.

Yazan pulled himself out of the hole he had dug and wiped his hair and face.

"They will not get far in this."

He stretched his hand out into the storm.

"Yazan, we have to go after him," Shimea grabbed his friend's arm. "We must go."

"Wait, wait."

Yazan shook off the cloak of sand and bent low to the ground. They both made for the supply wagon and hid underneath as more sand was churned up by the wind.

Baby grunted loudly as Yazan moved away and then buried her head in the sand again.

"Listen, listen," Yazan said as he coughed up the sand he had swallowed. "Yes, we will go, but they cannot go far and I know the next watering hole they will make for. It's three days away."

"Yazan," Shimea shook with anger. "If anything happens...." he clutched at Yazan's rough woolen tunic.

"Yes, yes." Yazan looked into Shimea's eyes. "We will get him back. Nobody knows this desert as I do."

Yazan dragged an old rug underneath the wagon and placed it as a barrier against the sandstorm.

"But now we wait."

Shimea the farmer had already planted the seeds of his brother's rescue. In his mind he prepared the sharp tools he would use to dispatch the men like so much chaff on the threshing floor.

"But one must live and talk," he told himself.

Shimea knew that David was different and that their mother was protective of him for a reason. The mother and son bond was a much more complicated and twisted one with David.

He would turn the soil around him bright red. He touched the ax from the supply wagon and adjusted the long knife that he kept under his robes. The farmer also knew that this was not a battle fought over a small, stony pasture but rather down large tracts of land between great powers with sharp weapons that dug deep into the soil.

The day after the storm Yazan said, "We go to the *wadi* at Hadramaut," and he took his stick and tapped Baby so she would kneel.

Baby shook her head at Yazan and pawed at the sand. She spat and kneeled to allow the two to climb onto the leather saddle.

The caravan camp was in chaos and nobody would miss the two boys; men and women had to reload cargo and find their belongings after the great storm had broken the camp's routine.

"We are two days away," said Yazan as he grabbed Shimea's arm and placed him in the back of the dusty and rugged saddle.

Yazan hit Baby's rump and with a high-pitched squeal of joy he left the caravan for the deep sands that led to Hadramaut.

"*Yellllllllaaaa yellllaaaa,*" could be heard far off in the distance and echoed back from a high plains dune. "*Yellllllaaaa yell la aaa.*"

The two boys disappeared into the desert, their water bags and pouches flying side to side as Baby raced along the great sands.

"This is where they will be," Yazan turned back to Shimea.

"I will kill them," Shimea yelled into the wind.

"We make a plan. Yes," Yazan said.

"We come upon them at night in their tents and slice their throats," Shimea said.

"Very good plan," Yazan smiled.

The *wadi* at Hadramaut was distinctive and large with many other branch *wadis* along its route: Dar, Amad and Bin Ali. It flowed parallel to the Arabian Peninsula about 200 miles from the coast.

"There are many places to hide, many *wadis.*" Yazan pointed to his tightly wrapped head. "But I know where these pigs will be. I know."

"Yazan," Shimea asked. "What's a *wadi*?"

Silence filled the desert as Yazan thought how to answer him.

* * *

The sand like the sea washed all around David.

The two ragged kidnappers walked on foot as they held the reins of the camels and behind them was David.

"Wait." The thin man stopped and put his finger in the air, divining the way forward. "We have the boy?"

"Yes," replied the dirty, fat thief. A large, leather belt hung loosely around his girth.

"We have the money?"

The rotund man quickly went for his belt beneath his dress.

"Yes," he chuckled to himself. "Yes."

He put his finger to his lips, "But I fear not for long."

"What do you mean?"

The camels stopped and spat before bowing their giant heads to chew the sparse vegetation. David flopped down in the sand.

"Once you have a plan."

"What's wrong with my plans you nasty, fat, little camel herder?" He glared at his long-time friend. "May the hooves of your camels be your bedfellows," he said.

The fat man looked at his friend.

"Well, Father was a one-armed beggar and Mother was something of a whore," the thief began. "No, I don't think there was a camel herder in the family."

"Oh, you fool," said the thin man before he stormed off.

"Camel herding?"

"Fool, all I am saying is that we can double our money."

David stood and looked up into the sun and sand.

"Can we hurry things along?"

"Hurry things along?" The fat man turned back. "Excuse me but we are busy."

"Listen." The other thief grabbed his friend by his robe. "We'll sell the little urchin."

"Wonderful, how much do good urchins go for these days?" He looked off into the desert. "And what is an urchin?"

He laughed and giggled, rolling the word urchin around his mouth, "Urchinnnnn."

The fat man did a little dance among the sand dunes. He stuck his toe in the sand and moved his belly in a crude fashion toward David. His eyes grew like saucers as he continued to move back and forth and swung his fat hips erotically. He put his fingers to his face and pouted.

"Little boy," he called to David.

"May your tent be full of camel dung!"

The thin thief smacked the other thief around his head and pushed him around the sand dunes. "What's wrong with you? Did your camel kick you in the head?"

He grabbed his fat friend and turned him toward David.

"Him, the boy, sell him to a slave trader."

"But the Moab priest?" The fat man was confused. "What do we tell him?"

"Yes, you're right." The other man walked off, his hands up in the air. "The reports we will write, our meeting each and every afternoon for tea in the garden."

He turned back to his friend. "You perhaps will write the reports of our thievery and deception."

"Not me, my friend."

"And have you ever seen me write on parchment, anything at all?" he said while he drank from his water bag.

"In the streets of Damascus while thieving and stealing," the fat thief said. "No."

"Do you think there will be any reports or files, any meetings, any afternoon teas with the Moab priest, my stupid, fat friend?"

"Do we need any help and directions as to where we are going," David yelled.

Both men turned toward David.

"Quiet. Nothing from you, boy," the thief yelled.

The plump man shook his head and raised his hands and with one finger made a circular motion with his head and then pointed to his confidant. He then shrugged his shoulders in apology toward David.

"So, my fine camel-breath friend," the leader continued. "Any letters or meetings or perhaps shoulder rubbing at the local smoking club planned with our dour, fanatical Moab priest any time soon?"

The fat thief looked down at the sand and kicked it away with his broken sandal.

"Well, perhaps not, maybe," he looked up sheepishly.

"Good. So he is sold to the next slave trader."

The leader looked off into the desert.

"And I know the perfect place, the dark place, the dark copper mines at Timna."

He looked back at the sun-drenched boy bound by rags and already beaten by time.

"He will die there."

Chapter 9
The Copper Mines

A warm Egyptian breeze blew along the Mediterranean and down the Nile, ruffling the Red Sea until it raced along the desert and finally stopped at the doorway of the small infirmary.

"I'm not so much a slave trader as a soul trader," whispered the old Egyptian nurse called Nebemakhet as he wiped the caked dirt and dust from David's limp body.

A lamp lit the small grotto where he healed the sick and prepared the dead. The shadows of the dead played on the cave walls while sulfur and black smoke hung over the nearby copper mines like a pall.

He dipped the cloth in a pan of water and began to scrub at David's face and body until the dirt fell away leaving clean skin in patches.

"More than that," he whispered to the unconscious boy, "I dig up buried souls."

The nurse felt the boy's limbs and put his old, rough hands on a shrunken stomach. He bent forward to catch a whiff of breath but looked curiously at the boy.

"Do I say the prayer for the dead?" He smiled. "Perhaps not."

The old man's face lit up the cave.

"Perhaps I will trade your old soul for a new one," he whispered. "I will make you a true artisan, a copper miner."

The Egyptian sat back on his stool, scratched his beard and looked around his small infirmary at the medicine and bandages, the pots and bowls and then out the rough entrance that looked down over the small hill that hid the great copper mines that stretched for miles in the desert.

He continued washing David's body and whispered a prayer.

The old Egyptian gently raised the boy's arms while washing downward, the water falling in pools on the cave floor. He washed his stomach and legs slowly in a ritual fashion.

"Yes, a new soul."

The Egyptian looked upon the boy's curly, red hair and angelic features.

"You have suffered much," he said as he continued washing David's body. "But there is more."

The old nurse turned and picked up a scroll that lay on a wooden bench. He unraveled the parchment and quickly looked around the poorly lit cave. The shadows that played on the wall convinced him that he was a great doctor who at Memphis soothed the great King Merneptah of his ills and cast spells that brought peace and health to the royal family. He saw himself greeted by clerics and servants loaded down with fruit and spices as he stepped off his papyrus raft at the Nile basin.

The old man smiled and looked at the mixture for the blisters on David's body.

A (remedy) for the removal of the blistering disease from any body part of a man: Pine resin 1, sfT oil 1, XsAjt balsam, cuttle-bone 1, ochre 1, soot 1, water. Grind fine, make a homogeneous mass, anoint in addition to that.

A desert wind mingled with the medicinal smells throughout the infirmary as the Egyptian continued to work.

"The Lady of Malachite will watch over you."

He wiped the boy's forehead.

"You must act in many roles: beggar, priest, warrior."

He pushed back the red hair.

"You will be a great actor."

The old nurse lit more myrrh incense which quickly filled the small cave. He picked up a torch from the cave wall and waved it over David, the sparks flying into the night air.

"For the Lady of the Dance will nurse you as she did the great kings in the guise of a cow and you will be reborn."

He sat down on his stool, wiped his brow and laughed.

"You will be reborn under the great King Merneptah and live in the shadows of greatness."

The Egyptian picked up a small scroll and began to read:

"Whatever he has found upon his path, he has consumed and his strength is greater than his spirit. He is the firstborn of

the firstborn; his existence is everlasting and his life shall be unto eternity."

The wind blew out the lamp and scattered the incense into the desert.

The old nurse shuddered and looked out into the quiet night. He thought he heard movement behind him but turned to see nothing but stillness. A drape inside the infirmary blew in the night air. All was dark.

"Hello," he called out.

He walked back into the depths of the small, hollow room and felt a presence. "Hello."

He looked at David and went to his side.

"Nothing will harm you," he whispered in the dark.

The drape then became alive in beautiful colors and hues that made the old nurse delight in what he saw; he was spellbound and reached out towards the beauty that he beheld.

He pulled back the silk drapes and beheld The Rose:

"My desert lover, you know not what you do for I am The Mystical Rose, the light of the burning bush that burns brighter than the sun. I am life and beauty while also withering death. I grew first in the garden only to burn disease from your body and be placed around your neck in the victory.

Fear not my blinding light for it nourishes the world. When he left the garden, it was I who remained to watch on high, guarded by the angel Zagzagel.

From the Tree of Life, I see all and will not let spirits or demons harm thee."

She came in the form of David's mother and without a word went to David's body. The spirit stroked his forehead and hair.

"You are mine and shall not die here in the dark. But you shall be forged here in the fires."

The old Egyptian, his eyes blinded, huddled in the corner rocking back and forth until dawn. The next day the face painter came to the little stone apothecary.

"Do not worry about me," said the old nurse pushing the face painter away.

He pointed at the bandages wrapped around his face. "I am old and only blind to things I cannot fathom."

He pushed the face painter towards David's limp and motionless body.

"Him." He trundled over to the boy. "He must know of the *Book of Going Forth by Day*."

The face painter looked quizzically at the young boy and then at the nurse.

"My old friend, Nebemakhet," she said.

"Old friend, please, no questions." He stumbled and held onto the table. "No questions."

The woman sighed and went about her work.

First she placed a large chest on a stone slab near David's body. The face painter slowly began to take out the contents of the chest with its 30 small compartments and the jars of granite and basalt, each covered in leather and with a pronounced lip for pouring.

She made white and black face paint from galena as well as green from malachite. Red ochre was ground and mixed with water.

The face painter took a drop of her finest oil pressed from the fruit of balanites and almond oil and began to mix them together.

"So," she remarked. "Another soul to save?"

"He is special," the old nurse said. "He is a king."

She continued grinding her mixtures. "He does not look like one."

"Ah, yes, those who cannot see."

He sniffed the air. "I smell irises, roses and cinnamon."

"Very good, then we soak them in oil." She stopped and looked at the small container of paste that Nebemakhet had been using to clean David's body.

"Old fool."

She threw his paste out the door and into the dust and dirt of the day. She picked out a small container of clay mixed with olive oil and almonds, which smelled like perfume.

"Clean your king with this, old man."

The face painter filled a wash basin with natron and salts.

"Keep this full and clean him with this."

She looked down on David's bruised and burnt body.

"He needs honey and I will make an ointment from red ochre, kohl and sycamore juice to help with the burns."

Nebemakhet smiled and was choked with emotion.

"Dua Netjer en ok!" he said.

"You're welcome," she said as she touched her old friend's shoulder.

"He is under my protection," he said.

The face painter began to grind red ochre with water for David's lips and cheeks.

"Yellow and orange for fingernails?" the old man asked.

"Yes, I will mix the henna."

The face painter spent another two hours working on David's body and face and carefully and methodically changed the desert rat into the boy king.

"There," she said as she took a drop of rose oil and placed it gently on David's forehead.

She stood back and looked at the boy.

"He is beautiful," she whispered. "Like a king."

"Bring me to him." The old nurse stumbled toward David.

He touched David's hand. "Yes, my boy, all will be well."

"But he will die here," the face painter touched her friend's shoulder again. "Here in the mines the weak die and the strong hang on by only a thread."

"He will overcome."

"No, he will die here."

The boy king was silent. His red hair was cut short and angled back from his face; his lips were full, his eyes beautiful, his skin glowed and he smiled a radiant smile that filled the small, stone room.

"He is not for this world," the face painter said.

"He does not fear such things," the old nurse said. "He will be a copper miner, a true artisan."

"What?" said the face painter as she looked at her friend. "Are you mad? Look around you, the sulfur rises in the air and we choke on it."

She began putting away her lotions and jars.

"This place is death."

"He will survive."

The face painter quietly put down her jars and looked at the old nurse. "How many men come into your little stone hospital?"

"None."

"And why not?"

"Because they are dead."

The face painter shrugged her shoulders.

"And so maybe he is strong. He will become a dark, dirty face with wild eyes and a broken back, an animal that just survives. Maybe he has workers who rally around his strength but they will die also. He doesn't belong here."

"He will become a copper miner," the old nurse said.

"He will become dead like the rest of these poor souls."

The face painter closed her chest with its leather straps.

"Who will protect him?"

She used her weight and bent slightly to tighten the last strap.

"No, it's better if you both come to Memphis with me. The horse and wagon will take us all."

The blind man's shoulders slumped.

"But...."

"The boy king comes," she said as she looked at the opening of the infirmary. "Bring the horses around," she yelled.

Quick footsteps were heard outside. The driver, dressed in black robes and wearing a hood, made ready the horses. He sat still and waited as two other men were brought in to lift David's body.

The old nurse seemed to watch as David was placed on a soft bed of hay in the wagon. Strong hands then lifted up the nurse to sit beside the limp body as they prepared to make the three-day journey to Memphis.

For an instant the driver turned his face into the light of the morning and the fat thief, the Little Scorpion who had sold David to the trader, showed himself.

"Driver, drive on."

One man slapped the rear of the horse as the wagon pulled away.

"Hey," yelled the Scorpion as he picked up the reins and guided the horses toward the stony pathway that led out of the copper mines.

"He should be awake by the time we reach Memphis," the face painter said. "Or he will never wake."

A wicked wind now carried the boy king across the desert, down to the Red Sea and over the Nile basin where the great city of Memphis stood bare to the Egyptian sun god Ra.

"Out of the star of Jacob will come the one who will smote us down," the Scorpion recited as he drove up and off the docks at Peru-nefer remembering what his teacher, the Moab priest, had said long ago.

He had asked to continue the journey and had succeeded in attaching himself to the face painter's house as manservant and driver.

"He is the one."

The driver looked forward at the narrow path that led to the outer city at Memphis.

"This dead boy king; he is the one," he thought to himself.

The narrow horse path gave way to workshops and trade houses that spilled out in every direction from the port. The dust of the day rose high in the sky.

The wagon slowed as people surged around them on the narrow path: a group of new slaves, barefoot, chained and headed for the marketplace, were let off from the docks for the workhouses. They chanted a slow, sad song, their dark skin dry in the sun and wild eyes glaring at all that was new in the great city that united upper and lower Egypt.

The driver took out his whip as they neared the wagon and shouted, "Away!" He yelled "Away!" again and lashed out with his whip.

A caged jackal snarled as it passed and clawed at the slaves. A boy with only a small stick maneuvered a baby elephant through the crowd.

The Scorpion dismounted and came to the rear of the wagon, his whip lashing out.

"Away, away!" he shouted.

Suddenly a quiet voice silenced the fat man.

"Wait," David said as he sat up in the wagon his hand resting on the side.

His face was pale, his eyes burning.

"Have you ever felt sorrow or pain; if you have, lay down your whip and know your master."

The driver seemed to act in slow motion, the whip crackling in the air one moment then stopped by an unseen hand the next.

"Come here, my Little Scorpion," David said.

The driver froze.

"I have not heard that name for many years," he thought to himself.

David was weak and reclined onto the hay in the wagon.

The caged jackal stopped his awful crying, the baby elephant stood with its trunk in the air smelling something magical, and the sweet, sad song of the slaves continued in the background.

"Come and know your master," David repeated.

The slaves made their way to the wagon and stood around it, protecting it from the noise of the day.

They allowed the fat driver to make his way through to David while continuing to chant their mystical songs and prayers and finally he stood in front of the boy king.

David was too weak to move, his painted face like the sun god Ra.

He put out his pale hand.

"Kiss my hand, my Little Scorpion."

He extended his arm.

"Kiss me and know your master."

"Who are you?" muttered the driver.

"I am the one your dead Moab priest calls Davooowd."

His eyes grew bright and his colorful face lit up.

"Do you think I did not know you — the face of a poor beggar's son."

The driver stood back in fear.

"All those lonely nights studying ways to kill me while learning of your enemy," David said.

The jackal cackled while the elephant trumpeted his joy.

"Kiss my hand and know your master," David said again.

The driver bent low and took David's hand. His mind went numb as the sun beat down in the marketplace. The slaves continued their lyrical chanting and moved away slowly as the market again stirred to life.

Later that night, David sat upright in a marble bath while servants poured milk and honey into the water. The face painter stood by while her maidservant mixed one part gum of frankincense, one part wax, one part morning oil (the sweet smell wafting through the chamber) and one part cypress grass.

The face painter nodded while the servant poured the potion.

"This will heal the scars."

She came close to David. The face painter held a jar and poured the contents into her hand: a restless scorpion that waited to do her bidding. She let it play on her palm for a moment and then tipped it into the steaming waters.

"I see all and will not let demons or spirits harm thee," she recited.

The water hissed and bubbled while the servants stood in attendance watching and waiting. Slowly the scorpion emerged from the water and went to David. Two more creatures came up from the bath of milk and honey and after crawling up David's hands and arms they sat on his shoulders.

"I see all and will not let demons or spirits harm thee," the face painter said again.

The servants repeated these words while the frightened, fat thief stood watching in the shadows.

"I see all and will not let demons or spirits harm thee," repeated the fat thief.

"The Scorpion King," said the face painter as she kneeled.

The servants kneeled as did the fat man, who was beginning to see what his role was. He must protect his king.

"The Scorpion King," said the face painter as she once again anointed David with rose oil.

"Now, my Scorpion King," she whispered. "No evil shall befall you but you must travel to the war town of Gibeah and be wary of your many enemies."

A servant whispered in her ear.

"Come." She clapped her hands twice loudly. "The Pharaoh's daughter commands us."

Chapter 10
Yazan

"A *wadi*," he looked back at his friend. "You ask me what a *wadi* is?"

He chuckled slightly.

"Yes," Shimea said.

"You are asking Yazan what a *wadi* is?"

"Yes."

"So you don't know what a *wadi* is?" Yazan laughed.

"No."

Shimea blushed, his ears bright red against the head scarf tied below his chin.

"And do you think that a boy, no a man, of your age should know what a *wadi* is?" Yazan asked.

"Yes," Shimea said.

"What is a *wadi*?" Yazan smiled. "My father once told me that."

He could not control his laughter and it rang out over the rocky high plains and desert ridges that they climbed down and through.

He turned back to Shimea.

"It's like your gulch, only larger, and water flows through from the mountains."

Yazan turned back to the desert as they started to climb the high plains. They traveled to 200 feet above sea level before they stopped.

"We will reach Wadi Do'an by nightfall. We camp outside the village."

Yazan drank from the water bag and passed it back to Shimea.

The boys arrived at dusk to Wadi Do'an, Southern Hadramautta region, high in the mountains with great cliffs of sand that towered over the high plains and desert floor. The sunbaked plains and rocky, narrow strips of trail led higher and higher to a village built into the side of the great cliffs.

Narrow mud huts jutted from the cliffs with windows like eyes that watched over the valley below. And they rose even higher until some huts seemed like they would topple into the sands below.

Yazan slowed Baby on the narrow trail.

"We rest here tonight," he said. He touched Baby softly and she stood on the trail. "We must stay outside and go in under darkness."

They picked a flat area with brambles and rough plants to bed down the camel and rest before night fell.

After Yazan took off the saddle, he gave Baby water from a water bag and allowed her to graze on the plants and bushes that grew in the rocky terrain.

She brayed and watched Yazan as he took off his blanket and laid it on the desert floor. He took out a date and held it high until she plodded over and took it from him.

"What's a *wadi*," he laughed and laid down on the camel hair blanket, his hands behind his head with eyes to the now-darkening sky. "A *wadi*."

Shimea, ever the farmer, was picking up the soil and rubbing it with his thumb and fingers.

"Very rich," he said as he looked down in the valley. "Very fertile, good rain."

Yazan was snoring and Baby was eating all that was in her reach.

Shimea looked down from the massive cliff tops and watched as the sun dipped low over their valley. His heart sank with the day as he thought what he might have to tell his mother, how she would wail and cry at losing her youngest child but he fought back those feelings and knew that he must find his brother if only to bring his body back to Bethlehem.

He turned his gaze back to the small village with its brown, sunbaked huts and little windows jutting out from the mountains. He felt awkward about being in a village again. He had known such small town life in Bethlehem — the running between blacksmiths and millers, and village women running errands, but that all seemed so far from him now. The farming fields and barns were lost to him and the deep, rich soil of his home was not his anymore.

The night air was cold and the mountain winds began to pick up. Shimea wrapped himself in his camel hair robe and thought, "I am no longer a farmer. I am an outcast."

There in the growing dark, he knew what he was becoming and this gave him strength. He imagined himself becoming a great tribal chieftain living off the desert while on an endless journey.

He breathed the mountain air deeply and remembered what his mother had said about the battles being fought all around him and knew now that this was true. Behind the highest walled city or in the deepest glade there was a large, powerful argument between light and dark. It had raged for centuries and those who chose to ignore it were fools. But how simple it was to live your life in ignorance, to pull the threshing board across the threshing floor, to bring in the crops, to drink beer and not worry about such things.

Deep in the valley the last sliver of light burned brightly.

Shimea turned back toward his campsite with a new powerful image of himself and knew he would find David.

At dawn Shimea and Yazan awoke to the sound of braying camels and men. Five men stood drinking and preparing their morning meal around a fire. Fresh bread was passed around and they were drinking a strong, local tea with sugar.

Shimea stood up quickly and reached under his robe for his long knife. Yazan rubbed his eyes in the brilliant morning sun.

The men looked at the boys and laughed while they continued to eat and talk.

Shimea blinked away his morning haze and refused to back down but the men continued talking calmly. One of the men pointed to the vultures that circled overhead and nearby.

"Dogs," he said.

He drank his tea and motioned for Shimea to take some tea.

"Eaten by now," another responded as he ate his bread.

The men were tall and full of muscle. They wore bracelets around their biceps and each carried a large scimitar tucked outside his robe.

"Come," said the one man as he motioned Yazan and Shimea closer to the fire.

The men's horses, fine and powerful Arabian mounts, were eating while two small camels tied to a tree were grazing on wild plants. Saddlebags, water bags and rough blankets were spread out over the hard plain like something from a lost adventure.

The camels brayed and spat.

"They can't ride far," Yazan whispered to Shimea. "They don't have enough camels."

Baby finally roused herself from a deep sleep and stood up, towering over the horses and two smaller camels. She tossed her head and snorted loudly at the small company.

"Where do you come from?" Shimea said.

The men busied themselves with breakfast and paid no attention to the questions. Laughter erupted over a small joke and one man spat his tea into the fire.

"He rode all the way back."

He laughed and wiped his mouth with his sleeve. He coughed a little and tears came to his eyes as he swallowed the wrong way. The others looked over, stood back and laughed at the large man.

He wore a black *keffiyeh* and flowing black robes. He was the tallest and although they laughed the men stood by in respect.

"You dogs," he laughed at himself. "I'll cut you and feed you to the vultures."

He wiped away his tears and quickly mounted his white Arabian stallion.

"We ride." He looked over the two boys. "*Ta'ala.*"

One of the other men grabbed Shimea and lifted him up behind him onto his saddle.

The leader motioned to Baby who was still eating plants and brambles.

"Take the beast."

Without argument Yazan moved to put Baby down on her knees and jumped into the saddle.

The horses flew past high plains, down narrow ribbon trails, then back along hairpin turns that with dust blowing up made it impossible to see. They rode mile after mile like this until they came to a gully that vultures circled. Some birds circled while others sat atop a carcass, large and clothed in the rough and dirty robes of camel pullers.

"He breathes no more," said the leader as he stopped and pointed to the body.

Shimea understood finally.

"They killed David's captors," he thought to himself.

"You are Sheba's men?" Shimea asked.

The only answer was resounding hooves that echoed off the rocky plains and fell again and again on the horse trails that spread for miles down from the mountains through the high country and down to the desert floor.

"What about David?" he thought. "Do they have my brother?"

His mind raced as he held tightly to the rider's waist.

Yazan struggled to keep up but then realized that the horses would stop at the next *wadi* for water and so he did not hurry. He felt happy for once and knew that his friend David was safe.

His life had been hard as a street orphan in Damascus. Both his parents had died, his mother Abal in childbirth, and his father Aban as a horse thief. But he was quick and survived in the streets when many did not. He knew knowledge was the key and so he outsmarted the local officials, ran faster than the old men he stole from and played innocent with the women who took pity on him and gave him food.

When an old camel trader whom he had stolen from caught him by his tunic, he could not slip out of the weathered man's grasp. This great, sun-drenched man with a large, white beard did not strike him but rather granted him a small amount of silver.

"I will give you some each day," the man bellowed as he held the dirty and ragged boy, "or teach you about my trade."

"Both," Yazan had shouted while still in the iron grasp of the camel trader.

The large man laughed and let go of the waif.

"Both," he laughed. He stared down at the lost boy, a skeleton in rags, and agreed.

He stretched out his huge, rough hands. "Both."

The little bag of bones stood back and looked up at the talking mountain, at his girth and yet the gentleness that shone in his bright, blue eyes.

Yazan felt calm that day as if he knew he were on a path that would save him from the life he was living. He understood he could not survive long without a helping hand. His body was hungry and sometimes he felt sick of all the stealing, lying and running he did each day.

Yazan thought back to Kalil the camel trader and the first story the old man told him while sitting in the open café drinking mint tea:

"Rajw al-hihuud min al-bil," Kalil began.

He told Yazan that the Jews were the first to have camels. They lived far up in the mountains and kept the best camels hidden from the Bedouin.

"Then on a raid in the mountains we found the Jews in their tents on the high plains. We slaughtered them and took the camels while other camels ran down the mountains. Then the Jews put out a jug of water hoping the camels might some day return."

"The Jews hope for camels," Yazan whispered to himself.

Yazan saw the larger-than-life Kalil bending over the small table in the market square.

He sniffed the desert air and could smell the tobacco from Kalil's hookah pipe, and he saw the trail of smoke as the great man stabbed his finger in the air.

"Abraham brought camels out of Egypt," he would say between puffs on the hookah.

Little Yazan sat cross-legged in the other broken chair, his dark eyes larger than cups of mint tea. The rug seller, his long, flowing camel hair robe blowing in the afternoon wind, stood at the entrance to his shop smoking and listening.

Kalil would have Yazan recite each part of the camel's body:

"*Sanam* is the hump, *Sulb* the back, *Gharib* the shoulders, *Farsam* the foot, *Burtam* the snout, *Shabib* tip of the tail."

Kalil would make Yazan repeat these simple things over and over again but the waif did it with joy and had the ability to sit at his master's feet for hours on end while he saw the others running in the streets. His young mind was quick and he desired only to learn more each day so that one day he could become a trader and escape the streets. He still stole bread and dates in the morning and perhaps an *Ajet Beythat* or *d'Abeen Ghorayebah* in the afternoon but now the shopkeepers only smiled. They knew where he would be and that he was an apprentice of Kalil the camel trader.

The boy's life was still hard; he slept in a donkey stall with straw and when he could steal incense he would sell it on the streets for a paltry amount of silver. Then he would have to hide his earnings or risk losing it to older boys with their steely knives who quickly became the thieves of the marketplace.

And so he learned:

"A camel can drink up to eight liters at once and 20 liters daily," he explained to Kalil. "When they don't have enough water they tear up, moan and stop grazing."

"And?"

Kalil looked at the skinny, brown child.

"And he cannot urinate," Yazan said.

The rug dealer looked over at Kalil and smiled as he turned back into his stall. Kalil took another puff on his hookah.

"What do you do if there is no water?"

Yazan looked away in disgust, "Not me. I'd rather rot."

"Hmm," Kalil said as he looked at his apprentice.

"Gather the cud, squeeze it for fluid or make tea out of the urine."

Yazan stuck his fingers down his throat and spat into the dirt of the narrow, dusty market street.

Kalil sat up and looked at his charge. "Camels will not find water or food," he said. "They are dumb and you need to know every watering hole and how many days to the next one, child."

"Yes, Master."

Yazan laughed as he remembered his master and slowed Baby down on the steep hills that came down from the mountains. As he came around the sharp turn in the road he saw Shimea and the guards off in the bush waiting and watching.

Three mountain lions were hunched over their kill, a large gazelle that was now dead with its neck broken.

Yazan dismounted, tied the reins around a tree and moved quickly toward the group while staying behind bushes.

"Do we want meat?" Yazan whispered as he slapped Shimea's shoulder.

"What?" one guard whispered.

"We can have meat tonight," Yazan said to the leader. "We approach as a single unit, all of us, and walk toward the lions. They will run and we can take some of the meat."

"What if they don't?"

"Confidence."

Yazan stood up and the others followed him.

"Walk straight, look at them." He moved slowly.

The men walked out of the bush and straight towards the feasting animals. One lion, his mouth full of blood and meat, looked up from his kill and waited and watched the approaching group. He flicked his tail and quickly made for the shade of a large bush. The other lions did the same.

Yazan quickly moved toward the kill, took out his long knife and cut off a large section of leg and shoulder.

The lions were pacing behind the highland bushes, hungry and impatient.

"Come." Yazan carried the bloody meat over his shoulder and made for the bushes. He turned to Shimea as he put the meat in a large cloth sack.

"My master Kalil did this with ten lions. I was there."

He smiled as the other men looked at him.

As the troop traveled slowly down the hill, the mountain passes gave way to the valley below and the horse trails turned into a narrow strip of cobblestone road.

A Rider suddenly appeared and flew down the valley road.

The leader raised his hands and made the small group stop for the horseman.

"This is Harrumbra Road and that is the Rider," one of the guards said.

He controlled his horse as it moved off the cobblestone.

"Harrumbra, the Assyrian, built these roads for his horsemen to travel," said the leader as he guided his horse back onto the stone road. "Even in war when two sides are in battle we stop and let him ride."

"Rider, that's his name," the other guard whispered as the horseman disappeared down the dust and wind.

Yazan and Shimea could not know that eight days before nine Riders had galloped out of the great gates at Asur and like great, dusty fingers spread out over the empire on their appointed rounds. They traveled as far as Lydia to the north, south to great Memphis and as far east as the Hindu Kush in India.

Shimea remembered that Obed, his grandfather, was a horseman and the stories he had told of Harrumbra's royal stables.

Obed's father Boaz taught him to ride and from then on he was never far from his horse.

He smiled beneath his *keffiyeh* as he remembered Boaz's 214-day training regime: trot, canter and gallop before a rider or even driver was on the horse, three times a day workouts then rest days. Interval training included three stages: the first two for strong legs and the cardiomuscular system, the third for pure conditioning.

Boaz was quick to add brief rest periods to the lower heart rates. He also added swimming and then rest periods.

Kings and princes came to Boaz from miles around and would use only him to train their war horses — rugged, deep-chested beasts with slow-twitch muscle fibers.

And so with this training Boaz's stable of horses could travel 1,600 miles, a distance that would take caravans three months to traverse, in a little over nine days.

Harrumbra's royal stables held hundreds of horses and they were used to travel across the empire to deliver royal decrees and letters to disgruntled governors and to quell minor disputes over food stores and legal disputes.

The horsemen themselves were agents of the king and treated with reverence by both Assyrians and the many tribes that bordered the empire. They came and went as they wished.

Along the vast routes were waystations all within a day or so ride from each other so that fresh horses were always ready and another Rider would carry the king's news far down the line and deep into the territory.

The men were a wild breed who did not need the shelter of a city or village but instead only a narrow road and mission. They were single-minded in purpose and welcomed the hardships and danger that lay on the roads.

They were born to ride.

.

Chapter 11
Obed's Code

Horse and Rider captured earth and sky at a gallop.

"Slow, my boy," Rider whispered to his horse.

A young Obed appeared around the highland turn and stopped in front of the waystation for rest: he had ridden 150 miles, completed two routes and now was turning south to Jebus and Judah.

The wind was warm and blew the trees and bushes gently during the late afternoon. The sun dipped slightly in the bright sky.

Two old men sat in front of an old wooden table drinking mint tea and regularly drawing from a hookah pipe.

"*Salama,*" one of the old men said.

Obed dismounted, led his horse to a tethering post and dusted his long, black robe.

"*Salama.*"

"Many layers of dust," the old man smiled.

"Many miles." Obed took off his gloves.

He was a rider in Harrumbra's service and could ride 1,600 miles in nine days along the paved roads and networks of the Assyrian empire.

"Come, drink."

The old man beckoned him in.

Obed peered into the darkness of the waystation and heard voices inside. The barn had a large, dusty rug that covered the length of the squat floor. The room was full of horse saddles, rope and hitches hung on the walls.

He heard Balto's loud laughter and the large man came toward the entrance dressed in black leather from head to toe. His belt was full of sharp knives.

Zarek cradled Hadad in a headlock and was dragging the man around while holding his mug of beer.

Obed stepped quickly into the darkened barn. Hadad released the other horseman.

"Obed," Hadad said as he looked up and smiled.

Balto turned and spilled his beer.

"What?"

He went for his knife beneath his long robe.

"I still don't have the silver owed," he said smiling.

Obed threw up his hands as the others went over to him.

"Gentlemen."

He slapped his gloves together and put them in his pocket.

"Beer," Hadad called out to the station clerk.

The clerk, an old man in a gray robe and colorful headdress, moved slowly and drew beer into a mug. He sat it on the table and returned to his calculation of food and water needed for the next leg of the journey for each of the horsemen. He opened the leather binder and picked up his goose quill.

"Little man," Balto said. "Always measuring."

Obed put his hands on the old man.

"Budil, my old friend," he smiled at the clerk. "King of the pages. How are the stores of grain and hay and barrels of beer?"

"Yes, the beer," Zarek said as he downed his mug.

"All is well," the station clerk said.

"Then another round for my friends," Obed said as he slapped the small man on his back.

The leather-clad horsemen were without home or hearth and so they pushed and shoved each other over thousands of miles of hardship smoothed over by a few mugs of beer and talk of long-ago relationships.

"Where are you for?" Balto asked Rider.

"Jebus and Cairo," Obed said.

He drank his mug of beer.

"Why?" Balto said, "We have no royal decrees or letter for them."

Hadad played with his yellow headdress.

"A woman."

He smiled and hit Zarek in the arm.

"The roads are not paved and they fight all the time," Balto said.

He yawned in the small bit of light that fell through a broken window into the dust-filled station house.

"Roads not paved," Zarek said. "You, child, go only where the roads are paved. Sweet child."

He laughed and hit back at Hadad.

"I know why he travels there," Hadad said.

"And?" Balto asked as he drank from his mug.

"He talks to his people, the Jews."

Hadad poked back at Zarek.

"What?" Balto laughed. "He's not a Jew; he is a horseman like us."

"They fight the Philistines or the Jebusites, and if not them, they fight each other," Balto said.

"They are my people," Obed replied.

"You're a horseman, one of the best," Balto said as he drank his beer and said no more.

The day grew long and light disappeared from the window, throwing the small waystation into darkness.

The station clerk lit a lamp that threw shadows over the men and their lonely lives that had been swallowed up by the great and single mission to deliver the king's message.

Obed had in his saddlebags a new royal decree, a deportation decree given to all governors: Those to be deported were chosen carefully for skills and abilities and sent to new regions where their talents were most needed. Scholars were directed to urban centers where their knowledge could be codified. Architects and builders were sent to build projects within the realm. Families were not split up and travelers were not sent in chains but rather were carried on wagons or horseback.

How strange, he thought, that these messages rule the land. He wiped his forehead.

"The outcasts carry the law."

He pushed himself up from the table.

"Well, that is life."

Another decree carried laws regarding women and property to all corners of the empire. Obed's letter bags grew heavier as more lands were taken and more laws were needed to keep together the ebb and flow of daily life in the frontier.

* * *

The next morning Obed tightened his saddle then made sure that both saddlebags were securely fastened with their leather straps as he did before each long ride. He spat twice and bent down to pick the earth up in his hands, something he learned from Boaz. He mounted his horse.

As he plunged ahead down the morning road something weighed on his shoulders and he turned to see the dusty road behind him. The cobbled narrows remained silent and calm as a breeze blew the bushes gently.

The wind picked up slightly and the fields whispered and moaned. The sun became hot and the day unfolded as it should with the wind at his back and the open road before him.

Balto would travel east to the Hindu Kush, Zarek would travel north and Hadad would ride back to the main post.

Obed's flight was straight and true. He rode at speed as he felt a gathering of expectations and watched as the wild plains seemed to open up to let him pass into another space and time that others would want desperately to follow but could not.

The rust-colored hills blended into the valleys to be broken only by the dark green vegetation that fought for its survival while the brush blew over the rough trails.

Obed's way was the way of the horse. His father's family had lived in Damascus and Boaz had become one of the best horse trainers.

He always kept his father's words with him: "Quickly gather your horses around you. If you meet an enemy and are alone then recite the horses' training for your mission will not be questioned."

He felt a presence.

"Is it Lamassu or Sedy?" he thought.

Rider had been blessed with his *Simtu,* his mission and destiny all wrapped up on the road that he traveled.

For him all that lay on the road had meaning: the stones, the bushes, the small animals and the birds all told a story of his fate. His religion was of the natural world. He had come by this through his outdoor life. Let the priests have their prayers, fasts and the reciting of hymns. He had his angels who offered him good things in life and demons who brought him misfortune.

A good ride was his salvation. Obed would not seek help from God directly; he knew it was not his place to seek contact through dreams or the spirit world rather he placed great emphasis on the natural world.

If the river or creeks gurgled in a certain way or the wind blew down the road at a certain time then all was right in his world. If the sun and moon favored his ride then he was safe from misfortune.

"Aye," he thought as he rode. "The moon came earlier last night."

He looked behind him on the road but again saw nothing.

Obed slipped back in time and was once again standing against the wooden fence while Boaz stood in the middle of the training ground holding the reins of a young war horse.

"Hey," Boaz yelled as he put the horse through his paces: trotting, cantering and galloping. "You lead them, you don't ride them," he said.

The dust rose up in the noonday sky as the horse snorted and flared its nostrils.

Obed put his hand up to his face against the brilliant sun.

"Yes, Papa," he said.

"Why do I say this?"

Boaz let loose the training line and looked at his boy.

"The bones and skeleton develop slowly, more slowly than the heart and lungs."

"We will make a horseman out of you yet."

Boaz ran around in a circle with his hands outspread.

"You see, I run without weight or fatigue." He motioned to his son. "Come."

They both ran in a little circle, Boaz holding onto the two-year-old Arabian, Bavryoon, his coat shining as they laughed. Like his ancestors the horse was bred for endurance with strong, slow-twitch fibers and a calm disposition.

"See, no strain, no injury, no lameness." His father stopped. "Then long after do we ride him."

"When?" Obed asked.

"In time," Boaz said.

"When?"

"Seven months."

The father laughed at his boy.

"Seven months," Obed said.

Bavryoon stood and watched the two then pawed at the ground with his hooves, bringing the dust up. He was 13.5 hands high and was only allowed to be part of the four-day horse trials after the many pleas of young Rider to his father. The other horses were three to five years old.

Early the next morning after Boaz had his sweet tea he went out to the stables and saw the men leading their new charges to the parade grounds.

He saw only five horses that he knew: Apsu, Anu, Arur, Tiamat and Kisawr, all fine young Arabians with good bloodlines. The rest were a bundle of energy that flowed from the stables and out into the morning.

"Hold," one of the trainers said as the horse reared up on his hind legs.

"Are the chariots ready?" Boaz called out to the stable boy.

"Yes, Master," he cried out through the line of horses that filed slowly up to the training ground.

"Make sure all is ready."

The morning mist still covered the ground and the sun warmed the backs of the horses' shiny, well-groomed coats. The army needed a steady supply of horses and many were brought from Damascus but few would pass the four-day trials. Most would become work horses and carry supplies to the front lines of war.

The smell of hay and dust rose up into the wind and the sound of old, worn chariots being pulled up the hill resounded off the high play.

"Watch!"

A stable boy jumped out of the way as the chariot in front of him came crashing back down the trail.

"Hey, stop."

Two stable boys grabbed the front end of the old frame.

"These are useless," one said.

"He uses them," the other said.

The boys pushed the rickety old frame up the hill and into the corral.

Boaz felt the morning excitement in his blood and quickly picked up his pace and ran up the horse trail to the wooden fence and the training grounds. Obed and Bavryoon were waiting at the gate.

"Papa," said the boy as he smiled and fed Bavryoom sugar from his pockets. "He is all ready."

"Slowly, slowly," Boaz smiled at his son.

He walked through the gate and into the training ground.

"The old and the new," Boaz thought as he looked out over the grounds.

The dust rose as the horses one by one were let through the gates and lined up. Ten old chariots, old ghosts from wars long past, were standing in a line. The ancient ones had wheels without spokes and the new ones had spokes already broken in places. They all were beaten and broken like old warriors but still somehow managed to move forward at pace.

On the bones of decayed chariots, the master horse trainer would build an empire. His horses would travel farther, rest longer and calmly engage the enemy in battle time and time again. His was the way of the horse.

While the dust blew up and the horses pawed at the ground and pushed and shoved their way through the narrow wooden gate, Bavryoon quietly and calmly watched the chaotic procession.

Boaz noticed this but did not say a word. A lead trainer came up and nodded to the man. He was a tall, slender man who wore a long white robe and had a red and white *keffiyeh* on his head.

"Horse master, may we?"

Boaz smiled. "Yes, Dadu."

Dadu turned and went about his duties, lining up horses that had been chosen the night before, helping the men with troubled horses and making sure that all was ready.

It was October and a gentle wind blew the dust around. The heat of many months had cooled and this was the time that Boaz liked to begin the four-day trials.

"Listen," Dadu shouted over the noise of the horse grounds. "Listen."

He held the reins of one horse, a beautiful Arabian 14.5 hands high. He raised his arms in the air.

"Listen," he called again. "We don't want a saddled horse, ones that have been ridden, nor do we want horses that are in good shape. Those must go now."

Dadu quickly rode behind the front lines and glare. He looked around and watched as four horses started slowly for the gate.

"We want only untrained horses," he yelled again.

Boaz watched carefully as the sun started toward its zenith and the wind blew the dust in the paddocks and barns that surrounded the horse grounds.

"There are no whips used and no spurs," Dadu yelled out to the others. "Drop the whips as you leave the gates."

He looked sternly at the horsemen. "No whips."

He wiped his mouth and took a drink from his water bag. "Today we cover only gentle hills, no steep slopes."

He looked at the horse master.

"Master?"

"Go," Boaz said.

Dadu turned to the crowd of men and horses. He smiled.

"Now tie your horse to a chariot, four horses to one." He guided his horse down through the lines. "Four to one."

His horse slowly walked through the ranks.

"Tie one horse to the front," he yelled. "It doesn't matter which."

Obed quickly tied Bavryoon to the front of one broken chariot and smiled at his charge in the morning sun.

"Go, boy." He patted his horse and gave him a piece of sugar. "Go."

Bavryoon whinnied and kicked up some dirt as he stood in place.

"Hurry," Dadu yelled among the fray. "Hurry."

He looked down the line at the horses that were now tied to the chariots and eager to run.

"We will trot for one danna slowly, no pushing the animals." He turned down the ranks again. "Mount the other horses and follow."

As the procession started Dadu had full control over the pace.

"Then we canter for 42 meters then gallop for 600 meters."

The slow parade of untrained, young horses took off with dust rising in the air, the sound of hooves hitting the earth and the wind blowing across the valley and high plains.

Boaz breathed in the morning air as he mounted his horse and looked out over his young charges.

"It's a good day," he thought.

Dadu's black and white Arabian charger ran alongside the chariots.

"No hitting the horses and no speed."

He pulled his *keffiyeh* over his mouth and nose against the dust and wind.

The horses soon began to understand the pace and were calmed by this so that there was less and less noise.

"When do we race?" said an eager young horseman named Balto who came up to Dadu.

Dadu smiled, "In 214 days."

"What? My horse can beat any of these," Balto spat.

"Not if it's lame," Dadu continued, "or it's not in shape."

They continued on the dusty trail at a slow pace.

"His father is a great champion."

"The horse master will tell you in four days how great," said Dadu as he pulled off the horse trail and let the chariots go by until he was at the back of the training procession. The horses were calm now.

At the half point marker, a white flag on a branch, the horses slowly made the turn for home: one filly was lame and one colt was too tired to continue. Both were disqualified from the four-day training and released from the chariots.

"Take them back slowly," Dadu said to the other horsemen.

Bavryoon was calm and quietly leading the four other horses behind him at pace. His coat was fresh, his eyes and nostrils open and he showed no signs of fatigue.

"In 214 days I could be dead," the young horseman said to his friend Hadad as they trotted behind the chariots.

"It's a four-day trial to see who will get into the endurance trials," Hadad laughed.

"Still, I could be dead in four days."

"I'll kill you," Hadad said with a smile.

The two laughed and continued down the horse trails at the pace set by Dadu. The workout and prescribed daily distances served only to discover horses that would become unsound, tie up or have behavioral problems down the road.

Bavryoon rode through these trials and obeyed each order with a calm, almost placid demeanor. The two-year-old led with his energy and his love of running. His deep chest grew in muscle while his heart and lungs became conditioned. But most importantly his mind became aware of the tasks at hand and there was a pivotal point where both mind and body understood and accepted the challenges that faced the horse.

Sixteen days later Bavryoon was ready to begin the 214-day endurance program. Fifteen other horses, including Balto's and Hadad's, also were allowed to begin the seven-month training.

Over the weeks and months not only were Bavryoon's skeletal system and heart and lungs conditioned but more importantly the horse's mind was brought to a place where he was confident that he could do the work.

In time Bavryoon would march for four weeks to reach a battlefield and still be ready to gallop into battle the next day. He was a war horse.

* * *

Obed was brought back to reality quickly as the day grew dark and heavy clouds blew in that seemed to close in on him. The wind picked up along the road and the air became cool.

"Have I done something?" he asked out loud.

"By the Duranki," he said out loud. "Earth and sky."

He quickly glanced over his shoulder but saw nothing except a dark cloud.

"Midday but dark as night," he whispered while galloping onward.

He looked behind him on the darkened road and for an instant he peered into another world; the trees and high plains bushes came together and formed a rounded opening, a gnarled tunnel of branches and thorns from which came a brilliant light.

"David," came the voice.

Bavryoon's eyes were wide with fright as he smashed down the trail.

"David, David."

Obed turned back again as the words floated over the horse trails and high plains. There on the dark road she appeared; The Rose came full of mercy and dark judgment. Her wings spread over earth and sky and a great cloak covered her except for her arms that were bound in black leather. A brilliant light followed her and burned away the gathering dusk.

"David," the voice called along the trails.

Obed did not look back again but instead pushed forward through the gray mist that had formed along the ribbon of road.

"Ride, boy, ride," he whispered in Bavryoon's ear.

"Ride," he said as the two crashed on.

* * *

Years later Obed kept in touch with his comrades from his wild youth and so he had access across the vast Syrian empire. Balto and Hadad often found their way off Harrumbra's paved roads to the dusty plains and highlands of Bethlehem and supped with their old friend while telling tales of growing new powers in the region.

On one such evening, a war horse galloped from Bethlehem and pushed further into the Persian desert. The animal gathered speed through the camel routes along the Euphrates Valley that stood in the shadows of the Egyptian empire, which bathed in the great Nile as the Mesopotamian empire did in the Euphrates.

The stallion followed a northern path past fields of wheat and barley that swayed under an angry sun.

As the horse galloped, the Rider's saddle bag flapped wildly. He held a letter from Nitzevet to her David:

I fear that shadows grow and cloud my vision like a pair of dark wings. These wings rise and let in only a sliver of light that lies on the land as a gray shroud, a shroud of war and death. Two thousand strong gather at Michmash and Gibeah behind Saul, ready with plowing shears and sharp instruments. We cannot bear any more hardship. Your father and your brothers have become a fighting unit and are at Gibeah now.

Oh, David, how I wish you were here but even I cannot protect you. War harms everybody.

Miriam, my friend, has secured you a station at Saul's war camp. I do not know what awaits but I am full of foreboding. I have felt that jealousy, anger and even hatred await you and surround the war camp.

There is a sickness of some sort that clouds my vision. I feel a false love will lure you into a trap. Do not take what he gives to you or at least be very careful of strange gifts.

You and Shimea are expected in Gibeah.

All my love to you both.

* * *

"Master," said the man as he bit his lip and shook his right leg and then collapsed on the rocky ledge.

"What," his friend whispered as he returned.

"Nothing," said the man whose face contorted in pain.

"Master, Master," he coughed while grabbing his leg.

The squat, heavily muscled man cradled his friend's head between the craggy rocks as the wind and rain grew in strength.

"We can get help here."

"No."

The sick man grabbed his leg as a sharp, powerful pain shot through his body. He tensed his leg as his eyes rolled into the back of his head. He convulsed in the mud as his legs kicked out twice and then his body went limp.

"Master," he whispered before he passed out.

His leggings were torn and the wound on his thigh became red and swollen. The bruise opened and there in the mud high above the sleepy town of Bethlehem a single black scorpion slowly emerged with its tail high and ready to strike. It crawled off the man's body and was motionless on the muddy ground.

The squat man wiped his face and briefly pulled away his hood to watch as the creature made for the cave entrance.

"No," he whispered. "Not here."

He grabbed at the scorpion and without a thought he put it into his mouth and swallowed hard.

He moved to a sheltered area and put his friend down against a grassy patch in between the rocks.

"I'll be back," he whispered.

He took mud from the ground and covered his face before pulling his hood low over his head.

"May two strangers sit by your fire on this cold night?" he called at the entrance to the cave.

Inside the cave voices were raised and the clanging of steel on rock was heard.

"Who asks?" Yazan said as he stood up and peered into the darkness.

"Strangers escaping from conflict."

"What conflict?" Yazan said.

Shimea came and stood near his friend. The wind and rain slashed against the rocks and the cave's entrance.

"All conflict."

"You can never escape," Yazan said.

"For one night," the stranger said.

"Come," Shimea said.

"Thank you," the hooded man said. "I will tell my friend."

He gazed upon Shimea's face and quickly turned from the firelight. He returned to his friend who still lay unconscious on the rocks and with great strength picked him up and laid him across his broad shoulders.

He walked into the cave and gently put down the injured man.

"You are brave to be out tonight," Shimea said.

The broad-shouldered man sat down and kept his hood on.

"As you are," he said.

"We have the company of brothers," Yazan said.

He watched the two men closely.

"Sick?" Yazan motioned towards the unconscious man.

"Just tired and hungry," the hooded man said.

"Take some soup."

Yazan passed a bowl to the man.

The man took the bowl and swallowed it quickly.

"Many thanks."

"Where are you from?" Shimea asked as the other men gathered around.

"We are out of slavery from Egypt," the man said.

"Ah, Egypt," Yazan said.

"Yes, we bought our freedom."

"Freedom," Yazan laughed.

"And where do you travel to?" Shimea asked.

"I am a farmer and so wish nothing more than fields of wheat and barley," said the man as he turned from the firelight so as to hide his face.

"The fields are wet with blood, my friend," Yazan said as he brought out his sharp knife and ran his fingers along the edge.

"And so you fight for your land," the man said.

"We kill for it," Yazan said as he played with his knife.

"Are you an army?" the man asked.

"Many come forward," Shimea said.

"Do you have a leader?"

He looked quickly at Shimea then looked away. The group of 30-odd men became silent as the wind picked up and slashed at the highlands.

The sick man moaned slightly while attempting to sit up but then fell back on the soft earth and closed his eyes once more.

"We lead ourselves," Yazan said.

Shimea looked down at the cave floor as the others nodded in agreement.

A man still dressed in his blacksmith apron moved forward from the rough crowd his forearms bulging.

"We do what we must."

"We don't need anybody," Yazan said.

The squat, muscular man, his head still covered with his hood, looked around at the intense yet purposeful faces of war.

"Brave," he said.

Shimea came forward.

"We are waiting for our leader."

Yazan cautioned Shimea.

"Wait."

"Where is he?" the man asked.

"He is coming," Shimea said.

"And then you fight?"

"Yes," Yazan said.

The other men became uneasy and restless with the conversation. They turned to their barrels of beer and one man threw a knife at the earth floor close to another's foot.

"Close," he said.

The other man stepped forward.

"Dead men don't need close."

The other men laughed and pushed the two away from each other.

"Another round!" another yelled.

They all filled their mugs and were deep in their drink.

"Why do you need the leader?" the man asked.

"We don't need your questions," Yazan said.

The other stranger pulled himself up slightly.

"Master," he said, "Master."

The group of bandits and thieves looked at the weak man.

"Master?" Yazan asked.

"He is sick," the hooded man laughed.

"Who are you master of?" Shimea said.

"I am king of the goats and sheep," the man laughed. "My farm is outside Damascus." He looked out of the cave. "This rocky terrain is much like home."

"You are far from home."

Yazan stood above the man his knife gleaming.

Shimea stopped him.

"They are our guests," he said.

"Guests," said Yazan as he turned in disgust.

"David treated strangers well; he welcomed those less fortunate."

"Davooowd," the man wrapped his mouth around the words. "Who is this?" he said.

"Nobody," Yazan said.

He kicked the dog that sat near the fire.

"He is a skeleton at the bottom of some pit somewhere."

"Stop," Shimea said.

"Well," Yazan said. "What should I say? It's the truth," he sighed and went to pet the dog who cowered in the corner. He buried his face in the pup's fur.

"Sorry, boy."

He petted the stray once more and sent him to the back of the cave. The men stopped their drinking and listened.

"David is alive," Shimea said as he looked at the rest of the men who came forward looking for answers.

At that moment a scorpion appeared on the cave floor. It crawled towards David and was motionless. The sick man woke up and took off his hood displaying his fat face. He looked at the creature on the cave floor and whispered to himself.

"*Nish-e aqrab na as rah-e ast, tabiyyat-ash hai,*" the fat priest said. "It is your nature."

He laughed and bent close to the earth watching the insect crawl on the rock.

"Ah, I know you, my little friend," he drew close. "Spending your days in hiding only to sting in the dark."

He laughed a sick laugh and then looked around at the strange faces that glared at him in the firelight.

"He is sick," said the other man. "Forgive us."

A loud rattling noise came from the back of the cave and the men turned their attention to it. The sound grew louder and louder as the pup whimpered and sprang from its resting place to hide behind a man.

"What is that?" the blacksmith called out as he walked further into the cave.

The loud rattling continued and on the cave wall they could see a shadow of a scorpion with its tail high and beside it a desert viper slithering toward its enemy.

Silence filled the cave as the men watched the game of shadows. The sick man laughed and giggled as he rocked on the cave floor.

Then another shadow appeared, that of a squat, muscular king dressed in elegant silks and bejeweled bracelets who stood between the two fighters. The scorpion and the viper faced each other ready to strike. The king reached out to each creature; the scorpion climbed in his hand and continued upward before sitting on the king's head like a powerful crown of protection while the viper coiled itself around the king's leg and continued upward until it wrapped itself around his waist.

"Shimea, my sweet brother," said the robed man as he stood up and pulled his hood away from his face.

As he wiped the mud from his face his long, red hair fell to his shoulders.

"It is I," he spread his arms out wide. "Come, brother."

Shimea stood dumbfounded as Yazan took out his knife.

"What trickery is this?" Yazan came forward. "I have heard of such stories in the streets of Damascus."

Shimea grabbed Yazan and held him. His eyes welled up with tears.

"Soothsayers and visionaries, false words, false priests," Yazan yelled at David.

"King of the sheep and goats," Shimea cried. "Oh my brother, it is you."

The two rushed at each other and hugged. They fell to the ground and rolled on the cave floor. The men huddled around the two and drank and cried as the brothers continued their embrace.

Yazan looked wildly at the sick man who had taken refuge in the corner.

"Scorpions and vipers," said Yazan as he approached the man. "What is the meaning of this?"

The man clung to the rock as Yazan came forward.

"I serve only my Master," he mumbled. "Nothing more."

"Who is that?" Yazan asked.

The fat Scorpion pointed to David who was now being wrestled to the ground again by his tribesmen.

"The Scorpion King," he said.

Chapter 12
The Desert Tabernacle

"You were in Egypt all the time," said Shimea.

"Yes, I told you," David whispered as they came close to the small wooden gates of the war town of Gibeah.

"Drinking wine and eating good food while we drank brackish water," Shimea laughed.

"And camel's breath for dinner," Yazan laughed.

Under cover of darkness Yazan, Shimea and David arrived in Gibeah just a few miles from the city of Jebus. The hilly town overlooked the high plains and rough lands that separated the two towns.

The night fires were lit and men moved supplies into a storehouse.

A long line of horses and donkeys were standing in the muddy streets while men offloaded grain and wheat sacks.

A guard called out from the lookout point.

"Speak thy name, boys," he called out in the night air.

"Shimea, son of Jesse," Shimea called out.

David hid his face as they walked near the gates.

"And my brothers for Saul's army."

The wooden gate opened slowly and the boys found themselves in the small village that was now the center of Saul's fighting army. He boasted 2,000 men, very few weapons and even fewer chariots.

The lit fires showed the etched determination on the faces of the farmers who had sharpened their threshing knives into weapons.

"Let's find shelter tonight," David whispered. "We will show ourselves tomorrow at daybreak."

Yazan looked at his empty purse.

"We are not going to be sleeping with royalty tonight, my friends."

"We are kings of the street crowned at the beggars' banquet," David laughed and slapped Yazan on the back.

"We shall find something," Shimea said. "Tell me of Egypt, brother?"

"It's all magic and medicine," David said, "It's like a mirage that brings you close but then disappears."

"You read Mother's letter?" Shimea asked his brother.

"Mother was always a visionary," said David as he led the horses through the pathways.

An old man wearing an apron and gloves appeared.

"War is good business," he said with a toothless grin. "I'll take the horses out back."

He led the horses away.

"No rooms at the inn but you can sleep in the barn."

He looked at the three boys.

"Travelin'?"

"Too far," David replied.

"Well, rest awhile." He rubbed his chin. "We can find you some stew and bread."

"We should walk the streets after," David said as he walked into the barn and put down his saddlebags.

"Why?" Shimea unfolded a thin blanket and placed it in the hay.

"We ask questions, we see things," said David.

Yazan yawned. "Yes, we should."

"If we are true kings, we must see our people…. be among them and listen to them," David laughed.

Shimea said, "Okay, king of the sheep and goats."

They ate a hasty meal prepared by the stable hand's wife and went out into the night.

"You, young soldier," said David as he spotted a man carrying his pitchfork and a jug of water. "How goes the battle?"

The farmer looked at the three.

"Like my boot up your ass, my boy, cold and hard."

The three walked on as Yazan pushed David off the narrow path.

"There is your answer, King David."

David's face turned red as he walked on along the muddy path.

"All in due time, my friends."

The night air was cool and the wind from the north came in. Fires were burning at each corner of the village and men stood talking.

"Our pitchforks against their steel," one farmer said.

David and Yazan moved closer to the fire and conversation.

"We can't continue," the other robed man said.

"We have to bring our farming tools to be sharpened. We are not slaves."

"I say fight or be slaves to them."

The men's spirits rose with the night fires. They drank wine and passed it around to all.

"Here and now," the man continued. He had a heavy beard and his rough, thin tunic hung over his broad shoulders.

"We stand and fight the Philistines."

He placed his threading tool in the dirt for good measure.

"How against their swords?" David asked.

The man turned on the group.

"We ambush them, kill them and take their weapons," he said.

"We need more like you," David said. "Words are the sharpest of weapons."

He smiled at the large man.

"What is your name?"

"I am Aron, son of Joshua."

"I am David and this is Shimea, sons of Jesse, and our friend Yazan," David said.

He noticed the man's rough hands and a knife tucked in his belt.

"You are a fighter, yes?"

Aron took a large gulp of wine and passed it to David.

"Yes, I am a scout for the Assyrians. They pay me to scout the Hittites and Moab lands." He wiped his mouth with his sleeve. "I cannot farm."

"Neither can I," David laughed. "But ambush, kill and take their weapons? That I can do."

Aron nodded his approval.

The night fires were burning low and the cold settled on the ground and in the muddy paths that lined the war town. Drunken laughter rang out over the paths and disappeared. Lamps were slowly put out as the men shuffled off to the warmth of their beds.

"Where will we find you?" David asked Aron.

"I have to report tomorrow."

Aron looked over and pointed to groups of tents that had been set up row after row to house the new recruits.

"Come with us in the morning." David looked out over the sea of tents. "We are going to meet with Saul."

The next morning a long line of new recruits stood outside the officers' tents in the morning rain. They came from all over each carrying a farming tool or makeshift weapon.

"Next," said the sergeant at arms as he pushed the men forward.

They were given a thin blanket and a leather helmet and were then rushed through and told which row in the tent city they were to be in. It had grown outward from the shacks and barns that filled the village.

David and Shimea stood shivering in the cold, damp air.

"Bloody rain," Shimea said.

"But it's dry rain," David laughed and poked Shimea in the belly.

Yazan came up behind the two with Aron who had his head covered with his hood.

"Too much to drink last night?" Shimea asked.

"Too much of everything," Aron said.

He kept his head down and his eyes on the mud that became thicker as the line of men stretched farther and farther.

"Next," the sergeant repeated. "Name?"

He did not look up from the parchment in his hands.

"David, son of Jesse."

The man in full war dress and with a large knife tucked in his wide leather belt looked up.

"Lion Killer," he sneered and drew his eyes up to David.

"I was there," Shimea said.

"I kill lions," Yazan said. "Well, I steal their food."

Aron looked on in pain and simply wiped his brow with his hands.

"I may be sick."

"Not here." The sergeant pointed. "The ditch is over there."

The sergeant walked over to the other officers huddled in the tent and they talked until he came back to David. The new recruits surrounded the fires trying desperately to keep warm.

"Next," said the sergeant as he pushed the new men up and shrugged at David's group.

"Go see Abner," he said as he pointed to the tents ahead.

"Next," he yelled at the men huddled together for warmth. "We don't have all day."

"Those blankets wouldn't keep a dog warm," Shimea said.

"I feel sorry for them myself. I want to take them home," Yazan laughed. "Poor little orphaned blankets."

"Please, enough talking," Aron said.

The village of Gibeah was a recruiting camp and a sea of tents and supplies flooded into every stable and side street. Farmers from both Judah and Israel came by donkey, horse and on foot. Women and children were put on wagons bound for the safety of camps far from the front lines.

"I smell opportunity," David said.

"War is death," Aron said as he picked his way through the mud and rows of tents. "I've seen it."

Yazan hurried after his three friends. "There must be 1,000 men."

He tripped slightly on a tent line but managed to stay afoot.

"More," Aron said.

"But the Philistines outnumber us five to one," Shimea said.

"Just numbers," Aron said.

Yazan laughed, "I like you, son of Joshua; I like you a great deal."

"Stay out of my tent," David laughed.

"Ha," said David as he looked over at Yazan. "I don't like big men, just the scrawny ones like you."

He grabbed Yazan and put him in a headlock.

"Lion food."

They scuffled until two soldiers walked past and glared at the boys wrestling in between the rows of tents that stretched from the village out into the fields.

"Boys play," one soldier said. "Men fight."

The group turned on the soldiers: Aron, Yazan and Shimea instinctively put David behind them and moved as one towards the soldiers.

"I'll rip your tongue out," Aron said.

Yazan quickly took his knife out from under his robe.

"Want to play?" his breath trailed off in the cold morning air.

David slipped quickly in front of his comrades and put his hands up to both parties.

"Now, gentlemen, plenty of time for fighting later," he said while pushing Shimea back as he tried to get at the two soldiers.

"Brother, not now."

"Save your strength."

The other soldiers backed off. They turned and walked away in the mud.

"I'll cut you so bad," Yazan yelled at the two as they disappeared past a supply wagon full of farm equipment that would be sharpened for war.

"We haven't seen a Philistine yet we are already at war," David laughed.

"Let's have at them," Aron said.

"You are one for war," David raised his hand over Aron. "I like this one."

Yazan slowly put away his knife.

"Reminded me of my alley days in Damascus with me slicing and dicing."

The group came to a row of tents guarded by four soldiers, two of them the ones they had had the altercation with. They stood in the rain with shields and spears.

"Morning, girls," Yazan said as he walked up to the soldiers and added, "Want to play now?"

He threw back his robes showing his long, sheathed knife.

"Anybody?"

He stared at the two men.

An officer walked up and into the tent without a word. The two soldiers stared straight ahead.

"Let them be," David said. He approached the two.

"Abner wanted to see us."

The tent was open and loud voices could be heard from outside.

"No, don't tell Zadok under any circumstances."

"Very well," said the officer as he walked out of the tent and went about his duties.

"Yes," yelled Abner, the captain of Saul's army, to the soldiers outside.

"The lion killer is here," one soldier said.

"Aye, good, send him in."

The four men filed into the small tent and stood around, happy to be out of the wet if only for a short time.

"David," said Abner, a tall, slender man with a large beard who looked sharply at the men. "Your father and brothers are already at the front."

"We should be there," David said.

"Just wait." Abner went and closed the tent flap. "You are all able-bodied men."

He looked at the drenched group who had not slept and had had very little to eat over the last few days.

"Able and willing?"

"Eager," said Aron with a large grin. "Eager is the word, sir."

Abner picked up a piece of parchment that lay on a wooden box. His tent consisted of only a makeshift cot, a bowl of water and many saddle bags full of parchment and letters. His spear and helmet were hung on a ring post.

He unrolled a map, put it on the small table and began to point at dots in different places.

"The Philistines are pushing in from the sea." He looked up at the men who gathered around the map. "To the east are the Moabites."

"Can we move north to the Euphrates?" David asked. "We could control the trade routes." He pointed on the map, "here and here."

"That's the plan but for now we have to worry about other matters," Abner said.

"Edom and Ammon are also pushing in from the west, no?" Aron said.

Abner looked at the two men. "You know well our troubles."

"I've heard some news and it is not good," Abner looked at the men. "But I need secrecy in this matter and men who are not tied to Saul. Men who are expendable."

"I can expend," Yazan said and smiled a wide, open smile showing rotten teeth.

"Eager is the word," Aron said.

David stepped up to Abner. "Let us serve."

"Good." Abner turned to the tent flap and opened it. "Get me some hot tea and grapes, olives and warm bread."

He turned back to David.

"Your men are hungry."

"Very." David said as he shook with the cold that was in his bones.

"Now where was I?" Abner picked up the dispatch again. "We had success at Jabesh-Gilead but this is different. We are outnumbered greatly at Michmash."

"Just numbers," Aron said.

Abner continued, "We have at most 600 slingers, 300 archers and very few chariots not to mention rusty farming tools."

He put down the dispatch and looked at the tent flap again.

"This is not why your men are here." He motioned them to come near.

"We have other news," he said as he began to whisper. "There is a rugged valley horse trail that leads to Michmash and a column of priests went down that road."

He brought the men in closer and looked at David. "They had the Ark of the Covenant with them as they said prayers."

"The Philistines have it," David said.

Abner bowed his head and looked at the floor, "Yes."

He rubbed his face.

"My dispatches say that they may have it but we have to know."

"So we scout today?" Aron said.

"No," David said. "Under cover of darkness. The soldiers don't have to know this, nobody does."

"Exactly," Abner said. "Your orders are to scout out the trails, find the Philistine camp and report back here."

Abner looked at each and every man. "Understood?"

"What if they have it?" Aron said.

"Report to me; do nothing," Abner said.

For a soldier who fought constantly for survival the real power came from the fear that the Ark generated. The acacia wood box was two and a half cubits by one and a half cubits and was gold plated inside and out.

The common soldier did not read or write and if he did read it was Aramaic and not the Hebrew spoken by the upper classes or the priestly caste, the tribe of Levis. A soldier was fearful of touching the Ark on pain of blindness or death. He wanted it close but not too close and he wanted the Ark as a weapon against his enemies. The Ark was a symbol of fear.

A soldier standing beside Abner's tent came up to the group.

"Follow me."

He walked toward a group of tents and turned to Shimea as he said, "You can all stay here."

The tent was larger than the rest and had a wooden table with a bowl of fruit. The makeshift beds were brought as they opened the tent flap and stood inside.

"Rest," the guard said as he walked away.

A small, slender woman lit a fire inside the tent and placed a heating plate over the fire. Another woman brought in plates of food and began to prepare it.

David and Shimea huddled around the fire while Yazan and Aron stretched out on the beds.

"Opportunity," David whispered to Shimea.

"What? To be killed by Philistines or blinded by the Ark?"

Shimea warmed his hands by the fire.

"I don't see opportunity here."

David was quiet and watched the fire heat the rabbit on the hot plate.

Shimea turned and whispered to David, "I see death here."

"Who are we, a group who doesn't belong?" Aron said.

"We have to make our way in the world."

David peeled an apple from the bowl. "Don't we?"

"Like this." Shimea moved closer to the fire. "On a mission like this."

David bit into the apple.

"Think of this as a scouting patrol, nothing more."

"Nothing more."

"Of course."

David threw back the hood from his soaked robe, allowing his red hair to fall to his shoulders. He took the last few bites of his apple.

"About the Ark of the Covenant," Shimea whispered loudly.

David turned on Shimea, "Stop worrying so much."

"What?"

"Did you ever think that we are alone now? Let the priest worry and carry around our anxieties and failures and raise them up through prayer. We have to live our lives, not huddle in the corners waiting for the next pronouncement from on high which may never come."

They both looked into the fire that spat and hissed with the meat on the spit.

"I miss Bethlehem," Shimea said.

"So do I," said David as he yawned and shook himself.

Before dawn, David and his small group of men made for the Wadi es-Suweinit, which was 10 miles north from Gibeah. Their horses' breath trailed off in the morning air as they trotted toward the rugged pass at Michmash. On either side were high, jagged mountains that fell 60 feet to the pass below.

"Slowly," Aron said as he took the lead.

He whispered as they approached the deep gorge. He looked down and over at the pass carved out of the rock.

"I wouldn't want to be caught going through there," said Aron as he stopped his horse and looked behind at the others.

"It's too dark," Shimea said.

"Do we wait till light?" said Yazan as his horse whinnied and pawed at the ground.

"I see firelight above the pass," Aron said.

"The Philistines are camped above," David said as he dismounted.

"Tie up the horses here," Aron whispered.

The men tied up their horses and began a quick run across the barren trails until they reached the outskirts of the war camp on the rugged hillside. They hid behind the rough brambles and bushes that fought to survive on the rugged mountain pass.

Two oxen attached to a wagon bellowed in the morning.

"We need that wagon," David whispered.

"Why?" Yazan said as he slunk below the bushes.

"That's not firelight," said David pointing to the light beaming steadily from the camp.

"Wait here," said Aron as he moved out from the bushes and ran towards the light.

The others waited in silence, the rain and wind whipping at their faces. The light seemed to flicker and then fade among the mountain paths. But then it became stronger and beamed warmth towards the men.

"The Ark," Shimea said.

Silence played upon the craggy mountain as light and dark fought over the trails and muddy paths that led down toward the valley. Dawn would soon break but now only faded light was scattered across the deep gorge.

"We need to move before daybreak," David said.

Aron returned breathing heavily with his robes soaked with rain and matted with dirt.

"It's buried in a shallow gully," he breathed. "One guard is standing, no, sitting half asleep with his helmet off."

"What do you mean?"

"He is sitting but he is as tall as we are standing. He is a mountain."

"How far away from us?" David asked.

"Five hundred yards."

Aron wiped his face from the rain and mud.

"No other guards?" Yazan asked.

"Not that I could see," said Aron who continued to breathe heavily.

"So we kill the guard and take the wagon, yes?"

David looked at the other men.

"I'll drive," Yazan said as he tightened his belt against his robe.

"I'll get close and first use my sling then slit his throat."

David took out his sling.

Shimea looked at the hillside as the morning broke.

"I will follow you and kill this giant once you have hit him with your stones."

Aron stood up quickly.

"I'll show you the path and then go with Yazan."

The group crouched low and ran toward the Philistine camp and the light that was breaking over the mountains.

David ran as close as he could get to the Ark and wagon and hid behind some brambles and bushes. There in the rain on the hillside as morning broke he lowered himself to the ground with a good view of the giant.

He closed his eyes and let the world slip away. All he heard was his breathing and all he felt was the wet, rough earth below him. The mountain faded, the rain slowed and the wind dropped so that all he heard was his heartbeat.

From his mountain perch high up on the hillside he gathered a pile of stones and then took the largest and rubbed it with his forefinger. He blew out his breath and slowed his heart again. The giant was sitting on the ground and was leaning to one side as if half asleep.

David took aim and fired. He hit his mark and then fired more stones until his pile was empty. The mountain of a man uttered a small cry and then slowly tried to rise to his full height. He came to his knees bellowed like a wild animal then slipped in the mud. His robes were wet and heavy and the giant struggled to move. He was slobbering and wiping away blood at his mouth.

Shimea came and stood over the mountain man and buried his sword in him as the sun came up over the mountains. Yazan led the oxen by the reins while Aron jumped onto the wagon.

The Ark lay in a shallow hole filled with rain and mud. It was covered in a rough cloth blanket. As Yazan approached the Ark he slipped and fell in the deep mud. He heard a rustling noise and peered up to see a great pair of black wings hovering over it.

The wings fluttered gently over the gold-plated box and the Ark's light flickered and faded over the mountainside with a Rose-colored hue that became the dawn. Silently the great dark wings fluttered over the Ark and disappeared.

In the next moment Yazan and Aron had the Ark in the wagon and the two oxen seemed to float slightly above the ground as they made their way through the deep mountain pass and steep trails.

The black wings slowly rose above the mountains and turned toward the oxen team and wagon that was pulling away from the mountain pass and toward the high plains and hilly fields of Judah.

David watched the vision and when he reached the wagon he took the reins and followed.

The oxen plodded for ten miles in the heavy mud until they reached the town of Kiryat Jarmin, a border town between the tribes of Benjamin and Judah. Here David watched as the dark wings circled above until landing on a small house on the outskirts of the tiny village, a quiet and desolate place.

"We stop here," said David, who pulled the oxen to a slow walk. "They are Hivites and tent dwellers here."

"What do we tell Abner and Saul?" Aron asked.

"We tell them the Ark is safe." David watched as the dark wings flew off and disappeared. "That is what we say."

Meanwhile Jonathan, son of Saul, scaled the rocky mountains and attacked a small outpost overlooking Michmash. His men had killed 20 soldiers before the breakfast fires glowed and his band of farmers scattered the new Philistine recruits after the Philistines saw the giant guard lying dead in the mud and rain.

Saul's force of 750 men stationed at Gibeah were given marching orders once Jonathan's dispatches were received while a small group of farmers was sent to confront attacks at Morgan. The main group traveled quickly through the Michmash pass and boldly went on the offensive against the much larger Philistine army.

A winter rain slashed at the chariots and horses as the Philistines made their way down the narrow, winding trail to the valley below. In the front of the column a chariot was stuck close to the cliff edge.

"Slow the line," an officer cried.

His horse raced to the front as the wind whipped his face. The chariot was wedged between two rocks and the horses were rearing up in fear.

"I can't hold him."

One man got down from the chariot and was holding the horse's reins.

"Can't hold him."

"Pull them back," the other man yelled into the rain.

The Philistine archers were assembling on the valley floor below.

"Archers," one officer yelled. "Assemble here, archers!" he yelled and stood to face the oncoming Hebrews.

The Philistine archers were cut down from behind with hammers and farming tools before they reached the line.

"Archers," he yelled again into the wind.

A group of 40 archers managed to fight their way to the line.

"Archers ready!" The officers pointed towards the Hebrews. "Let fly!"

The bowmen pointed their arrows into the cold, winter rain and let loose their hell.

The Hebrews saw the arrows and clung to the rocky walls of the Michmash Valley, escaping the brunt of the assault. But screams of pain resounded throughout the small valley as some of the arrows found their mark.

Suddenly from above a crashing sound rang off the mountainside as a chariot and its team of horses came hurtling down to the valley floor. The horses were wild-eyed in fright. One man screamed as he fell over the cliff.

Wood and bones splintered at the bottom of the trail while a line of archers was crushed as the chariot hit the rocks below and thundered across the valley leaving blood and death in its wake.

The Philistine officer above slowed the column and could only look down and watch as the men were swarmed by the Hebrew farmers.

"Hold the line!" the guard yelled.

More archers came to the line but slipped in the mud churned up by the rain and blood.

"Hold," he cried into the wind. "Now!" he yelled.

Another rain of arrows took flight.

Above the valley the chariots were turning back and were no longer a threat. The horses were slowly guided by men as they made their way back along the mountain trails.

"We can't have them killed," said the officer as he turned toward the men. "Another day, another battle."

The Philistine army was in chaos during the attack: they fled the theater of battle to the west and east but found themselves under attack from the villagers and farmers who let out their frustration and anger on the occupying force. The archers were caught from behind as the Hebrews surrounded them.

"Quickly!" Abner yelled.

He led his horse through the blood and went at a line of soldiers with his sword.

Saul turned and threw his large spear at an archer, which penetrated the shield and gouged the man's eye.

"Follow me," he yelled as he charged the line of men.

The Hebrew clansmen forged a ring of death around the trapped Philistines and Saul's men quickly set upon a line of archers who were trying to ready their bows against the lightning assault. They killed them with knives, pitchforks and hammers and soon were slipping in the growing pool of blood.

The cries of the wounded and dying spread out through the valley and upward toward the mountains.

David yelled at the farmers around him as he stood in the large mud bowl of death.

"Kill them and take their swords and spears."

He stopped a Philistine in his tracks with a hammer to his head and as the man dropped picked up his sword.

"Kill and take their weapons," he yelled again.

He pointed to a breach in the Philistine's wall of spears and men.

"There."

He ran towards it. In that instant he saw his soldiers, like himself, lacking the tools they needed and the direction they desperately sought.

The farmers stood behind him with hammers and handmade knives waiting for direction. He could feel their eyes on him and he knew that he, the outcast, would lead the rough farmers. He was again a child leading his father and brothers out of harm's way and then he would be a working member of the clan. He would have what he desperately sought: the love of his tribe. He was without emotion, the perfect war child.

"We attack here."

He sprinted towards the line of soldiers with his sword held high.

"Kill and take. Kill and take," was the resounding cry the Hebrews used all up and down the narrow valley.

The few charioteers that had made it down the mountain pass fled quickly as they could not maneuver in the thick mud.

Aron jumped onto one chariot and quickly cut the man's throat. He looked back to see the last few chariots turning and heading west out of the valley.

"Buggers," he whispered to himself.

He ran back to join David as he fought his way through the Philistine line.

"Rally to me," David yelled. "Rally here."

Shimea, Yazan and Aron came to his side while many others followed. The men stood around him with a pile of spears and swords lying in the blood-soaked field.

Abner and Saul looked at each other and then laughed as they viewed the carnage that surrounded them. Saul went over to David where he towered over the bow-legged, red-haired cherub who wore a savage smile.

Saul put both his hands on David's shoulders in front of the men.

"A true warrior," he said.

"My king," said David as he bowed his head.

"Tonight we sup; join us at Gibeah," Saul said. "We have a family of travelers who will entertain us."

Saul turned with a smirk on his face and left the battlefield. Aron wiped the blood and sweat from his eyes.

"I don't trust him."

Shimea put his arm over David's shoulder. Yazan stood with a big grin on his face surrounded by dead bodies, limbs and men groaning in pain.

"Just like Damascus in the back alleys."

He put his long knife under his robe.

"I'd hate to meet you in Damascus," David laughed.

The Scorpion stood a little way off from the rest his sword held high in the morning sun while the rays glistened off his bald head. His robe was covered in blood. He looked around at the swath of blood he had made while standing with one leg forward and the other back in a warrior's stance.

"My stinger," he breathed, "Made of the finest Damascus steel."

He took his sword and wiped off the dripping blood with his robe.

The men trudged through the mud and moved on toward the rugged path that lay before them in the late afternoon.

"I'd hate to meet *him* in a Damascus alley," Yazan said as he walked on.

The small company of men laughed at this and the heaviness of war left their shoulders.

The Scorpion walked slowly behind and looked up at a rocky, windswept cliff as the sun slowly retreated from the valley and highlands. He smiled and picked up a broken box that lay in the mud.

"It was in a place like this I can imagine," he said catching up to David.

The Scorpion ripped three pieces of his robe and began to wrap them around the box.

"What?" David said as he shielded his eyes from the sun.

"With the wind blowing high up on a cliff. This is where he would want to talk with his people."

He continued to wrap the box.

"Who?" said David.

"Yes, he would talk with his desert people on a rocky cliff and lift up their spirits." He pointed to the ledge. "See, up in the hills."

David and his small band of men stood in the valley and looked up as the sun dipped below the mountains.

"The desert tabernacle, the windswept meeting place."

"The Ark," Shimea whispered.

"What do you know of The Ark?"

The Scorpion touched the broken box.

"If you are unqualified to touch or even look at the Chest of Testimony," he said, "You will die."

The men gathered around the Scorpion and sat down on the rocky desert floor. He began again:

"Those who bore the light box were forbidden to touch or look at it and it was covered with three layers; the first was a cover of flax, the second of goat hair and then a thick animal hide over this."

The wind blew across the plains and blew sand off the cliff tops that swirled in the air before it disappeared.

"This is why he traveled with your people."

The Scorpion waved his arms at the desert.

"So that he could feel the desert wind and you would not forget your roots."

"How do you know this?" David looked into the Scorpion's eyes.

"A Moab priest many years ago."

Yazan started to build a fire to keep the cold desert air at bay.

"Go on," he said.

The Scorpion looked at David, "You will know what to do."

"But how do you know so much?" Yazan said.

"I sat at the feet of a mad man," The Scorpion said, "and was taught the deep ways: the ways of the Tabernacle and The Ark."

As dusk fell around the men a scorpion appeared out of the broken box and then another and another.

Suddenly the box was on fire and the Scorpion dropped it while vipers and scorpions flowed from it like water in a stream. The box opened and its bright flames shot into the air. The men had to turn away from the brightness.

"Yes," The Scorpion said. "I have no power here. It burns away all vipers and scorpions in its path; all evil and darkness are banished by its power."

The men huddled together in fear but soon stopped and watched as the light disintegrated and it turned back to what it was, a broken box on a battlefield.

Chapter 13
Saul

"Do I kiss him or cut his throat?" Saul thought about David.

Torches were lit in the king's stone garden. Shadow and light played upon his jaundiced face as he turned toward his family and guests. Michal, his daughter, and Jonathan, his son, sat on a stone ledge while generals gathered and drank in small groups.

The night air smelled of jasmine. Saul, long and lean in his chair, stroked his beard and leered at the women who came and went with jugs of wine and beer.

"Listen," he called out to nobody.

"Abraham, Moses," he whispered while taking a large gulp from his goblet. The old ghosts seemed to flicker to life and turned their cold, dark features toward the new king of Israel.

"Oh yes, I will protect The Ark."

Saul gnashed his teeth and saw invisible spirits in the night. The king became aware of eyes like daggers upon him and sat up. He waved to his guests and then turned away.

"Children of light and dark," he muttered. He smiled at the generals and their men who now filtered into the small stone garden.

He nodded to Abner, the host of the guard.

"Who holds the tribes greater than himself?" he thought as he stood up quickly. "Where is David and his small band of brothers?"

He looked around.

"No, my king," a servant said as he looked but did not see the young warrior.

"Ah." Saul clapped his hands and a family of travelers appeared. "Tonight we have a small story to entertain us."

He clapped as two men and a little boy came to the middle of the garden.

"Quiet now," Saul said while putting a long, bony finger to his lips and then pointed to the travelers.

Michal, dressed in a silk gown of green and gold, came and sat at her father's feet.

A servant clapped twice and silence filled the stone garden. A tall wisp of a man emerged from the darkness, all in black and with a limp. He dragged his twisted frame to the middle of the garden then threw his dark cloak to one side.

The crowd stopped and watched the stranger half in sympathy, half in disgust.

"Welcome, my friends," he bellowed with a voice much larger than his tortured limbs would suggest.

"Welcome to this game played over earth and sky."

His cloak ruffled in the soft summer breeze.

"Welcome to the power of magic, the very trick of the tale. Welcome the players, the white and black."

He threw back his head and laughed.

"Raise a cheer and damn the blood-soaked ending."

He drank from a goblet and beckoned the crowd to drink. A loud cheer rang out after he toasted the crowd wildly and spilled wine on his cloak. He then put his fingers to his lips and bent close to the crowd.

"I say welcome to the battle twixt light and dark but now as I take my leave I request but one thing."

He looked darkly at Saul. "Let us play these games no more but rather drink or be damned."

He bowed.

"My king, ladies and gentlemen, a tale twice told of regret."

He bowed again and turned from the audience.

Two men sat down in the middle of the garden, a jug of wine between them. The small crowd was hushed while they watched the men in the flickering torchlight.

One man gulped the wine nervously and began, "She comes only at this time of night, the trees cracking and the wind blowing."

"Oh no, she haunts the waking hours also," the other said.

He drank from the jug as well.

"She preys on weakness; she waits for the right time to strike."

"Evil, I say then, evil."

The other man laughed.

"She is thinking of ways, weaving her stories."

The swarthy man grabbed his friend by the tunic collar and pointed upward.

"Do you see it, the web? Look how it shines."

The small audience settled down, relaxed and also looked up into the night air. The women held their men close to them.

Saul sat in a cold sweat. His skin was sallow and his breathing heavy. He looked at the young David as he and his men quietly entered and sat down. A wide sneer ran across Saul's face as he observed them.

Jonathan watched his father while Michal sat spellbound. Saul put his hands to his chest and muttered something.

The swarthy man began again, "See how the spider attracts the eye, her terrible beauty."

He stood up with the other man by his side.

"Come and see what loss and regret look like."

"Childish nonsense," Abner whispered.

"Shuuushhh," Saul said. He pointed his bony finger, "Look."

"I don't see the spider web," one soldier said.

The traveler began again, "Come and feel the pain of loss, come and see how your actions have set into motion a stream of loss. Years of trouble and turmoil, the loved ones left broken while you push on without thought or care and nothing to hold you down."

He wrapped his hands around himself.

"Look how she slowly wraps herself around the loss."

The audience sat still, each understanding how alone they were. They huddled together trying to forget the spider web. The guests were quiet as they felt their shortcomings and lost loves roll away in some dreadful game of chance.

Saul sighed heavily and wiped his brow.

"But you continue throughout the years not thinking of your actions, not understanding that the ones you made long ago are catching up to you."

A single torch glowed and a small waif appeared wearing nothing but rags and heavy makeup.

"Child," said the swarthy man who looked at him. "It is too late for you to be up."

"Yes," the other agreed.

The young boy stood in silence holding the torch. The audience was transfixed.

"The road is pitch dark and only the narrows of pain are open," the boy said.

"Nonsense. A good night's sleep is all you need," the man replied.

The child laughed at the man.

"Well, away with you."

The man turned from the boy. "Go away."

Then the two men followed the boy's gaze as did the audience and stopped in fear of what they saw.

"The web," the swarthy man gasped.

The web was now complete and heavy with its black netting and sad memories.

The waif continued to laugh at the two men.

"Poor souls, do not worry about me," he said as he watched the two huddled together on the stone floor.

They looked up at him and then down at the ground as they hid their heads in fear.

"Poor souls, do not worry about me. It is too late for you."

The audience became lost in memories as the cold night air wrapped them in a communal cloak of regret. The family of travelers stood and bowed to the small gathering.

Saul wiped his face and eyes.

"I must meet them. I must meet the child."

A servant went to the travelers and begged them to come over to Saul.

The man-child walked slowly to Saul while combing back his long, black hair.

"You had us all gasping," Saul said while he beckoned the boy.

The soldiers and generals clapped and drank more wine.

* * *

LATER THAT NIGHT

"My regret is not laying eyes on him first," Jonathan whispered in his sister's ear, his flowing cloak dancing gracefully in the summer breeze.

She pushed him away and laughed. "Whoever are you talking about?"

He turned and brought his full lips close to her face, "No one then, a mystery man."

"Oh, I like a mystery."

She sat down on a bench in her chamber while her handmaid started to brush her long, auburn hair.

Saul had picked the largest house in Gibeah to be his post during the war campaign and his family moved with him.

"But," she motioned her lady away. "I don't have time for one."

"What do you mean?" Jonathan asked.

"Dearest brother, we women work," she smiled. "I've tended to the animals, sorted and carded the wool once the goats were shorn and spun wool today," she giggled. "And you, what pray tell, have you been up to?"

"Oh nothing much."

He sat down on the wooden bench beside her. "Conquering the Philistines, retaking The Ark, small things."

She put his hands on his leather breastplate.

"Wasn't it father and that mystery man who did such things?"

"We warriors don't quibble about who has done what; we all pitch in."

The breeze blew in the small stone garden and light penetrated the darkest corners of the room.

"Miriam," Michal called. "Please make sure that the flax is dry before you use it and we need more pomegranate for the dye."

"More tunics and lovely cloaks for you," said Jonathan as he picked up his sister's flowing tunic and smelled it. "Just the thing to capture a mystery man."

She playfully slapped his beautiful face. Michal put her bracelets on her slender wrists and then put her necklace around her neck. She took her large, leather belt and gathered her *halug* up around her waist, its fringes at the bottom dancing with excitement, and then let it drop gracefully to the earthen floor with its deep, rich rugs that were in every room of the house.

She smiled at herself in the mirror and thought, "Simple and elegant like the princess of Egypt, not the she-devils who live along the Euphrates."

Her face is what many a man had fought over but none of them excited her.

"He makes my heart race fast as the wild ponies who dance across the desert," she thought to herself.

Jonathan looked at his sister and kissed her on the cheek.

"Beautiful but I saw him first."

He looked at himself in the mirror before quickly applying some eye shadow.

Later that night in the stone garden a soft breeze blew in from the desert, deep valleys and rolling hillsides. Torches were lit. The guests, generals and the few old men who ran the town of Gibeah mingled and drank wine and beer.

Jonathan and Michal stood alone looking out over the balcony and down into the street.

"Any sign of him?" Jonathan said.

"Who?" Michal replied.

"Our mystery warrior."

Saul's war house was the only place he had in which to entertain but could invite only a small number.

"He may come," she said, her voice trailing off as she watched soldiers drinking in the street and walking to the center of the village.

"Your yellow *halug* is beautiful." He said, "It brings out your lovely eyes."

"Stop." She wiped her eyes. "Father has been so brave and he finally is getting the respect he deserves."

"Look around us." Jonathan waved his wine goblet. "He invites generals who before laughed at him; he commands 3,000 strong, yes."

"Yes, it is his time and ours."

She looked at him as her tunic blew gracefully in the breeze.

"Our time to fall in love."

"This is not a palace of love; it's a war town," she laughed.

"Why not fall in love?"

"You are such a child."

Michal put her head on Jonathan's shoulder.

Saul came to his children and laughed while he drank from his cup.

"I see you are entertaining our guests."

"Ugly soldiers with bad breath and beards," Michal said.

"Honey, just try," Saul towered over Jonathan. "And you also Michal."

The three looked at each other their eyes glistening with humor and they burst out in laughter. The small crowd of men looked over at the balcony.

Saul turned to his company.

"The family curse," he said. "Too many bad jokes."

The generals laughed and nodded their approval. More wine was brought to the table already laden with fruit and meat while a harp player struck just the right chord.

Saul gave Michal and Jonathan a knowing look as he took his leave.

"Try," he said.

He wiped a smudge from under Jonathan's eye.

"I wonder what it would be like at Egyptian court," Michal said as she turned back to her brother.

"Excitement, intrigue, sex," Jonathan whispered. "All of what we don't have here in this puddle."

"I imagine servants bringing you down secret passageways to beautiful rooms."

She moved away from the guests and back to her post at the balcony. "And splendid clothes made of gold and silk."

"And sex."

"Yes, my little child, lots of that too."

"Did I mention sex?"

"You might have," she continued her watch over the balcony.

"Beautiful boys and girls together."

David and his men entered and filled the small stone garden. Yazan entered first in a brash way while Shimea followed behind him laughing. They had already been drinking beer in the street. Aron walked in under a somber cloud and headed to get more beer.

David stood in the doorway, his wool cloak dancing in the summer breeze. The Scorpion stood slightly behind his master and seemed to disappear.

"The warriors are here," Saul said as he walked to the group. "Come lads and drink."

He went to David and grabbed him by the forearm, "Welcome."

David returned the hospitality, "My pleasure."

Yazan walked to where servants began pouring the wine.

"We are small here but we are mighty," Saul laughed as he motioned around the stone garden. "Please come and sup."

Jonathan and Michal remained near the balcony.

"The heart is a hunter," Jonathan whispered.

"Shush, you silly boy," Michal said. Her eyes glowed.

"Father is upset," said Jonathan as he turned to Michal. "I think he does not like our young warrior."

Michal moved her gaze slightly.

"I've seen that look before," she said. "He is somehow jealous or angered by something. Did they fight?"

Jonathan put his finger to his lips and talked softly, "They say David hid The Ark but has not told father."

"Ahhh," Michal cast her eyes to the balcony again.

The 12 tribal chieftains gathered around Saul's home like a desert storm. Samuel the prophet sat in the corner watching the night. Judah came down from the high country, his robes blowing in the night air and his royal blue breast plate emblazed with a lion's head.

Reuben, Simon, Levi, Zebulun, Issachar, Dan, Asher, Naphtali, Joseph and Benjamin came from the wild desert with flashing smiles and holding their wine goblets as if they were hard-fought territories won with brute force and blood. Some were dressed in animal skins while others still bore the blood of battle. They swam in a sea of wine and boastfulness.

Dan clamped his shoulders on Zebulun.

"You fought like a warrior today."

"And you fought like an ass," Simon said. He moved toward the two wide-eyed and drunken. "Your men did not protect you and you were exposed."

Dan laughed and poked Simon in the chest.

"Follow me, my friend, follow me."

The rest of the chieftains laughed at this.

"Always first," said Joseph.

"What would a shepherd boy know," Dan laughed. "Where is the next ewe?"

He pushed his loins out back and forth, spilling his wine. "You'll look after her."

Levi, the only chieftain in a white tunic, turned away from Dan so as not to get his new tunic dirty.

"Not happy," Dan said to Levi.

"Keep your vulgar ways to yourself," Levi smiled at Dan.

"Ha, I saw you today your eyes wild with excitement and bloodstained hands, priest."

David watched the circle of men as they drank their wine and lied to themselves with old and new war stories in the cold desert air.

Dan spotted David out of the corner of his eye.

"Little whelp," he called out. "You and your men fought bravely today."

Aron moved toward Dan. "Whelp, is it?"

Dan lifted his goblet as if to avoid a charging bull.

"Slowly, friend," he said.

David waved Aron off and walked toward the drunken chieftain who towered over him and still carried his sword around his great leather belt.

"Whelp," he laughed. "Why don't I take a branding iron and whelp you?"

Dan put down his goblet and looked at David who was moving forward.

"Maybe the little whelp needs a lesson?"

"Maybe," said David as he continued forward.

The Scorpion went for his dagger under his tunic and Shimea moved closer. Saul stood back and watched from the balcony, a smile on his face.

The 12 tribesmen, even without the Philistines, would fight themselves to feed their bloodlust. Dan, wearing a breastplate with a lion inscribed in relief, took a step and then was looming over the smaller yet muscular David.

Dan breathed deeply as he stood watching for a moment of weakness. He moved a little to his left and to his right his arms out and hands open. David was a statue, eyes glaring.

Dan raised his hands and quickly picked up David in his bear hug. He patted him on the back and put him back on the stone floor.

"You are a warrior, my friend," he laughed. "No whelp."

He grabbed his goblet and swung it around for all to see.

"To David, son of Jesse." He looked all around him and eyed the twelve men. "The Lion Killer."

The men took up their wine and toasted David as he stood in the middle of the crowd.

"To the Lion Killer," Simon said.

Levi watched the redheaded man in front of him with his bright eyes and the way he stood.

Levi turned to Joseph.

"A man to follow?" he said.

"Perhaps," Joseph replied.

David looked around for his wine goblet and shouted.

"Listen, my brothers," he called out. "Tonight we raise a goblet to our King."

He watched everyone and raised his glass. Saul stumbled slightly and looked up as if from a daze.

"We come together, Judah and Israel, united in blood against our enemies and to bear witness to our anointed King."

He raised his glass and gulped briefly, "King Saul."

The cries went to the rooftops and back as Saul was toasted late into the night. For a moment the tribal chieftains put down their anger at one another and their battle for territory and banded together as brothers against the desert night.

Levi stood back a little and with a smile watched David. More soldiers and part of Saul's guard appeared in the stone garden. David was lost in the small crowd that huddled around the first real battle that belonged to the twelve tribes.

Saul drank in his victory and his face became darker. Michal drew her brother close to her on seeing her father.

"We must protect him from father."

She bit her lip.

"So you can bed him?"

"We must protect the future, child." She tugged at her brother's tunic. "Father cannot keep the tribes together but he can."

Jonathan looked at David, "He can do just about anything."

"Mind out of the gutter," Michal laughed.

He pinched her bottom.

"We are all there; it's just that some of us look up once in a while."

He laughed and sauntered off to fetch more wine.

David cautiously looked in Michal's direction and she smiled and then looked away.

"Comely but not beautiful," David thought.

Yazan brought another glass of wine to David.

"Here, my brave fellow."

David took the glass while being crowded by the soldiers who had just arrived.

Shimea came forward spilling his drink.

"We grow restless," he said. He gathered Yazan and David close. "Saul drinks more and his visage becomes muddied as if he plays with a dark secret."

"He drinks, what of it?"

David put his hands on his brother's shoulder.

"Nothing," Shimea said as he stumbled and laughed. "I'm drunk."

Saul had a few soldiers around him and they were deep in whispered conversation.

"So," one said.

"In the morning all will be made clear," another said.

"It's The Ark we are talking about."

Saul loomed above his crowd with his face a dark and nasty knot. Aron stood just out of the circle listening. He had his hand on his dagger under his tunic. David observed Aron and caught his attention. He shook his head and Aron retreated.

David looked over at Michal who was also watching her father. He bowed good-bye as she returned his gaze and smiled.

Yazan grabbed at a poppy seed cake and figs while Shimea finished his wine. They quickly walked toward the entranceway.

David headed for Saul's group. He walked straight through the men and they parted as he went up to Saul.

"My King," David began. "We thank you for your hospitality but we bid you good night."

Saul looked down on David.

"So soon?" He spread his arms out. "Stay, enjoy the night air."

"My lord, I must excuse myself for my men have drunk too much and do not behave well in such society."

"Warriors who cannot hold their drink," Saul said.

He laughed loudly. The others around him followed in unison.

"Does Bethlehem send me women?"

"Bethlehem sends you the finest cuts of men," David replied.

"Yes, yes. I mean no harm." Saul downed his drink. "More wine," he yelled.

With a great heave of his arm he launched his goblet out over the balcony and into the night air.

"How far can you throw, my boy?" Saul said as he turned to David.

"My Lord, you have the power to make things disappear, not I."

Saul looked down at David.

"Yes, you are right."

Michal came forward and took her father's arm.

"Come, Father." She took him around the waist. "Your daughter is cold."

She smiled at David.

"Leave the men to themselves and their drink."

Saul took delight in his daughter's touch and was led back to the stone patio.

"Why bother?" Yazan said.

"It's impolite not to."

David turned, his tunic flowing and walked out of the stone garden followed by his men.

Saul watched as the group left.

"Who is this David?" one soldier asked.

"Son of Jesse from Bethlehem," Saul said while still looking at the entranceway.

"I don't like him."

"Hmmm, neither do I," Saul agreed.

"Still, there is something there," another said.

"He and his men did well at Michmash."

The soldier drank more wine.

"Many did well," Saul said.

"You, my King, fought like a lion."

Saul drank from his goblet.

"We all did."

He turned his face away from the torchlight.

"Luck," the soldier said. "He was lucky."

"Killed a lion once with nothing but a slingshot," Saul whispered to himself. "Will he use a slingshot on me?"

The soldier turned toward Saul.

"You are our King, anointed by Samuel and loved by our people."

"Yes, yes," the King said hastily.

Saul had disappeared from the conversation and was now busy talking to shadows.

"He haunts my dreams."

He walked to the balcony and looked out over the war camp with 30,000 men, horses and farm animals huddled together against the night. Saul yawned and quietly moved to a corner of the balcony.

"I can offer my daughter as a wedding present or send him to his death. A scouting detail into enemy territory perhaps," he thought.

He rubbed his hands in the cold night air. The guests were now retiring for the evening and as they said good night he remained standing on the stone balcony.

"Yes, good night."

He waved them out and away. The war camp was still. The war chariots thundered in his mind while the sharp spears cut at his confidence.

"I am no king," he muttered. "I am a killer."

He saw a lone figure walking on the mud trail that snaked through the camp. The figure walked toward the stone house and seemed to look up into the night.

Saul froze with fear.

"He has come to cut my throat."

He dared not breathe so as to give himself away. The night guard turned and walked down the road again following his evening duties with a spear over his shoulders. Saul twisted his face in disgust at himself. His two guards stood in the entranceway of the garden.

"Why do you haunt me so?"

Jonathan had followed David out, his smile lighting up the path homeward.

"You were brave," he said while pushing up to David.

Shimea started to draw Jonathan back but David put his arm on his brother.

"My father was drunk."

"We all have our weaknesses," David said.

"He hates not knowing," Jonathan said.

"The Ark, you mean," David said.

They walked out into the air and the sounds of the army camp settling down for the night took over. Fires were lit, men sang drunken songs and the animals moved sleepily in their pens and stalls.

"Not just that."

Jonathan wrapped his tunic around his neck in the night air and hurried to keep pace with David.

"He seems jealous of you."

"Why do you tell me this?"

"Because we think you need friends."

David stopped in mid stride and looked Jonathan in the eyes. Their gaze met and they smiled at each other.

"You and the lady Michal."

"Yes."

David put both his arms on Jonathan's shoulders.

"Friends."

"Yes, friends."

He quickly looked around and then disappeared into the shadows.

"Be careful with this family," Shimea said as he caught up with his brother.

"Yes, brother."

The men continued on to their row of tents and bid each other good night.

At dawn a ram's horn blew loud and clear over the war town of Gibeah. Twelve priests stood in a line, their garments of white flax blowing in the breeze as they faced the soldiers who were gathering at the sound of the horn. The men came for prayer.

The Scorpion pulled his robe close to his body against the cold morning as he walked slightly behind David talking to himself.

"Their tunics worn to atone for killing, the pants to atone for sexual transgressions, the turban to atone for haughtiness, the breastplate to atone for errors in judgment, the ephod to atone for idolatry," he mumbled to himself his eyes on the ground.

The soldiers quickly made for the center of town where a high altar was built and one step below stood the military priest wearing white robes and a jeweled crown.

The Scorpion continued his morning sermon, "His golden garments were not sewn but rather woven of one piece of linen. And the bottom of his robes had bells and was a rich, red pomegranate."

The Scorpion continued with a darting glance at the war priests on the altar.

"*Shesh,* six."

The Scorpion looked down at the mud remembering his teachings by the Moab priest so long ago.

"The six threads each garment is made of."

Yazan and Shimea walked closely listening.

The Scorpion looked out over the crowd, "And they shall make the ephod of gold, sky blue, dark red and crimson, and twisted linen."

He continued to look down at the dark mud that covered the camp.

"And they shall make the breastplate of judgment the work of an artist."

Aron joined the men and yawned as he tucked in his dirty tunic and maneuvered his robes to keep out the cold.

"Why all this over clothes?" Yazan asked.

"The very clothes themselves are holy and give sanctity to those who wear them," The Scorpion said. "They are garments of the temple."

Other men joined the group as they moved toward the crowd that was gathering. The twelve priests stood facing the altar and the soldiers stood behind them watching and waiting.

"He is the Anointed for War," The Scorpion said as the priest moved slowly up the steps.

The war priest walked up to the altar and turned to the soldiers. He spread his arms.

"Now you have gone out to battle against your enemies and have seen horses and chariots and people more numerous than you and were not afraid of them; for the Lord your God who brought you up from the land of Egypt is with you. When you were approaching the battle, I came near and spoke: 'Hear O Israel you are approaching the battle against your enemies today. Do not be fainthearted. Do not be afraid or panic or tremble before them,' and you were not."

The twelve priests loudly began their prayers so that all could hear across the camp:

"Blessed art Thou O Saviour of Israel who didst quell the violence of the mighty man by the hand of thy Lord and gavest the host of strangers into the hand of Saul and his armor bearer! Shut up this army in the hand of Thy people Israel, and let them be confounded in their power and

horsemen; make them be of no courage and cause the bold-
ness of their strength to fall away and let them quake in their
destruction. Cast them down with the sword of them that
love Thee and let all those that know Thy Name praise Thee
with thanksgiving!"

The war priest began his story:

"So Saul established his sovereignty over Israel and fought
against all his enemies on every side: against the Moab,
against the people of Ammon, against Edom, against the
kings of Zobah and against the Philistines. Wherever he
turned he harassed *them*. And he gathered an army and
attacked the Amalekites, and delivered Israel from the
hands of those who plundered them. The sons of Saul were
Jonathan, Ishvi and Malki-Shua. And the names of his two
daughters were these: the name of the firstborn Merab
and the name of the younger, Michal. The name of Saul's
wife was Ahinoam, the daughter of Ahimaaz. And the name
of the commander of his army was Abner the son of Ner,
Saul's uncle. Kish was the father of Saul and Ner, the father
of Abner was the son of Abiel."

Saul appeared and went up to the altar and the army camp
erupted with cheers. Yazan, Shimea and Aron jumped up
and down and yelled wildly at the scene while David smiled
broadly. The Scorpion stood silently behind David.

Judah looked calmly upon the scene from his chariot.

"Will this united front hold," he said to his armor bearer.

Saul stood beside the war priest and bent his head as the war
priest blessed him and said:

"Therefore stand! Have the belt of truth buckled around your
loins; put on righteousness for a breastplate and wear on
your feet the readiness that comes from the good news of

YHWH's Shalom. Always carry the shield of trust with which you will be able to extinguish all the flaming arrows of evil. And take the helmet of deliverance along with the sword given by Spirit, that is, the Word of YHWH; as you pray at all times with all kinds of prayers and requests in the Spirit vigilantly and persistently for all of Yahweh's people."

Two nights later The Scorpion stood in the shadows of the quartermaster's tent as he kept his ear to the barn door where Saul and his men whispered.

The bald warrior priest kept one hand on his little stinger tucked into his robe.

"What of him?" Saul whispered.

"He is a good warrior," came a reply. "The people like him and come to know of him as your servant."

"They sing his praise?" Saul said.

"Yes, my King."

"Even over my victories?" Saul asked.

"Yes, he is one with the Lord."

The Scorpion tightened his grip on his sword.

"He is one with the Lord," Saul said slowly. "One with the Lord," he whispered.

Saul was lost in his hatred.

"I could win a thousand battles and take town after town but his name would still be over mine."

Saul gritted his teeth and smashed his fist into his glove.

"His songs would be greater than mine." He breathed harshly. "I see no relief."

"A scouting mission perhaps," another man said. "He may never come back."

Saul turned back to the group of men.

"Yes, perhaps."

The Scorpion released his grip and turned away quickly from the dark whispers. He returned to the small house that Saul had given David and his men and stood outside for a long time listening and watching the night by torchlight.

"Master," he whispered.

The Scorpion walked around the house bending low three times and then took a stick and made markings in the mud and sand around the tiny dwelling.

"Oh, Sekhmet, one who tightens the throat,
Protect this house and Master as you protect all from evil.
Lady of the Burning Sands,
Sekhmet, Mistress of Terror!
May no enemy find me,
May no harm approach me,
Your sacred fire surrounds me,
No evil can withstand Your Eye."

He walked three times more around and then stood in the cold night watching the war camp that was fast asleep. He entered and went to each corner of the front room where the spears and armor were kept.

The priest sat cross-legged in the middle of the room quietly rocking until he fell into a trance.

"Sekhmet," he whispered in the dark, "Sekhmet."

He continued rocking and coughed. He covered his mouth and continued coughing in the dark. He then repeated his prayer:

"Lady of the Burning Sands,
Sekhmet, Mistress of Terror!
May no enemy find me,
May no harm approach me,
Your sacred fire surrounds me,
No evil can withstand Your Eye."

The Scorpion continued coughing and began to choke on something. With his hand on his throat he fell prostrate on the threadbare rugs and began to roll in agony across the hard floor. He grabbed his throat with both hands and his face began to turn blue. He sat up and hit his back.

"Sekhmet," he gasped. "Sekhmet."

He fell to the floor again and was able to breathe slightly. The Scorpion lay quietly for a long time regaining his strength while staring at the ceiling. His eyes transfixed on something crawling above him.

Finally, he put his hand to his mouth and began to pull something from his lips. He held a small scorpion in his hands and watched the insect crawl down his robe and disappear into a corner. The priest did this seven more times until each creature had buried itself in a corner of the room.

He took a sharp stone from his pocket and began to draw a circle in the middle of the room with a woman's face adorned with a crown in the shape of a scorpion on top. He bowed his head to each corner and continued rocking.

"Master," he breathed once more before he fell asleep in the darkness of the small war house that was all that stood against Saul's poisoned mind.

* * *

A few days later Michal gasped as she took the game of Senet into her hands.

"All the way from Memphis, from Egypt."

The warrior priest smiled. The desert sun flooded into her room and scattered the darkness from the fat Scorpion's mind and so he would watch over her, quietly sitting in the corner soaking in the warmth of the sun.

"I hear everyone at court plays it."

Michal hugged the game to her chest.

"I asked a trader to bring it," The Scorpion said.

Michal sat down on her bed and drew her handmaid to her side.

"You play it on the board or can even scratch it in the sand," he laughed.

"I heard that even the highest of the high play it," Michal said and started to unwrap the game.

She stopped and looked at the bald priest.

"Is it true that boys there paint their faces and do their eyes and hair?"

"I hear it is true," Sarah the handmaid giggled. "The boys do it."

The Scorpion looked at the two girls as he sat cross-legged on a heavy reed mat.

He smiled, "Yes."

The girls flew into a fit of laughter.

"Jonathan would be perfect for Egyptian court," Michal said through tears of laughter.

Sarah grabbed Michal's arm and held her hand to her mouth as she shook in a fit of giggles.

"Maybe you could get him in at court," Sarah said to the priest.

"And he is a brave fighter, smart." Michal tried to control her laughter. "I guess he has to be wearing that eye blush."

The girls let out another howl of laughter and held onto each other. The Scorpion bent his head low as his face lit up with joy at the girls' laughter.

Michal tried to control herself as she began to unwrap the game and the papyrus fell away. As she did this, a scorpion slid out of the paper and fell onto the bed. The girls shrieked and moved quickly to the edge of the large mattress.

"Shush," the priest said as he went to the bed.

"It won't harm."

He picked up the tiny insect and put it on his thick, black robe. The scorpion crawled up his sleeve while the girls watched in horror.

"They are not evil but rather protect you from evil."

"Is it from Egypt?" Michal said with her knees up still at the corner of the bed.

"Yes," the priest said. "They are all the rage at court."

He took the insect, put it on the floor and watched as the scorpion crawled into a far corner and disappeared.

"See, nothing will harm you now."

The priest sat down in the middle of the room and looked at the two ladies.

"This game is not about chance but fate," he said as he looked at both of them. "Perhaps we play later?"

"No, now," Michal said.

"Yes, please," Sarah agreed.

"We should wait," said the priest as he put up his hands.

The women resumed their interest in the Egyptian game. The priest took the board and spread it out on the floor.

"We have 30 squares laid out in rows of ten." He pointed out the rows. "Some squares have symbols others do not."

The women drew close and finally sat on the floor overlooking the board.

"*Senet* means passing." He picked up the knucklebones. "And so we see who passes through good and evil spots on the board."

He threw the knucklebones on the board. At that moment Jonathan stepped into his sister's room.

"And the first one to be blessed by the gods passes into the after world," the priest managed.

"Games of chance," Jonathan laughed.

He looked at the sun flooding into the room and the blue drapes that Michal had put up.

"Yours is the best room in this drafty old house," he said.

"And now it's protected," Sarah the handmaid said.

"Oh?" Jonathan said.

"We have an Egyptian scorpion on guard."

She looked into the corner of the room.

Michal grew brave.

"Yes, brother, they watch us day and night straight from the Pharaoh's court."

"Priest?" Jonathan said.

He removed his breastplate and handed it to a guard who stood in the hall.

"Life is a chance."

Jonathan laughed.

"Yes, I suppose so."

He moved into the room, picked up the knucklebones and rolled them on the board.

"Where is our David," he asked. "We can roll our lives away at the chance."

"It's more about fate," the priest said. "We should play another time."

"David is right behind me," Jonathan said. "He was getting a new tunic."

Jonathan looked behind him to see David appear, his eyes on the board game in the middle of the floor.

"A game of chance," David said as he came in and sat down in front of the game.

"More of fate," said the priest as he grew exasperated.

Jonathan laughed and also sat down.

"'Tis our fate to play."

"Close the door and drapes then," Sarah said.

She stood watching while a guard closed the drapes and then left the room.

"Isn't this fun," Sarah smiled. "What trouble can we get into?"

"Sarah," Michal laughed.

David's eyes gleamed as he looked over the board at the different Egyptian symbols that he had no understanding of but that seemed to have an energy and tonality that he felt and absorbed.

"You pass between good and evil and onto many different and exotic adventures," The Scorpion said.

The four drew closer as they felt the mystical board pull them.

"Maybe we should play later," the priest whispered once more.

The Judean sun set low over the hill and highlands and the bedroom grew still with only the thick blue drapes heaving in and out with the evening breeze. The war camp seemed to disappear as did the mountains and hills; the soldiers' voices and the animals in their pens all seemed to lose their importance and the foursome breathed into the intoxicating world of the unknown symbols that lay before them.

"Be very careful," the priest whispered as the sun disappeared and the drapes heaved once more.

"Go first," Michal said to David.

She handed him the knucklebones. David threw and watched as the priest put him onto a square.

"Here," said The Scorpion as he placed David's piece on a brilliant blue sun with bright yellow clouds.

"Come," said the priest as he drew David close. "Look."

A young David touched his satchel and walked quickly on the stony path that lay before him. He did not make for the market but went across the deep Boa Valley where the farmers had spread the terraced hillsides with grapes, figs and oranges. The sun beat down and spread its rays over the orchards and trees that dotted the rough landscape.

As David walked and as the sun grew stronger, a dark storm grew. He looked up at Mount Gilboa and saw a brooding cloud hovering over the mountain. He ran through the fields holding onto his satchel as it flew by his side. Then he stopped as his thoughts swirled around him; he sat under a large tamarisk tree that gave shade to those thoughts.

"The Sons of Light and the Sons of Darkness," he thought as he pulled out papyrus scrolls and started to read:

"For the Instructor, the Rule of the War, the first attack of the Sons of Light shall be undertaken against the forces of the Sons of Darkness, the army of Belial: the troops of Edom, Moab, the sons of Ammon, the Amalekites, Philistia and the troops of the Kittim of Asshur. Supporting them are those who have violated the covenant. The sons of Levi, the sons of Judah, and the sons of Benjamin, those exiled to the wilderness, shall fight against them with [. . .] against all their troops when the exiles of the Sons of Light return from the Wilderness of the Peoples to camp in the Wilderness of Jerusalem. Then after the battle they shall go up from that place a[nd the king of] the Kittim [shall enter] into Egypt."

David put down the parchment and looked out over the fields and valleys drenched in sunlight. He put his hands up to shade his eyes and wrapped his head scarf tightly around his hair.

In the distance on the stony path, dust rose higher and higher in the air and Rider flew down the plains.

As David looked over the valley, earth and sky were tied in a hot, dusty knot. The dust rose higher and higher as the traveler made for Egypt. The sand and thick air turned the peaceful valley into a furnace. The dust continued to rise on the trail as Rider charged up the steep hillside through the inferno and came to a halt on the path close to where David sat.

Rider, dressed in a purple silk robe and purple headdress, put his hands on his two empty water bags on either side of the great, white Arabian horse. He moved his veil from his mouth.

"Lord of the Sheep," he called out.

David looked at the pathway and laughed.

"Lord of the Horse," he replied.

"The messenger for Pharaoh Thutmose III begs to know where he may find a watering hole."

"They are few in Bethlehem but travel ahead and you will be replenished."

"Come closer, my friend," the messenger said.

David rose and went to the path. The messenger put his arm on his jewel-encrusted saddle horn. His beautiful robe blew in the breeze as his horse whinnied. His spurs were made of the finest and sharpest iron. The whip was also jewel encrusted and had two rams' heads that came together in a ferocious roar. His eyes were clear and bright and he smiled a beautiful smile that put the dust and heat at bay and cooled the hot valley.

David took a piece of flatbread from his satchel and offered it to Rider. Rider's smile was an oasis. It was a calm that the boy had never felt before, not in his father's house with his hostile brothers or in the village with the mocking peasants who threw their disgust at him. Oh how he longed for such peace. Tears ran down the young boy's face as he looked at the beautiful Rider.

"I am the message," Rider whispered as his horse reared up and he disappeared in a cloud of dust.

David looked around as the wind echoed across the dry plains and trailed off into the high country. He felt empty and turned to make his way back to the village but then saw Mount Gilboa brooding in the distance.

He was drawn to it and began wandering toward the mountain paths that his mother had shown him. The trails and rough bush were his secret garden: he knew that his journey would not be along the sweet and easy ways that some traveled but rather through the narrows of pain.

Each step up the high country made him feel more clear headed, lighter and stronger. He recalled the line of lepers and how sad and lonely they had looked.

"Only the ninth leper turned to thank us," he thought. "Did they make it across?"

He secured his satchel around his neck and closed the leather strap. The wind and rain came down and he looked up as his face became wet. He felt welcome with the wind and rain, his father and mother, the high narrow paths, hearth and home. Each broken step and the forgotten path were an old friend receiving him after a long journey.

When he finally turned back, a gray veil covered the land and above a battle of light and dark raged over the mountain.

* * *

David shook himself as if out of a deep sleep.

"What?" Michal said.

David handed her the knucklebones in silence.

"Come look," the priest put her piece on the board. "Aye," he said. "Faraway lands."

Michal looked away and shivered in the cold night air. She wiped away her tears and did not speak.

"Perhaps we should stop."

The priest looked around the room.

"No," said Jonathan as he gripped the knucklebones and threw them on the board.

"Look then," the priest said. "Across the great seas to another land, another place."

Jonathan looked over the board.

The Rose came full of mercy and dark judgment, over the sleeping Moormund, patriarch of Greythorn, on the Isle of Burton.

Her breath became the very mist that clung to his hazy memory.

"You fools have learned little of compassion," she whispered through the dark labyrinth of Moormund's mind.

"The wicked ninth has caused much turmoil, this sending young Arlemay away so many years ago."

He drifted in his disturbed sleep, moving imaginary, heavy chains that bound his bloodstained hands and feet. He turned his eyes up only to look away from the brilliance that immediately blinded him. The cold stone floor became a refuge where he kneeled.

"I know, I know," the prisoner pleaded, grasping at straw with broken and bloodied fingers.

He nervously swept his hands over a long, dirty, gray beard and scratched his deep powerful chest before reaching out and clinging to the dungeon wall in terror.

"Please, I beg you, enough."

He trembled as he stood hunched against the cold stone wall, his face in his hands as the white winged vision rose momentarily only to vanish in the dawn of the new day.

"What? What have we done?" Moormund cried as he sank to his knees. "But it's not too late if we go back and undo the Laws."

He cried, "We can get our Arlemay back from the wilderness."

He fell weeping.

"He's not so wicked, not so bad."

Moormund breathed deeply and saw himself once again on that day: two horsemen galloping down the cruel coast as the wind blew up. The sea was angry, the sky brooding.

Bru grabbed a wineskin that hung over his saddle and quickly drank from it, gulping the wine until it spilled over his black cloak.

"Steady," Moormund urged.

He looked over at his second eldest son as they made for the town with the wind lashing at them.

"Steady," Bru laughed. "There is the world to be taken by force not steadfastness."

"You must learn when and how to take things," Moormund yelled into the wind.

"Like that little runt Arlemay."

Bru wiped his mouth with his sleeve.

"Send him away. He eats too much and even the dogs howl in laughter at him."

Bru's arrogance and cold heart could not be contained. They both slowed their mounts.

"He is your younger brother, only a boy of nine."

"He does not ride. He does not hunt with us. He is weak and as the old laws tell us, 'Ye may set forth one child so that the rest may live. Whosoever is weak shall be cast out as the wicked ninth.'"

The wind and rain swallowed the two voices. Moormund let out a deep nightmarish scream.

* * *

The priest sat up straight.

"These visions are not to be understood by us, they just are."

He looked at the four young people before him.

"Maybe we should stop and put the game away."

Torches were being lit in the cold hallways and a servant came in to light the torch in the room and build up the fire that had burned down to a few coals.

"But somewhere these are peoples' lives," Michal said.

"Yes and their hopes and dreams and heartbreak."

"And they have no meaning in our lives?" Jonathan asked.

"Only what you take with them," the priest said.

"But we can take wisdom from many places," David said slowly. "We learn from fools and kings."

"We learn about the community and how to live," Sarah said.

"Yes," the priest agreed.

"We should continue the game," David said.

"Yes, we should," Jonathan said as he wrapped his tunic around his shoulders for warmth.

The two ladies pulled a bearskin rug from a great chest at the end of the bed and pulled it over them as they sat in front of the game.

"It's my turn," Sarah said as she looked at the group.

She smiled and threw the knucklebones.

"Into the wild," she laughed and her brown hair fell around her face. She winked at David.

The priest motioned to her as she landed on another square that was black.

"Lady Michal," a voice called. "Saul asks you and your guest to sup with him tonight."

"Yes," Michal said. "Tell him yes."

"Lentil stew," Sarah whispered as she stared at the board game.

"Roughly chop the cilantro. Scrub the carrots then cut them into chunks. Cut celery into chunks, including the leaves."

She breathed deeply over the game as if it were a deep pot.

"I remember my mother's recipe," she recalled.

She drew her hand over the game and then smelled the stew.

She began again, "Chopped cilantro, carrots, celery stalks, olive oil, onion, garlic, red lentils, pearl barley, stock, cumin, hyssop or parsley, sumac and bay leaf."

The others drew near and breathed in the magical ingredients that held them all spellbound.

"I'm ravenous," David said.

He and Sarah looked at each other.

"Just for lentil stew?" Jonathan laughed.

"For many things," David said.

"Then we go," said the priest who bent to stretch his calf muscles.

Sarah began to cry, her long, brown hair falling around her shoulders as she held the bearskin rug against her.

"What's wrong?" David asked.

She wiped her eyes and stared at the board game.

"We can be so cruel to each other," she sobbed and David held her.

Michal and Jonathan also came to her side. The soldier appeared in the hallway.

"I fear your father is not well," he said as he fidgeted with the sword at his belt.

He bent closer to Jonathan.

"He has limped for days after the battle and talks of strange things."

"Thank you," Jonathan said as he walked with Sarah toward the great staircase that led to the floors below.

Saul emerged from the darkness dressed in black and limping from his battle wounds. The four stopped and watched him half in pity half in disgust as he walked past them and into the larger sitting rooms.

"Welcome, my friends," he bellowed with a voice larger than usual. "Welcome to this game over ancient earth and sky."

"Father," Michal said, "You have been drinking."

She came to him and put her hand on his shoulder.

"Welcome, the very trick of the tale, welcome players black and white."

Saul threw back his head and laughed wildly.

"Come inside, come inside."

He walked past and into the hall.

He turned on David as more guests arrived in the hallway.

"Are these the sweet faces that will calm my soul like harp music?"

He laughed and beckoned the men into the room. "Or do they cut me down like lambs to the slaughter?"

"You are the anointed one, my King."

David looked at the other guests entering.

"Yes, yes." Saul drank deeply from his wine goblet. "Raise a cheer and damn the blood-soaked ending."

He drank again and some men cheered as they walked into the hall.

The King bent low and put his bony fingers to his lips, "I say welcome the battle twixt light and dark but now as we sup I request one favor."

He drank from his cup again and shook his finger at David.

"Let us not play these games but rather drink and be damned to hell."

Michal went to Saul and sat down beside him helping to arrange his tunic and sit regally.

"You drink too much," she whispered.

"Not enough, my sweet one, not enough."

A young girl sat down and picked up a lyre that she began to play, the soft notes soothing the troubled guests.

A young boy who stood beside her, started to chant slowly:

"Adah and Zillah, hear my voice; you wives of Lamech, hearken to what I say: I have slain a man for wounding me, a young man for striking me. If Cain is avenged sevenfold, truly Lamech seventy and sevenfold."

Servants brought plates of figs and dates while others carried large jugs of wine and placed them on the wooden table.

The soldiers sat on one long bench while the officers sat at another and watched as more plates of food including lamb and beef were brought in.

"My sevenfold," Saul whispered while watching the boy sing. "To his seventyfold."

He shot the simple child a dangerous look.

"You mock me even in my house," he turned to sit up but was held down by Michal.

"Try the lamb, Father."

She broke off a shank bone and placed it on his plate.

"Dear lamb," he looked at her. "You know not what burns me, what haunts me."

"Not tonight," she said.

He seethed and watched the boy continue his lament:

"If Cain is avenged sevenfold, truly Lamech seventy and sevenfold," the boy sang sweetly.

"My seven to his seventy," Saul bellowed as he drew his dagger and buried it in the wood table.

The boy looked up as Saul looked down at his feet. A few soldiers stood up but then quickly sat down.

"Please, please," Jonathan stood up. "The boy's song rang true and we feel deeply."

There were whispers of appreciation for the song and the men went back to their enjoyment.

The boy huddled in the corner while the girl began to stroke the lyre's strings once again.

"He did not tell us of The Ark until the priest went to him," Saul began.

Jonathan and David sat across from Saul where the generals and chieftains were also engaged in their entertainment.

Saul eyed David as wicked thoughts rummaged around his wine-soaked head.

"He kept it from us, from me, for his glory."

He tore into a piece of lamb. As he did so he felt for his dagger beneath his tunic. The touch of the cool bone handle and sheath calmed him somewhat.

"I could give him everything and he would still take more."
He bit deep into the lamb. "He kept The Ark for his glory."

"Father," Michal said. "How is the lamb?"

"Yes, yes, my lamb, fine."

His eyes were glazed.

"Father, are you well."

"Dear sweet lamb, yes, of course."

The bone handle felt cool and warm at the same time.

The players continued to play while the men disappeared in
a world of food and drink.

Jonathan bent close to David.

"I love you so I tell you it's not safe here."

"Why?"

"Father grows more obsessed with you."

"Obsessed?"

"He sees you usurping the crown."

"I need no crown."

David gulped his wine and looked around at the battle-scarred
faces of his tribe.

"That is the problem," Jonathan whispered into David's ear.
"You must leave here."

David watched as his men drank the night away.

"And those loyal to me?"

"They travel with you," Jonathan put his arm on David's sleeve. "I would join you if not for my duties here.

David looked into Jonathan's eyes.

"I know this, my friend."

Saul slammed his fist on the wooden table, while his mind reeled in drunken and perplexed thoughts.

"No, don't cut his throat, better to, better to…."

The king looked around at his guests with a blank stare.

"Father?" Michal said.

"Banishment," Saul whispered. "Banishment."

He lifted his eyes to the ceiling and quietly rolled the word around his mouth, "Banishment."

Saul smiled.

"Hiding The Ark means banishment," he laughed to himself. "Seeing himself higher than me means banishment."

He rubbed his hands together.

"One hundred to my ten is banishment."

"Yes, yes, my dear."

Saul took Michal's hand in his.

"All will be well."

Saul took another gulp of wine and sat back in his chair. The noise around him and the boy's quiet chanting to the lyre music now calmed his turmoil. He looked across at Jonathan and David deep in conversation.

"Like love birds," Saul thought.

He turned away and smiled at some guests.

"No, don't worry," he whispered to himself. "All will be done before the two cocks can go gaming."

The king began to play with the dagger that lay on the wooden table, caressing the handle over and over.

The Scorpion moved close to David, inching his way through the wall of laughter and drunken men all the while eyeing Saul.

"Master," The Scorpion whispered.

He had been keeping watch over Saul as the night grew long.

The Scorpion put his hand on David's shoulder, "Master."

Saul pushed forward from his chair unbound with renewed vigor.

"Banishment is David!" he screamed.

He grabbed the dagger's handle and flung the weapon skilfully to bury the knife in the opposite wall.

The Scorpion moved in front of David. Soldiers stood up and began pushing each other. A group of guards came to Saul and surrounded him.

"Banishment is David!" Saul yelled again.

David ducked under the table and was grabbed by his men as they left quickly.

"Go quickly," Jonathan yelled while trying to keep the soldiers at bay.

The guards quickly took up the chant.

"Banishment," yelled one armed man.

"David is banished," the drunken men yelled, some laughing and some wearing dangerous smiles.

"Banishment, banishment!" Saul continued yelling as the cock crowed uneasily in the new dawn.

Chapter 14
Banishment

I Samuel 23, verse 14:

"And David stayed in the wilderness in the strongholds and remained in the hill country in the wilderness of Ziph. And Saul sought him every day but God did not deliver him into his hand."

Yazan and Shimea watched over David as he slipped in and out of consciousness. The fat Scorpion lit a fire in the cave as the band of men hid in the highlands from Saul's men.

"Hold him down," Shimea said as he tried to restrain his brother.

"He will hurt himself."

The two men tried to keep David from hitting his head.

"I am hunter and prey," David spat. In his sun-drenched mind the blood rushed in his veins and his eyes were steady on the horizon as he pushed his stead faster over the dark strip of barren wasteland.

He rode for hope and despair, he rode for passion and pain, the passion for his God and the pain of banishment. He rode for revenge and regret, the revenge in his heart and the regret that filled his soul.

His flight was straight and true down the narrows of pain. Shadows played upon the cave walls as his red hair blew about him.

"Banishment, you know nothing of banishment," he whispered as he galloped up the rounded hillocks of cracked red earth toward the winding narrows that now turned inward daring him, demanding him to go further and deeper into a web of treacherous and mangled underbrush.

A cold, black wind swept over the silent stone forest: the ancient trees with their broken branches leaned forward in anticipation waiting and watching as they held the sun back from its appointed rounds throughout the wicked glade.

"Such coldness," David shuddered as he continued. "Have I lost my way?"

He looked up at a darkened sky. "Midday but black as night."

He shrunk from the forest and looked up once more.

"Cold-hearted orb, what do you want of me?"

His mount reared in fear.

Outside the cave, the long trail of 200 men clouded the horse path for miles. Brush and sand blew as silence gripped the baked plains. These were the outcasts who followed David. Each man and horse, donkey and camel were links in a chain of isolation.

"You know nothing of me," he yelled into the wild.

He rode hard through the tough, dense brush that littered the high plains not knowing or caring about the mass of desperate humanity that followed.

Donkeys brayed and spat the hard truths of traveling in the wild.

"What do you know of banishment?" he whispered to himself as he crashed onward.

"I've suffered a thousand times more than banishment."

He dug his sandals into his war horse and felt the breeze blow through his rough linen tunic as a late afternoon wind picked up.

"Paupers who believe they are above me, town drunkards who laugh and you think your banishment will harm me."

The Scorpion wrestled with David on the cold earthen floor as he kept his charge from hurting himself. Shimea and Yazan watched knowing their turn would be next in the coming days and nights.

David guided his horse through the mountain trails that lay before him. The rich, red earth gave way to a stony path surrounded by twisted and broken trees, their horribly malformed branches reaching out along the path pleading for redemption.

"Is that it?" David let out a wild laugh into the wilderness. "The very trick of the tale the hunter and prey. I welcome this, the players, the white and the black."

The fat Scorpion held David close as he continued to talk gibberish.

"I say welcome to the battle twixt light and dark."

He sat upright on his mount.

"Banishment from a father's love, banishment from brothers' love, this is pain."

David breathed heavily and sighed.

"You do not know what true banishment is," he said as he turned his horse around and stopped on the thick broken path. "You play at it while I live here with my heart and soul. I am banishment! I am pain! I was raised on it, spoon-fed it through the years. It was in every meal I took, every grain of salt."

"I swallowed it daily," David yelled at the forest. "I am the King of Banishment."

Silence greeted his onslaught. He breathed the forest deeply and calmed himself.

"So this is my lot to stay in the brooding dark only to emerge that much stronger."

Aron took his turn and watched David. He gave him water and tried to feed him soup without success.

David hid his face from sight and tucked his chin under his keffiyeh as a storm blew up from the mountain pass.

Dark anger and judgment swept the earth and sky.

"This twist of fate," he whispered.

"Steady," David cried into the wind. He patted his war horse and pushed on.

The mountain pass closed in on the traveler as he slowly turned in the twisted labyrinth.

His horse lost its footing and whinnied in fear as it scrambled back from the edge of the cliff and onto the stony path.

"Good boy."

David did not look at the canyon below but rather sighed in relief as rocks fell off the edge and were heard far below in the deep gorge.

"Good boy."

He smiled slightly as he saw a Rose-colored light far off in the distance but was lost too quickly in darkness.

Slivers of light fell upon the mountain from above yet a gray fog hung from the sky and served to highlight the game of shadows that played upon the cliff tops.

David watched from his rocky perch but soon moved on toward a great stone staircase sculpted out of the mountainside.

He breathed heavily as the air became thin and looked up at the narrow way that wrapped itself around the mountain.

"Steady," he called to his mount as the horse took its first tentative step upwards.

"Upward, boy."

David patted his trusted mount and they ascended as one. He leaned close and whispered comfort into the animal's ear.

David blinked his eyes in the darkness of the cave as ghosts appeared before him.

"What is this Black Sabbath, this unholy night?" David said.

He saw shadows charging and reeled back to soften the blow.

Thunder and lightning raged over the mountain pass.

His horse dug his hoofs into the rich, red earth.

"Hold!" David yelled into the wind.

He steadied himself and gathered all his energy. He made ready to charge but something held him back.

"Anointed ones," he shouted. "I will not fight you!"

He felt his horse move as if they were struck from the side.

"Hold!" he cried into the wind. "Hold!"

He felt another charge and was thrown to his right, almost losing his leather stirrup.

"No," he shouted into the howling storm as he and his horse faced the whirlwind head on.

"I will not tilt at the wind and sand. I will not battle you," he yelled into the darkness.

"Anointed one, I will not fight here."

He struggled but managed to stay on his mount.

"Take some water," said Shimea as he made David drink from his water bag while helping him sit upright.

David looked at his brother and smiled.

"Where are we?" David asked as he looked out over the plains.

"Mount Nebo is to the east," Shimea pointed. "The Dead Sea to the south and the Jordan River is four miles to the west."

"The village sits in the middle," said Joab, Saul's former captain, as he walked into the cave.

"Are you well enough?" Joab watched David.

"Today we ride."

David stood up and put on his tunic and boots.

Below them was Jericho. Heavy clouds battled the sun as David's men made their way down the winding trails to the village.

Rays of light filtered through the gray sky and brought into high relief the shades of light and dark and the lush Jericho palms and life-giving spring Elisha.

As the wind beat about the small party David's emotions came tumbling down. He did not see the town for what it was and he could not see beyond the length of his sword for the lepers in his head.

"I say this battle twixt compassion and dark judgment."

He galloped onward. In the heat and wind the stone walls and fences seemed conjured by the very desert itself. The rough, thick walls were the skeletons of straw and brick.

"We must stop for water." The scout led David downward. "Ein as-Sultan Springs."

"We need food and water for the horses," shouted Joab into the afternoon breeze as he approached the party.

"David." He rode beside him. "I thought wolves or bears had you."

"They did."

Both men laughed.

"You're sure?"

Joab put a hand on his friend's shoulder.

"You will make a fine nursemaid one day," David laughed.

"I am already."

Joab smacked David's horse on the rear as it galloped off.

"Stay by him," Joab said quickly to the scout. "Protect him with your life."

The horses and camels whinnied and snorted as if to take in the momentary coolness.

Joab looked off into the distance.

"We need to reach the wilderness by nightfall."

The captain of the guard drank from a water skin and looked worriedly at David.

The horse slowed to traverse the steep, stony path but then charged up the hill in one final gallop.

"Haw, haw," David yelled as he spurred the animal forward.

Two guards dressed in light battle armor, leggings and leather breastplates, knives at their sides, approached the outcast.

"The villagers will tell Saul where we are," said one scout who pointed in the direction of the small oasis.

David's eyes burned with a passion brighter than the harsh sun.

"They can tell him what they will. We need to rest."

The barren landscape stretched for miles around the Dead Sea while only silence gripped the plains. An afternoon wind blew across the sands and toward the rough hamlet. Working dogs barked as they darted from one patch of shade to the next.

"We must survive."

David watched the jewel in the desert as a hunter stalking his prey.

"Philistines will rob and rape, why not us?"

He looked back at the wolves that followed him: mercenaries, malcontents and petty thieves chomping at the bit for blood and money.

"Let us hide our true selves," said David as he positioned his scarf to cover his nose and mouth. "With a Philistine's raid on this outpost."

The horsemen quickly gathered their energy and flew down the hills and valleys.

"Burn the huts!" Joab cried as he killed a man walking toward him.

David ran straight at another man, trampling him in his thatched doorway. The men circled the village and began systematically burning the huts. The women screamed but were cut down as they ran.

"Take all the grain!"

A shower of arrows fell upon more men as they approached the bandits.

"Burn it all!" David cried with his voice full of fury. "This is my gift to you, Saul."

His voice ascended with the rising smoke and wind. The wails of women and children rang out. The robbers looted the stores and strongholds of the town. Donkeys and camels were loaded with supplies.

Out of the bloodshed and carnage walked a young boy, full-lipped and beautiful, the sun spiking behind him to create the image of a golden crown. His lovely legs seemed to carry him effortlessly through the fog of this little war. Although each of the bandits saw him not one would touch the man-child as he approached.

David turned to see the boy but was blinded by the sun's rays that for a moment seemed to cast a divine light over the child.

David charged. He first cut the boy down at his legs. A scream rang out as he fell to the ground holding his leg. David dismounted, his eyes never leaving the golden child.

"All of the children."

He walked over to the wounded boy and slashed his other leg as the men watched.

"Not a boy or child will be left to hunt me down."

He stood over the poor child and without hesitation took his sword in two hands and struck his breast and then the slender neck.

David turned away and said nothing as he mounted his horse. The fury in his mind raged as he tried to calm himself.

"Strike at the heart without mercy," he thought. "Saul's sons and their children must not have a hold in my kingdom."

He saw himself cutting into the flesh of Saul's line: Abinadab, Malki-Shua, Ish-bosheth and even the girl Merab was not to be spared. He felt Saul's noose closing on him.

"We can eat and drink again like men, not like animals," one thief laughed nervously as he strapped jugs and water bags onto a tethered ass.

He slapped the animal's rump and caught up with the others as they formed a path toward the outreaches of the tiny kingdom that stood in the shadows of the great Egyptian and Mesopotamian empires.

"What will become of us?" he whispered as he wiped his brow and peered up into the angry sun.

The man shook his head and disappeared into the sands as the great line of animals began a slow march into the unknown. The trail of bloodshed and tears lingered on the wind.

"Now we disappear and wait out Saul."

David breathed heavily as he took off his scarf and wiped his mouth. He drank lustily from a water jug.

"Hurry," Joab yelled. "We must make the hill country by nightfall."

The train of horses and donkeys heavy with supplies slowly moved deeper into the wastelands. Whips flew as the call of men pushed the line forward.

"Hawwry!" cried the horsemen as they guided the beasts over the sun-drenched land.

Two scouts rode hard for the hills in search of camp.

David nervously glanced up at the silent blue sky. He looked back at the smoking huts before galloping off into the desert.

The stone walls that hugged the land and kept the sheep from straying slowly disappeared. The men entered the wasteland of sun and sand.

"A simple farmer," one of David's company said to himself.

He turned back to see the last stone field. "I should have become a simple farmer with a wife and children."

He struck the donkey again and shuddered as the next stony hill grew larger in front of them then gulped water from a jug and swung it back on his shoulder. He closed his eyes and dug his thighs into the animal forcing it on.

He coughed up dust and spat it out.

"A simple farmer," he cried to the cruel sands that swept him along.

Later that night the air was thick and hot. The two scouts had found a hole in the wall between the mountain ranges that was hidden by trees and brush.

David settled in a rocky nook and looked out into the night sky.

"And what now?" he sighed.

"You will continue," the voice whispered.

"Hunted like a criminal, like an animal."

"This is your wilderness but you will see beyond."

"My eyes burn with hatred. I cannot see beyond this cursed wasteland."

"Many places will burn but you will survive."

David looked out upon the quiet desert and rubbed his tired eyes.

"I will bend but not break," he thought.

Laughter rang in his ear. Then he heard his mother's voice in the desert wind.

"My boy, my David," said Nitzevet over the desert sands and straight to his heart.

He blew a kiss to the wind and watched the night fires languish in the late evening while composing a letter of regret to her:

"Oh, Mother, how I regret this battle between Saul and me, this war.

Am I doomed always to be an outcast? From youth to manhood, I have always been alone. You know how my brothers treated me, how Father never accepted me as his flesh and blood. How the goat herders and drunks of Bethlehem taunted me without rebuke from my father. Why?

Why, Mother, why do I feel so alone, so unworthy?

What is it inside that demands that I am so different, so totally alone and separate from other men?"

Chapter 15
The Desert Tent

Grail, a prince from Greythorn Castle and the Isle of Burton, with his traveling companion Squire Polo travels to the East in search of adventure....

Mount Gilboa's hills stood smoking from the fires of war. Below the craggy mountain and deep in the Beit Shean Valley, the desert wind whispered of King Saul's death. The fields spread far over the plains until they merged with the pale blue sky under the harsh Judean sun. Wild rust-colored flatlands stretched far into the valley only to be broken by thorny, gnarled plants scattered over the rough trails.

Grail continued at speed upon the ribbon of dust, headed for the small village of Hebron. A letter of safe passage written by Champendeau, hastened him onward.

"How old and rough is this land as if some ancient potter had molded it from clay," the pale knight wondered to himself.

He slowed his horse and looked behind at the trail of dust that was his companion Squire Polo atop their beloved donkey Flag.

"Well, Sir Polo," he called out as he turned his head to face his squire.

"How is our Flag today?"

His charge fell backward and landed on the stony trail with an unceremonious thump. The knight rolled his eyes and dismounted quickly to help the fallen lad.

"Polo?"

"Y-y-yes?" said the red-faced boy as he stood and dusted himself off.

"What are you doing?"

"A sound made me turn back."

"Polo," the knight intoned firmly, "Remaining on your mount despite distractions is of the utmost importance to a horseman."

He reached down and gently lifted the fair-haired child back onto the donkey. He swatted Flag on his rump and the beast trundled along.

"Here is money to find lodgings for the night. You may go ahead and secure our beds at the village."

"Yes, Master!" Polo's cherubic face beamed.

Grail laughed.

"On second thought, it might be better if we stay together."

"Yes, Sire," he replied meekly.

"And Polo?"

"Yes, Sire?"

"Stay on your mount."

Grail felt the hot wind on his face and heard Champendeau's burly laughter ringing out like shards of sunlight in the tall shadows of Mount Gilboa.

"You will find food and lodging under your fingernails, my boy. Olive gardens, sweet food and wine await the weary traveler."

He slowed to wait for Flag who brought up the rear.

"The old war horse," he thought to himself.

Moormund was father but Champendeau was mentor.

Truly my guide, he thought with gratitude and a hint of sorrow. That damned old man sensed abilities and greatness in him that no others could even begin to recognize. He understood the knight's need for perfection, his absolute hunger for challenge.

So he nurtured this with an intense regime of training and schooling. In time few would be able to equal the young man's skills and he remained matchless in matters of duty and discipline. Only one matter of the heart marred his perfect record and he held that pain tightly and deeply so it would never hinder his prowess as a warrior.

"With great gifts come great responsibility," the general had taught his student.

The apprentice and the old war horse campaigned in the rainy hills of the Brodish lands.

Mist played havoc along the banks of the Bromain River and kept the two armies spellbound. At the final battle, the warrior prince outmaneuvered his enemy by traveling up and down the banks until the enemy became weary with confusion and wet with despair. Then, during a daring night raid, Grail's men crossed the river and slayed the sleeping soldiers.

The Brodish king surrendered unconditionally.

The young knight allowed the King to remain in his seat of power while taking the best warriors as slaves. After good service in the army the men were able to buy back their freedom three years hence as citizens of Greythorn.

Grail's name became both feared and revered. In these dangerous times a whisper of his name could open the major crossroads for trade in the known world.

Eighteen months after the campaign, Greythorn had expanded its lands by 250,000 square miles and men were sent to the frontiers to manage and settle new villages and lords were given new lands to rule over.

Grail returned home with his grandfather's body and a trail of 20,000 men, soldiers, women and children, exotic animals, oxen, goats and sheep — all spoils to the victor. He however returned to Greythorn not as the conquering hero but as a grandson in mourning.

Royal guards with the king's purple flag swept down the field road.

"Stand aside," cried one soldier as the men crashed forward.

Grail's remembrance of youth past was violently shattered by the onslaught of horse hooves.

"Next I'll be falling off my horse like Polo," he chided himself harshly.

Flag brayed bravely at the intrusion and showed yellow teeth through her bit. Grail held his rein tightly.

A solemn procession of four beautiful white stallions, each with the royal seal on its headdress, trotted within sight. They cut a wide swath across the plain. In front and behind were heavily armed guards.

The dust on the trail rose up and for an instant smothered the sun in a sad gray pall.

Ner, captain of Saul's host, rode slowly in front of the procession. The King, the anointed one, anointed over Gilead and Ashurites and Benjamin and all of Israel, lay dying. He was mortally wounded, his long hair and beard matted with blood. His eyes looked into the distance. The chariot bearing King Saul was heavy with sorrow and slowed to a stop.

In the middle of the chaos, David tried to stem the tide of blood flowing from Saul's wounds. The guards looked on with stern blank stares.

He noticed the pale white knight on the road and then returned to his sad business.

David had Saul's head cradled in his arms while the King took his last breaths.

"Too much blood," David whispered as he looked at his hands and wiped them on the gray robe that hung from his light breastplate.

The chariot lurched forward and began its sad march as the horses trotted woefully. A sea of red spilled onto the horse trail. A light summer rain fell over the mountains and through the valley and washed Saul's greatness into the Sea of Galilee.

Grail looked behind him and up at the fires that still burned brightly on Mount Gilboa.

"Remember this day, my boy."

"How have the mighty fallen?" Polo asked innocently.

The procession continued down the holy road until it stopped under a tamarisk tree on the way to Jabesh.

Grail's journey took him to the hills of Ammah through the wilderness of Gibeon and finally to Giah. As he rode through the small villages and towns, he heard the wailing of men and women and understood that a great loss had befallen them. But even in their pain they remained strong and beautiful in his eyes. The men were sun bleached and sturdy, the women exotic and wistful. Sorrow and mystery cloaked these people yet their God walked beside each man, woman and child under the harsh desert sky.

At sundown, the two travelers stopped at a squat, two-storied inn. Grail walked through the palm-lined entrance, found a table and sat down.

"Greetings, traveler," a young man said. "And welcome. What may I offer you?

"Hot soup and your bread," Grail said as he looked at the boy. "Much has happened today?"

The young man looked back at his sister, a tall girl with long, black hair who was behind a wooden bar making food.

"The Philistine archers," the boy looked down at the floor in shame. "It is a very sad day. Our women cry in the streets and our men rail at the King's death."

"You will rise again," Grail touched the boy's tunic. "I sense greatness in your people."

"And how is that, stranger?"

"In your bearing."

"What is your name, sir?" The boy looked up at the large knight.

"Grail."

"Gr-a-il?" he played with the name.

"I am Second Samuel, son of Samuel, and that is my sister Hannah but don't worry about her."

"Where is First Samuel?"

"He is sick in bed."

Second Samuel's gaze met Grail evenly. "But I look after the inn."

"Good."

Grail handed his saddlebags to Polo. As he stretched his aching muscles and relaxed into the wooden bench he noticed across from him an old man and his students gathered together whispering urgently.

The man held out a worn leather satchel and intoned across the wooden table.

"In the cave," the sage whispered. "I must tell Zadok."

"How can this be after 1,200 years?" he whispered reverently. "The scorpion and the desert viper."

The wise old man stroked the leather bag and motioned the others to join him. The five black-robed men moved away from the table in a flurry of whispers and rustling robes.

Grail returned his eyes to Second Samuel arriving with his meal followed closely by young Polo who eyed the plates eagerly.

Philistine archers were drinking loudly in the corner.

"And smote him down," a large soldier bellowed across the floor.

He pretended to take an arrow from a quiver and fired it into the air over and over. He laughed loudly while continuing his barrage. The soldier aimed in Grail's direction and let fly an invisible arrow.

"What do we have here?" the soldier cried. "A guest in our land."

He looked at the large man dressed in a light tunic and cloth pants, his golden hair hanging to his broad shoulders.

"A stranger and his girlfriend."

"I'm no girl."

Polo began to stand but Grail's strong hands held him in place. He looked at the soldier and smiled a cold, hard smile.

"A stranger without a tongue," the soldier continued.

"No," Grail replied, "A stranger who is to be left alone."

"Where are you from?" demanded the large archer.

"Across the seas."

"Ah, a fisher of men."

"Grail is no fisherman," Polo excitedly yelled. "He is a great knight."

Mybad, the Philistine captain of the guard, stood back, hands on his hips and began to laugh.

"Where have I heard that skinny little voice?" he said through his amusement. "It sounds like my boy."

"My nephew," Grail introduced Polo in an apologetic fashion.

"It is difficult to make men of them. Some are not worth their salt," said the captain as he settled.

"I have no salt, however, if you are a gambling man," the knight raised an eyebrow and gave Mybad a grin.

The captain looked back at his soldiers.

"That I am, sir."

His soldiers turned with interest eyeing Grail cautiously.

"So! Is he a fighter?" one of the soldiers asked.

"Is he a fish fighter?" another laughed.

"What do you have in mind?"

"I'll tell you. Let us arm wrestle for the boy." Grail eyed the drunken man with shrewdness. "If you win, he is your slave for a fortnight."

Mybad laughed loudly and drew near.

"That is a bet I'll take."

He stumbled while looking back at his comrades.

"If I win, he is my slave."

"Done."

Grail looked at the lad.

"Have no fear, Polo."

The boy looked beseechingly at his uncle.

The captain rolled up his sleeves with his bulging forearms on display.

"I'll show this fisher of men how it's done."

Second Samuel looked up from behind the wooden bar.

"We don't want any trouble."

"This will be no trouble at all, my boy," Mybad sneered. "I'll be quick about it."

Grail rolled up his sleeve and faced the captain of the Philistine guard with a respectful bow of his head. "Come and hold us steady, Second Samuel."

The young innkeeper held both men's elbows in place upon the bar.

"Ready...Steady....Go!"

The two men were evenly matched. Their faces showed strain, one losing advantage as the other took it. All eyes were on the two large men.

"Look, the stranger is winning!" a slight man in a long, brown smock and sporting a rather prominent gold tooth yelled out in dismay from the party's table.

"I put ten shekels on the fisherman," another shouted out.

"I'll hold the money," the one called Patch-Eye yelled.

The focus shifted to the one-eyed soldier who began taking the money and scratching down bets.

Grail and the Captain battled back and forth each desperately seeking a weakness in the other. Their faces became red with strain, their arms locked in a ferocious contest.

"Come on!" both Polo and Samuel screamed in unison.

With one last great effort Grail began his final assault.

"The fisherman *is* winning!" cried out the man with the makeshift crutches, barely sitting in his place in the corner.

The crowd pushed as close as was safe to the Herculean battle. Slowly but surely Grail began to move towards victory. He'd let up a little and then force his arm down, let up a little and then down again. The knight was clearly in control.

Sweat broke out on the Philistine's face. Grail made his final move and with a quick jerk pushed the captain's arm down solidly onto the bar.

Patch-Eye got to work doling out the winnings.

"A fight well won."

The captain rubbed his arm and slapped Grail soundly on the back.

"Drinks for all!" Mybad ordered with a laugh.

"You better get upstairs and rest," Grail whispered to Polo with a wink.

"Yes, Master," he said as he quickly disappeared behind the staircase.

"That fisherman gave me quite a catch!" the one-eyed soldier said rattling his heavy coin bag.

"He is not just a fisherman," a soldier who had remained quiet during the contest commented solemnly. "He has royal bearing and military training."

"Let him rot in the sun for a while," said Patch-Eye as he continued counting money and pocketing coins. "That will cure him."

Grail quickly downed a shot of a clear liquid and patted two or three men on the back as he headed upstairs away from the now-crowded inn.

Polo appeared in the darkened hallway held firmly by three men Grail did not recognize.

"We mean no harm," a young soldier whispered as Grail pulled his dagger out of its sheath.

Polo's eyes widened in fear.

"Unhand my squire," Grail said.

"It is important that you accompany us into the desert," the soldier said. "We are King David's men and no harm will come to your boy. We have horses waiting. Come with us now."

They slipped quietly from the small inn and disappeared under the cloak of darkness. They flew past wells and huts and soon found themselves far from civilization. Although the paths were treacherous the three horsemen handled them expertly as a cool breeze blew in from the coast.

The four men and the boy continued until the road began to follow the coast. The waves from the sea broke heavily on the beach below and the horses traveled down toward the water on a steep and narrow path. Soon the wet sea air rose up and splashed the men's faces as they galloped along the coast.

The horsemen came to a steep hill and worked their way down to an army camp on the shore of the Sea of Galilee.

"Halt," the stern-looking soldier said.

He stopped his horse and came around to Polo's side. The sound of donkeys braying and camels spitting became louder and louder as they approached. Rows of tents were illuminated in the moonlight.

Fires were lit at the end of each tent row and men huddled around them, some standing and talking while others looked at the fire. Whispers of battle spread over the camp in a wave of nervous emotion.

"At dawn," one soldier said.

"A few days," said the other.

"The Ark will have a place to rest."

"We have wandered for too long."

"It will not be easy. They say that blind men could guard Jebus."

"David will find a way."

"Who goes there?" came a voice from the dark.

"The Lion of Judea," came the reply.

The party emerged from their night journey and entered the camp. Barefoot servants flashed inquisitive eyes and then disappeared. Two soldiers led the horses and Flag to be watered and fed.

The men walked down narrow rows between tent stakes and supplies that led to the main campground. In the middle of the encampment stood a majestic tent larger and taller than the others and beautifully wrapped in reds, browns and orange. Nine large torches surrounded it with two guards at the entrance. Spread before the tent was a long wide archway that extended along the sand.

"Holy," Polo whispered as he took in the desert splendor.

"Quite an adventure," Grail whispered to the boy.

A woman approached the men with a flask of water.

"Tsk, tsk, this young one will need some food and hot mint tea," she said as she gave the soldiers the water and led Polo away.

"Come," the soldier said, "It is time."

He guided Grail toward the great tent and walked by his side as they passed guards and entered David's world.

"So let the players play," Samuel whispered as he arranged his robe and disappeared into a quiet corner.

Inside the massive tent a fire burned and a robed, bearded man sat at a large wooden table. Its legs were carved with bygone battles and in its center a beautiful rose was engraved. The table was large enough to seat 24 and was segmented into green and white sections. Six men sat on each side and at the end sat a squat, muscular, bearded man making their number 13.

Grail recognized him instantly as the one who had accompanied Saul's death procession in the Beit Shean Valley.

"See what brilliance surrounds him," Samuel nudged his quiet disciple. "Watch and behold."

David cut an apple. As his gaze turned to Grail the knife slipped and a drop of dark red blood dripped into a beautiful blue goblet adorned with golden Hebrew inscriptions that had been resting at his hand.

The inscription read: "There shall step forth a star out of Jacob and the Messiah shall rise out of Israel and shall smite the corners of Moab and break down all the sons of Seth."

Samuel watched intently. His followers gasped but the old prophet smiled with pure and growing joy. He quickly reached for the sapphire blue goblet and it disappeared into the shadows.

"And so it will be," he whispered to himself.

"Grail, a precious legacy."

Zadok the high priest quietly kissed his shawl and silently looked on.

A rush of wind blew into the tent and a heavy rain began to fall upon the desert camp. Outside, men's voices rose as if in prayer. The soldiers spread their arms wide and rejoiced, raising their faces toward the Rose-colored sky.

The atmosphere in the tent became festive. Servants appeared from the shadows serving grapes, olives and cheese.

"You are the uh, how do you say," David began in a deep desert accent. "The pale knight on the road?"

He turned brilliant brown eyes toward his guest.

Grail bowed.

"Yes."

"We are," he said, pointing to the men at the table, "Joab, Abishai, Shimea, Aron, Jehoshaphat and Zadok. We are desert tribesmen."

"And I a simple traveler," Grail said with a respectful nod.

"Yes, yes, drink some wine." David clapped his hands heavy with rings and bracelets of gold and a servant emerged with a goblet of wine.

"We have found a note on your belongings from Samuel to your Champendeau."

"My grandfather. It was written many years ago."

"Samuel is one with the Lord. It is good."

Samuel's eyes glowed in the darkness as the fat Scorpion sat at his feet with a few disciples of the old prophet.

"What balance does this pale king hold?" David wondered.

David swallowed grapes and put some cheese on flatbread. A new goblet was put before him. He drank deeply.

"How far is your home?" he asked.

"Over the seas," Grail replied. "The Isle of Burton and my ancestral home Greythorn."

"Greythorn?" he said slowly. "Maybe I should visit your Greythorn one day?"

"You would honor us."

"But why are you here?

"To see new worlds."

"New worlds."

The strong desert man thought for awhile and then wrapped, "New worlds," around his tongue with his deep accent.

"But you are a fighter, a military man at your Greythorn."

"Yes," the knight replied, "But we explore."

"Explore, yes, I see. We are too busy battling for territory for this exploration," David said.

His men let out a chorus of sad laughter at this remark.

"I witnessed the fires on the mountain," Grail said.

"Yes," David said. "A sad day, but if tears saved our people, I would always cry to fill the void with water."

The broad-shouldered man stood up. He wiped his eyes and went to the tent door. The others stood watching and waiting for his command.

Zadok stood up and motioned to a scribe who sat behind the men.

"Tell it now and write this down."

He motioned to all.

"Lest ye forget this day that there will be many pretenders to the throne of the King of Kings. But there is only one king and he alone with his powers will draw a line of succession. His light will shine through the darkness and it is his line that all men will want to branch from, the King of Kings. They will beguile you with tales of great knights and men who claim to be children of God. Be not fooled. For only David's love will create goodness and his blood will be that which men will hunt for down through the ages."

Zadok finished with a flurry and turned to the scribe.

"So it shall be this day as the light floods in from the darkness."

The high priest looked sharply at the men before him.

"Dare not question the truth of The Ark of the Covenant or the beauty of your music."

Zadok rose from where he sat as a harsh judgmental wind blew through the tent and ruffled his thick camel hair robes. He raised his hands in fear and prayer.

"Jebus is yours."

"And the pale knight in our midst?" David said.

As the two men left the tent Zadok spoke, the wind whipping his long, white hair.

"Take him to Jebus with you. Let him touch the hand of God and it shall pass that he will bring light to his world through you for they will build a strong nation down through time and with our enemies all around us they will stand by the City of David."

"He is a clever military mind. I feel it," David replied.

"Use all that he knows of war," Zadok agreed.

"Cleverness like a fox," said David as he drifted off in thought. "Always watching and waiting for the perfect time to strike."

"Think more about your great vision and not so much of this pale war chief," Zadok counseled.

"We will teach each other," David countered. "I sense greatness in this stranger, this tightly wound man who is lost among the sands. This desert fox."

Zadok sprang up and shouted, "Oh my sweet David, why ask these questions? Why think about it? You and you alone are the Ninth Shepherd, the foundation of Israel."

At Zadok's words, The Ark shuddered and opened wildly as it flipped in the wind and a burning light jumped from page to page.

The wind howled around the two men. They held each other and quaked in fear as the sandstorm surrounding them rose to full force for a terrifying moment before subsiding.

David shook the sand from his robes and began to walk and as he did rose petals flowed gently from his footsteps. The flowers were carried on the wind while his men looked on in amazement as the Rose Petal King calmly surveyed the troops.

Some soldiers bowed their heads as he walked while others turned away with tears in their eyes.

The Rose shed ancient tears for the dead and dying, the suffering and the lost.

As her tears fell on the sweet garden floor, a slight rain fell over the city of Jerusalem and further into the City of Palms. A lone Bedouin looked up from his desert camp and cried as rose petals fell in the soft summer rain.

He picked a rose and then blew the petals on the wind. Through the northern gates of the city of David, a breeze blew across the Temple that caused Zadok to cover the pages of the Talmud and the veil that covered Queen Zenobia lifted slowly as her smile shone brightly over the desert sands and further out to sea and across the shores to Greythorn.

As The Rose held her head up and continued to cry the waves grew high and light danced across the cruel sea. The fields of wheat and barley swayed under an angry sun.

The Great Hall of Lower Light was ablaze with a relentless light that found its way into each and every dark recess.

As the rose petals blew on the wind over the garden, one by one signal fires lit up the mountain ranges below.

The breath of The Rose pushed David as he traveled at speed.

"Our hopes and dreams rest on you heavy as the deep sand that lies before you," she whispered.

The royal flag bearers and entourage were far behind gathering up courage in the valleys below.

The Rose then took up her sword and commanded the light bearers as they waited dutifully with quivers full of light.

Her piercing gaze lit the mountain post fires that David and Grail crossed.

"Stand guard!" she whispered at the top of the last mountain post.

The war horse reared on his hind legs as the two riders crashed on into the darkness.

"Hold!" Grail yelled through the wind and snow that surrounded him. "Hold, Arserbarb."

"Let them to their business," Princess Rose whispered. "It is theirs and theirs alone."

The mountain fires down in the valley were dwindling and giving way to darkness but rose up with her precious breath.

David rode on through the wind and cold never stopping, never looking back. He took hold of the reins with renewed energy and felt his youth in his veins. The mountains around him seemed to give him safe passage and he heard a rumbling from above.

"David," came a whisper from above. "Be strong. You will be King."

The whisper grew louder.

"King, you will be King."

He remembered these haunting words from his youth. David threw back his cloak as he drove onwards.

"King."

He laughed wildly into the night.

"Kill a father, become the Goat King."

"The ruin of all of us," he thought.

David pushed his horse further and faster towards the Stone Pillar Pass.

Suddenly a menacing cloud passed over the moon and total darkness took hold. The cold mountain air was still and then a rush of foul wind blew up over the pass. David stopped and from his great cloak took a wineskin and drank greedily.

"Too much blood," he thought to himself.

He spurred his mount onward but felt a freedom take hold of him. The broken silence had smashed the bloody shackles that had held his father's legs and pushed open the iron prison door that he had closed on him so long ago. He was free. No longer would ancient wrongs haunt his mind and hold him from the future.

He rode swiftly with renewed vigor.

The tears of The Rose flowed once more as the clanging of swords rang off mountaintops and down through the valleys so that the entire kingdom resounded with the grim sounds of battle.

Finally on the ninth day King David had the upper hand. He brought his sword high, its great bejeweled hilt glistening in the sun ready for a death blow.

David did not rejoice. He heard the mountains whisper, "You are the rightful King."

He did not falter or hesitate but rather brought down his sword firmly and laid it decisively on the barren rocks.

"Hold!" he thought to himself. "Hold!"

At that moment a dazzling Rose-colored light came bursting upon the sky so that David had to shield his eyes from its brilliance.

The Rose appeared in white and seemed to hover over the rocky terrain while her entourage of light bearers began shooting arrows of light to all parts of the dark kingdom.

She was bathed in brightness and had wings that shielded David from the brilliance that burned so that the rocks turned to lava and slowly started to move down the pass.

The light bearers continued transforming the sky into a dazzling display of color while thunder sounded in the distance. As the light storm slowly subsided The Rose unwrapped her wings of mercy.

David remained motionless on the rocky path humbled by her presence.

She hovered above with two light bearers by her side. In one hand she held a terrifying scorpion and in the other a black viper.

She looked on as the light bearers shot more arrows into the now-burning sky. Trumpets sounded and King David's entourage led by Grail made its way slowly up the last torturous mountain pass.

The shouts of men could be heard down in the valley as the entourage gathered speed and the world of court came closer to the site of the magnificent battle.

The two light bearers tugged at Princess Rose's wings like children losing their patience.

The Rose kept her eyes far off into the distance. Then as she slowly took her leave she breathed one word, "Compassion," which lingered on the air as she disappeared.

Grail hung back at the tent respectfully allowing David time to finish speaking with his men. He approached him carefully in hopes of engaging the King in conversation. He gasped and gaped, mouth open, head shaking in disbelief, as he noticed the black creatures issuing from the great man's footsteps.

"A home, a home," Samuel sighed with joy from the depths of the tent.

Tears rolled down his face for he knew in his soul that soon The Ark of the Covenant would have a resting place, a home.

The Scorpion and the disciples cried with joy and looked at each other.

"Come," the King called to Grail, showing no reaction to the astonishing event that had now subsided.

The two men stood and surveyed the desert landscape. The battle camp was strewn with scorpions that had fallen during the heavy rain. In between the rows of tents, in the open parade grounds near the animal paddocks and around the general's quarters they covered the great sands.

"Is this treachery or divine?"

Grail struggled to keep calm.

He walked beside David through the camp. With a start he thought of Polo. Was the boy safe here? He then remembered the kindness of the old serving woman who had given the boy tea.

"I'll wait for now," he thought.

Straightening his shoulders in an attempt to regain his composure he turned to David.

"Do you value organization or individual ability?" he asked.

"You tell me," said the Scorpion King as he spread his arms wide.

Grail squinted into the morning sunlight and began, "The layout is uniform and rectangular with paths laid down around the general tent."

Grail quickened his pace as he talked.

"This marching camp is larger than usual but still has the same patterns," he commented, remembering the familiar battle camp he and his men made each night as they pushed further into unknown territory.

He pointed to his left and right.

"Senior officers' tents, marketplace, standards and payroll, there and there and there."

He continued not daring to look at David for fear of stepping on another sacred insect.

"Each soldier knows his place in camp and keeps his animals close to him regardless of how many camps are made?" Grail asked.

"Yes," David smiled.

"The cavalry is kept close to their units in camp," Grail said as he walked on to reach the outskirts of the square and parade ground.

His eyes were squinting in concentration as he began marching and measuring each step. He paced off 200 feet averting his eyes from the scorpions.

He finished his measurement and looked up.

"Soldiers," he called to two guards who stood near the posts.

"Move those two yellow flags 100 yards to the east and west."

The guards looked at David who nodded.

"You need to keep enemy archers and javelins away and you and your men need more room to position and to train."

"Yes," David said as he smiled at Grail and continued walking with his guards past the long row of tents.

"You are clever like a fox who knows his way through danger and back to his lair."

Donkeys and camels brayed in the sun as men loaded them with water and supplies. As David passed the soldiers he smiled and slapped one large man on the back.

"Barack," he called. "Tame that beast of a donkey."

He laughed as he continued through the laughter of his guards.

A fighter pushed Barack's large bulk toward the spitting animal.

"Kiss that tonight," he teased.

David laughed loudly at this while moving onward through the hot lines of the camp.

"The entire camp covers one-half of a square mile and so I would say that you have 30,000 to 35,000 men here."

"You know well the battle camp."

David walked on.

"Come, my cunning desert fox," he smiled. "Tell me why the camp is of such importance."

"It is home and attack at once. It gives the men strength to know their place wherever they may be or how far they travel."

He walked on quickly, banishing thoughts of desert insects and his always thorny relationship with Lady Beth.

"Go on."

"Even if you retreat hastily the soldier knows that there is a camp, there is a place for him that is safe," Grail's voice trailed off. "A home."

"Every warrior needs a home," David agreed.

They walked in silence measuring their difference and their likeness.

"Order and structure are key and not the abilities of one man," Grail revealed.

"Organization is important but my men are from many different tribes. They resist the rulings of one king," David began.

"Soldiers need order and discipline," Grail replied.

"We need the heroics of individuals this day," David began. "We are upstarts in a land where great powers, the Egyptians and Mesopotamians, rule."

"You fight a guerrilla war?"

"We fight with desperation," David laughed.

"I am the known to the Egyptians so they leave us alone for now. They are busy with other matters so I'm free somewhat to do what I wish. I am a bit player in this desert game."

"You know your strengths and weaknesses before you take the field," Grail agreed.

While David surveyed the landscape the knight quickly looked to see if the scorpions were still flowing from David's feet.

"Maybe it was the sun, a heat stroke. Something in my mind that waits for the fever to attack me," Grail hoped.

He knew only too well the heavy toll of a lonely heart. Although he fought them, his feelings for The Rose and Lady Beth ambushed him in moments of weakness.

"No rest, no retreat."

In matters of the heart there was no training, no scaling of walls, no orderly marching, only a blind lurch through uncharted territory, sometimes bliss and sometimes hell. The lack of control brought on in him that which he feared: uncertainty.

So he escaped. He battled the foul weather, sickness, crippling disease and even death. Leading 10,000 men into a marching camp of death was easier than talking to Lady Beth.

"Give me war, not love," he thought as a dark cloud settled over his mind.

The war camp was love and home and yet Grail knew that his skill at war masked his weakness. The sword could not speak to the heart yet its cold blade kept him warm. His battle shield defended him and kept him safe from what he could not articulate.

He also knew with a growing certainty that each unknown territory that was won, each tribe that fell to his sword, served only to build a higher wall around his heart. He drew further and further away from the real pitched battle, the assault that began each day anew as the lonely rider endlessly galloped around Greythorn without reason or tongue to tell.

"You taught me well," he whispered. "But not the things I needed to learn."

He laughed bitterly. He felt like a straw man full of muscle and empty hope. He put his hand on his dagger and like a warm blanket the blade calmed his thoughts.

David watched the handsome figure of the blond warrior.

"What of your family, do you have a wife or wives?"

Grail cast a furtive glance at David.

"Does he read minds as well as give birth to scorpions?" he thought.

"Come tell me of life at court at your Greythorn," David asked.

"My work is done on the battlefield," Grail replied.

"And mine in the bedroom," David laughed.

Grail's pale features reddened as he kept straight on the path.

"You are a strange fellow, my dear knight," David began. "You know so much about war and seem to know nothing about life's finest gifts."

"Emotion clouds the mind."

"But emotions and ideas drive greatness."

"War is not great; it is simply to be won."

"Ah, but how do you win a lady's heart, how do you spring a trap for her and lead her to an oasis before you can take her for yours?"

Grail walked on ramrod straight until finally he held up and waited for the bow-legged king to catch up.

"I don't know, my lord," he sighed. "I don't know."

"Well then," David laughed. "My desert fox will teach me order and discipline and I'll teach him to climb the ramparts of the female heart."

"That would be fine," Grail replied quietly.

He turned a corner to watch a lizard enjoying a sun bath on a rock. The knight made a quick movement toward the cold-blooded creature, snapped his fingers quickly and watched as it skittered away.

"The desert fox."

He smiled as he wrapped a light, tan-colored tunic around his head. Perhaps he could learn something from these people of the hot sands that had so taken hold of his imagination.

The captain of war loosened his reins. Grail's head was dizzy from the heat and he thought back to the times with Lady Beth.

A hunting horn rang through the dense woods surrounding Greythorn. The sounds of rushing hooves and men's voices came from the depth of the green velvet darkness.

Far down below, Grail appeared out of thick brush, his clothes full of burs.

The thick forest glade shielded Lady Bethlehem from harm and from time itself. She danced and laughed, her brown skin glistening as pure gold shines in the light of truth.

She stepped down from the waterfall and onto a stone ledge where two lion cubs fought playfully over her clothing. Her handmaid Juliet, a young girl, sat clutching her knees in awe of the forest.

Lady Beth first placed a diamond pin through her flowing hair and tied it up with a wave of her hand before smoothing the green satin gown that she slipped over her head. Juliet then took snow white fur boots that the lion cubs were tearing at and slipped them onto the lady's feet.

Near a stream below Lady Bethlehem's vantage point, Grail made his way through thickets. Aserbarb followed slowly behind pausing from time to time to drink.

Grail stood facing the stone ledge and waterfall from the opposite side. He wiped his forehead in the afternoon sun and looked up to see the figure of Lady Bethlehem against the stone cliffs.

As their eyes met Grail felt the kiss and the watermark she had left on his lips those 20 years ago.

"Hunting?" Lady Bethlehem asked from above.

"Yes, my lady," he answered softly, "But not on the right trail."

"Aserbarb seems to be leading the way."

"Yes, my lady, he knows the forests around Greythorn better than I."

"Remember when you called me Boots?" She let out an intoxicating warm laugh and motioned him up to her vantage point.

Grail felt dizzy as he climbed up to the stone ledge. He was brought back with each step through the forest to a youthful time, a simpler time of faith and love.

"Boots," he laughed nervously, "You, my lady, did a great deal of damage to many a young knight's confidence. You could outride, outfight and beguile us all."

Lady Bethlehem's outstretched hand and warm smile steadied his nerves.

"You always played the hero so well," she said.

Juliet sat down behind them.

"And now?" he asked.

"There is little time to play." She sat on a carved stone chair. "There are powers at play that are destroying the kingdom. Your King and brother need you. Have you talked to him since your return?"

"No," Grail said. "We are to speak tonight."

"Forget the past and any misgivings about his love and respect for you."

She smiled as she added, "And Princess Rose has grown into a fine lady."

"I am glad for her."

"The Princess has powers that even I do not understand."

Lady Bethlehem leaned closer to Grail, "The Kingdom's fate may rest in her hands."

"Princess Rose?"

"Watch and protect her with your life," Lady Bethlehem said quietly.

"I will as I always have."

He looked down at the forest below.

"Any word from Bru?"

Lady Bethlehem looked up from her chair.

"Not these nine years."

She picked up one of the lion cubs and stroked its face.

"Be warned that all is not well and you must help your King."

Grail turned to Lady Bethlehem, took her hand and kissed it.

"Yes, for you and your forest I will bury the past and fight and defend."

As he kissed her hand he recalled their bright young days together. Greythorn had echoed with the laughter of young love as Rolf, Lady Beth and Grail walked down the halls and out to the archery range.

"They will marry someday," Lady Fan whispered to her husband as the two passed the young couple. "See the way he looks at her."

"What, Rolf and Lady Beth?" Lord Fan asked as he fussed with his tunic.

"No," she tapped his shoulder. "Grail and Lady Beth."

"Are they not brother and sister?" he asked while continuing to walk in his soldier's way, ramrod straight as if still on parade.

"Whatever gave you that idea?" Lady Fan gasped. "Lady Beth is no relation."

She looked over at her husband who was charging off to another battlefield.

"Why do I bother?"

She smiled as she heard their laughter ring off the courtyards.

"Riding bareback and hitting all targets," Beth yelled to the two boys as she hurried across the quadrangle to the royal stables. Her long, red hair was tied up in a ponytail and her eyes caught the sun sleeping and so brought warmth to all she met.

The guards smiled at the inseparable trio as the barn door opened.

"Hello, Rum," Beth said to the blacksmith.

"Aye, my lady," said the small man who smiled showing two missing teeth. "Fine day for a ride."

He placed the long calipers in the fire and wiped his hands on the black apron. "Sam," he called out. "Get Lady Beth's horse ready."

Rolf and Grail entered the stables and took their saddles from their bunks and walked towards the back of the stables. Grail and Beth looked at each other in passing with the young boy becoming shy and glancing toward the straw of the stable floor.

"I'll hit twice as many targets and it's bareback.... as in no saddles.... remember?"

She laughed at him as he held onto his saddle and raised his eyes.

"Forgot, Boots, that you wanted to lose today," he managed.

He put his harness around his neck, placed the saddle back and continued toward the back of the barn.

Rolf looked at the two and rolled his eyes at this puppy love play.

"You are both going to lose today because all you do is stare at each other," he said as he threw his saddle down.

Rum had to turn away to hide his laughter.

"I think not," Grail said as he brought his horse out of its stable.

The horse trotted slowly up to Beth and put his face in her hand while she rubbed his ears.

"Come on," Rolf said. "Are we going or not?"

"We're going." Grail grabbed his arrows and quiver from his wooden locker before leaving the stables as did Rolf and Beth.

The morning air blew cool and sweet over the archery range as the three galloped toward the yards.

"I'll go first," Beth yelled as she stopped at the first entry gate and set herself steady.

She slung her quiver over her shoulders, took the bow in one arm and dug her cloth boots into her mount's quarters. At the start she held the reins in her teeth as she spurred the animal on.

She flew around the course gracefully, jumping over water traps and wooden logs, her eyes wide and calm. The horse obeyed her verbal and physical commands to the letter.

"Gentle," she whispered to him. "Go now."

She made each turn look easy and hit target after target in the bull's eye. On the last jump the horse came up slightly short in the water trap and she missed the middle of the target.

She stopped at the end of her run and patted the animal before turning toward the two boys.

"Well," she smiled, which lit up Grail's world.

"Not bad," Rolf trotted to the entrance gate. "Not bad, but watch this."

He kicked at the horse's hindquarters and off he went over the course.

He held the reins tight in his mouth and made the jumps quickly. As he finished he slapped his thighs in frustration.

"Two misses," he quickly dismounted and threw up his hands in disbelief.

Grail thundered out of the entrance and with masterful ease guided his charge over the distance, riding low on one side while hugging the horse's underbelly with his feet and letting fly his arrows to the heart of each target.

He would change his side as he turned and then change again so that he was always in perfect position to hit his mark. It was both terrifying and beautiful to watch.

"The battle-axe next," Beth called out as she led her horse back to the stable.

The two young men looked at each other and laughed.

"More like the games room for cards," Rolf laughed.

He threw Grail another look.

"I have to see my father so I can go over the rounds with him; you play with the battle-axe."

"Not me," Grail said sheepishly. "I'll go where you are."

"No you won't, fool." Rolf took Grail's horse by the reins. "Your job is to follow your wife."

"Not my wife."

He pushed Rolf and hit him in the shoulder.

"She will be one day," Rolf called over his shoulder as he took the two animals back to the stables.

Grail kicked at the ground as he wandered through the yards by himself and then scrambled to catch up to Beth. She stood waiting for him at the stables and without a word started walking by his side.

"So," she said.

"So what?" he rejoined.

"You are the finest rider I have ever seen. Ever," she exclaimed.

"It's nothing," he said as he looked down at the gravel. "Grandfather taught me."

"Grail," she cried out. "Lots of people learn things; they don't learn to ride like that, not as if you and the horse are one together."

"It's just practice that's all."

He turned red and looked away.

"You are such a baby," she said.

"I'm not."

He threw a glance at her.

"Oh that was mature," she laughed. "I'm not," she mocked him. "Am not."

"Rolf wants to play cards now," he said changing the subject.

"Aren't we going to play?" Beth said quietly.

"But Rolf wants..." he said.

"All right, go and play with stupid Rolf," she said.

She turned toward Grail and left him quickly, but her smile never did. He smiled as she walked away and she never realized how much he cared for her.

Chapter 16
David at Hebron

Joab, captain of the host, rode in front of King David's entourage as they neared the town of Hebron.

Grail as was the custom now rode beside David on his left while David's chariot was kept behind for ceremonial purposes.

It was noon and the sun rose high in the sky while the dust and wind swept across the dry, rocky plains.

"We shall gauge their will and desire," David said as they neared the small town.

"Meaning?" Grail asked.

"We Israelites hate kings; they hold too much power," David began. "Saul was allowed to be king because we needed a strong man against the Philistines."

"Then how did you manage before?"

"We were mere tribesmen with leaders and elders, prophets."

David rounded a turn and picked up speed racing down the narrows as he often did. Grail kept pace as the two men outraced the entourage causing Joab no end of frustration.

David and Grail raced through the small village and beyond before turning and cantering back to where the King's men had stopped and waited for his return.

"You disapprove."

David looked at Joab.

"No, King, I wait."

Joab took off his gloves and tapped them on the horn of his thin, leather saddle. "We all wait."

He spread his arms and motioned to those about him.

David laughed.

"I will write a poem for my Joab, Joab the Frustrated."

Joab chuckled, "That will have to wait. First we must gather an army then you can write, my King."

Joab turned to the soldiers. "Go knock on every door and tell them to gather in the town square to hear the King."

He clapped his hands.

"Go!"

"He is right but I cover my nerves with comedy," David told Grail. "Why should a king have to beg for men but a king must do whatever is needed to protect a kingdom, nothing too low or high? So I am here with arms out as a simple beggar."

Grail nodded his understanding.

"Good," David said as he walked off with his jaunty energy, wrapped his headdress around his long hair in the manner of a street beggar and looked back, his mischievous eyes laughing.

"A king should never be afraid to be what he has to be: beggar, thief and sage."

He came back to where Grail stood.

"If he thought himself as above and detached then he will be just that, cut off from reality."

Soon a crowd of men both young and old gathered to hear David. They were farmers and hard working men with little time for rest or play and wore rough tunics and headdresses to protect themselves from the harsh sun. The fields needed tending yet they also knew that the Philistines posed a great threat to their security now that King Saul was dead.

Joab clapped for silence as the crowd grew and David stepped forward, his white robe blown by the desert winds.

"Men of Hebron," he cried out.

He seemed to grow in height and the David of a moment ago was now replaced by a pure passion.

"The arrow that struck down Saul is still lodged in my heart."

He drew out the imaginary arrow.

"I bleed for all of Judea and Samira but I will take out the arrow, let the blood spill on the ground and weep no more."

He threw down the spent arrow.

"I will do all this for you but in return you must unite behind my shield. You must put down the farmer's hoe and pick up the weapons of war against the Philistines."

He glared at the men in the crowd who came with ambivalence.

"Who among you dares defy your King? Who among you has little to fight for?"

The men murmured approval at this.

"Are we not fighting for our very survival? Is this not a time for harsh measures so that one day soon we can come back to the sweet waters of Jordan in peace."

He stopped for effect.

"I will take this arrow out of my heart but what will you do for your King?"

The crowd stood and shouted its approval while other men came running to join the gathering.

"I will take this arrow and bleed for you my people but what will you show me?"

The men yelled back and waved their farm tools, shields and rough weaponry in the air.

"Let me take the arrow out to heal the wounds but only with your strength can I go forward."

The crowd became excited at this.

"I will build my kingdom on this arrow of pain, this arrow of hurt and loss, but you are my soldiers, you good men of Hebron."

He raised his fist in the air.

"You are my arrows that must never fail must never quiver in the face of pain or death!" he shouted. "Fly to the very heart of the Philistines and let them know that David's arrows will strike relentlessly!"

He continued, "Good men of Hebron be my sharp arrows so that I may build a kingdom, a kingdom that will unite all of Judea and Samira. This I ask of you today."

The crowd erupted and the farmers, blacksmiths and tinkers followed as soldiers guided the men forward in a line and took down names to enlist the new recruits.

Chapter 17
King David's Head

"Do we help those miserable Jebusites or pray all day?"

Bru, Grail's older brother who had also traveled to the east, bellowed as he appeared from his tent. He quickly fastened his leather belt and swung his sword over his head and shoulders.

"As-salaamu alaykum wa rahmatullah," came the answer from the heavily armed leader.

He smiled a cold smile.

"Peace on you and the mercy of our moon god Allah."

The braying of donkeys and sobbing of men echoed off the stony hillside of Wadi al-Qura, a village along the valley between Syria and Yemen as it awoke to the harsh light of day.

The goats and sheep tread carefully. Camels started for the water hole braying and stamping their hooves.

"Yes, yes," Bru said as he mounted his horse and threw the bag of money at the leader. "Here is enough money to make your moon god glow."

He turned toward the men.

"Half now and half when we get to Jebus," he yelled to the crowd. "And more for King David's head."

He faced the men who were mounting horses and gathering weapons.

"David has no men, no real army," Bru shouted.

"He thinks his god will save him from ruin," he laughed. "These Hebrews have no business there except to die."

Bru wrapped his *keffiyeh* around his face and looked down the long line of carts and wagons that his wild group had led over the barren wasteland.

The slaves traveled in horse-drawn carts with wooden bars that let in only misery and death. Twenty-five slaves and three armed guards per wagon made the journey in a five-mile line of dust and death.

Bru's brutality had preceded his army of mercenaries so that young and old men alike would willingly join to spare the women and children. At each village, livestock was taken, war chests looted and often the fires of grass huts could be seen for days across the plains.

Far down the line a disfigured man with black teeth took a stick and rattled it against the cage.

"I know you and your brothers," he sneered as Bru trotted by.

Bru looked up into the sun and shielded his eyes. He slowed his horse to look at the wretched piece of humanity.

"Brothers kill brothers but you won't be king."

The man rattled his cage again. Bru lifted his glove to strike.

The foul man drew back from the cage.

"I know you; I know what you did with young Arlemay and how you wish Grail dead."

"Guards," Bru called.

"Wait," the ragged skeleton said.

He drew near the cage.

"I can be your servant for I know of the Oracle at Toad's Hollow."

He grabbed the bars and pushed his face between them. "I can move heaven and earth and the tides themselves."

Bru's horse whinnied and shook its head with dust and hair flying into the air.

"We will see, my ugly fellow," Bru said as he spurred his mount down the long line of wagons.

"How can he know of Arlemay?" Bru thought as he galloped up the line.

His mind was flung far back to that day.

Bru grabbed a wineskin that hung over his saddle and quickly drank from it, gulping the wine until it spilled over his black cloak.

"Steady," Moormund the patriarch urged. He looked over at his second eldest son as they made for the town with the wind lashing at them.

The two horses galloped down the coast as the waves crashed on the beach.

"Steady," Bru laughed. "There is the world to be taken by force not steadfastness."

"*You must learn when and how to take things,*" *Moormund yelled into the wind.*

"*Like that little runt Arlemay.*"

Bru wiped his mouth with his sleeve. "*Send him away. He eats too much and even the dogs howl in laughter at him.*"

Bru's arrogance and cold heart could not be contained.

They both slowed their mounts.

"*He is your younger brother, only a boy of nine,*" *Moormund said.*

"*He does not ride. He does not hunt with us,*" *Bru began.* "*He is weak and as the old laws tell us ye may set forth one child so that the rest may live, whosoever is weak shall be cast out as the wicked ninth.*"

The wind and rain swallowed up the two voices.

That night Bru sat over his fire drinking heavily and thought of the Oracle at Toad's Hollow.

"Bring that creature that I spoke with this morning," he said.

"What do they call you?" Bru said when the man arrived.

"Gore," he said. The man slouched toward the tent while holding onto a walking stick and then fell into a heap near the fire.

Bru looked on in disgust.

"So?"

"Dear Master, I beg your indulgence for David's story is only the half of it, the better half no doubt, the one that brings light to our brooding world just as the sun illuminates the cold yellow orb. But we must leave the heat of the east and visit the cold, deep coves off the shores of our home, the Isle of Burton. Yes, we are a desperate people still hunting and gathering our fears. David gathers courage across the seas while we listen only to the wicked wind whisper of the danger through our barren rocky fields."

He sat up still leaning on his walking stick and breathed heavily. His bad breath became the very mist that clung to Bru's hazy memory of his past.

"But oh how we love the shadows, the depths that we live in, the depths that we relish more than the sun. We are the shadow people. Revenge and regret are all that we know."

"Moormund, our King, lies in his sick bed with wild visions strutting across his dark mind while his sons a brood of nine bicker and squander what hope remains for our future. We are returning to our folklore days, the days of the Bear:

The bear sensed that we were not a strong people. We did not plant and harvest. We roamed like animals. The bear knew we would not last so he hunted the hunter. He watched our warriors bathe in the blood of animals and sing at night without looking toward next winter. The bear knew that there would not be another winter for our people. He would track and kill us just as we did him. We were no better than those we tracked and killed. We belonged to the bear. We had no soul."

"And so I chose to follow you into the east. Why? Perhaps to escape the visions that haunted Greythorn and tore the fabric of our lives. These visions rose each night and raged over the land louder than a wild boar caught by our hunting dogs. It rained down fury but not some unknown dark fury, some evil, but rather our shortcomings that rose on the wave of the great sins of the patriarch and father, Moormund."

Bru's eyes glistened in the darkness and he drank from his goblet.

"Ah, but you don't know what was said to me at Toad's Hollow, do you, wretch?"

Gore tried to rise to a normal sitting position but his limbs were not strong enough.

"A brother shall be rewarded in battle across the seas," he breathed.

Bru became quiet and looked at Gore in the firelight.

"Are you some demon come to haunt me?"

"I am just a simple man," Gore said. "Your servant."

"And what of Grail?"

"Your brother must find his way," Gore said.

"Never."

Bru let out a laugh and threw his goblet into the fire remembering the past.

"Never," resounded through the Great Hall of Lower Light.

The two boys Bru and Grail dashed through the ancient ill-lit room with wooden swords.

"That's my gold coin," Grail said.

"Never!" Bru yelled.

"Be good or here you stay," laughed Dramoor as he maneuvered through the Great Hall of Lower Light with Grail and Bru on either side of him in double headlock.

The Great Hall of Lower Light was an ancient room at Greythorn where Grail's grandfather, Champendeau the Great, had spoken about the three essentials of ruling: Courage, Faith and Honesty. The old warrior had traveled far and uncovered the secrets of the east bringing back a treasure chest of exotic spoils, the greatest of which was a magnificent table that could seat 24 and had a beautiful rose engraved in the middle.

"The soul of the world," he would laugh as he stroked the beautiful wood finish.

Champendeau and his forefathers who now lay entombed in the walls of the ancient hall seemed to flicker to life in the brooding dusk and turned their cold, dark faces toward the brothers warning them of the coming struggle.

"We will," came Grail's muffled answer.

"No, we won't," Bru countered.

"Aye, then here you stay."

Dramoor winked at a servant girl and skipped past her down the hallway with the boys in tow.

"Let me go," Bru cried.

The trio passed wild boar roasting on spits in the kitchen on fires that were lit for the coming feast that night.

Dramoor let go of his brothers and rubbed his hands in delight while looking around the hall.

"Tonight we celebrate."

Grail combed back his golden locks and stuck his finger in his ear.

"Where is Father?" he asked.

"With some men doing business with the Horites king."

Dramoor clapped his hands and a servant brought wine to the three royals as they sat down.

"If only our Arlemay could be here," Dramoor took the wine and poured three goblets but poured sparingly in one.

"Watch it."

"But I don't train until tomorrow."

Grail looked at his glass and acquiesced.

"You must be ready at all times," Dramoor said as he passed the wine to Bru.

Bru laughed.

"Arlemay wasn't surviving at Greythorn let alone in the hills by himself. That boy will never be seen again."

"I miss him." Dramoor drank and looked around the fire-lit hall. "But tonight we celebrate Father's birthday."

"He could come back," Grail comforted his big brother.

"Where are the two wild boys," said Dramoor looking away as he hid his feelings. "Where are my crazy lads?"

"Running wild upstairs killing each other," said Bru as he drank from his goblet. "One can only hope."

"What is it going to be like when you become a priest?" Grail blurted out.

"No more headlocks," Bru laughed.

"I don't mind them so much."

"I'll be right beside you when you get in a muddle," said Dramoor looking around as a loud noise came from the hallway.

The Great Hall of Lower Light was alive as servants scurried around and prepared for King Moormund's birthday celebration.

Exotic dancers and entertainers practiced their arts while tables laden with delicacies from the east were set out row on row.

Roma and Riga dashed into the hall wooden swords in hand and faced off against each other. They both wore the same colored tunics and no one could tell them apart except save for Dramoor.

"That is my gold coin, Father gave it to me."

"It's mine."

"Never."

The servants backed off as the boys began to sword fight. They danced upon the cold stone floor and soon headed down the hall near the main entrance where actors from a traveling group were rehearsing for tonight's play.

"Mine!"

"Never!"

The boys ran down the hallway forcing a servant to spill a tray of food and then overturned a table to get into a defensive position against whoever the next invaders were.

The actors stood up and began to quickly engage the two new players.

"Enemy spies behind the lines," one called out.

"Catch them."

"They will pretend to be of the royal family but they will cause ruin."

"Call out the White Knight."

Roma and Riga laughed as they were pitted against the troupe. They held their position and dug in deeper behind their make-shift barricade.

The actors huddled around each other and looked over at Dramoor who smiled and in gesture bid them to continue. Bru turned away in disgust and drowned himself in his wine goblet.

"Maybe they are royalty, members of the family cast to distant shores only to return," one actor shouted.

Bru and Dramoor suddenly paid more attention and watched the play unfold.

"We must capture them and interrogate each warrior," called another actor.

"Never!" the boys shouted in unison.

"Take them alive."

The actors ran around the table but were cut off by a strong counter thrust from the boys.

"Look," one actor cried. "It grows dark around them and the seas are heaving upwards."

"The battle between light and dark," cried another.

"Perhaps they control natural things?"

"Can we learn from them?"

The actors circled the boys and began to talk about the warrior knights.

"Two knights but only one can be king."

"They grow apart and soon fight each other."

"Never," came the battle cry from underneath the table.

The audience grew now with servants and other players at court shaking with laughter at each "Never" shouted out.

"They become locked in pitched battle for the kingdom," one actor continued.

The actors made a desperate attempt to unearth the two by reaching under the table but to no avail. Two wooden swords flew up in the group's direction.

"Never!"

The cry reverberated throughout the hall as the audience joined in and howled with laughter.

A hush came over the crowd as the actors devised a new strategy to dislodge the warrior knights.

"I sense these knights have been to different lands."

"Blown by the winds of change," another actor replied.

Roma and Riga both forced themselves to break wind loudly, which echoed through Greythorn's hallway.

The actors and audience laughed hysterically as they plugged their noises and gagged in mock terror.

Dramoor laughed loudly as Grail followed his big brother's every move. Bru turned away and sneered as he looked off into the corner waiting or wanting something to appear.

"Mother would not want this," he said quietly.

"Little ones," Dramoor bellowed, "Out with you now."

The twins emerged from their hideout as the crowd dispersed and the acting troupe held a discussion about the night's entertainment.

"Now listen," Dramoor began. "We are all going to sit down at the table and go over how to act tonight when Father returns."

"Just let them slit their adorable little throats," Bru sneered.

"You're the second eldest, why not act it?" Grail shouted back.

"All right, go and play with real daggers, boys," Bru said as he gulped his wine. "Don't miss the eyes."

Grail's face burned as he heard Bru speak.

"Brave talk with your little brothers," he challenged.

"And what would you know about that?" said Bru staring at his younger sibling who stood almost his height.

"You are supposed to protect those who are weaker not make fun of them."

"Are you now?" said Bru moving closer.

"Grandfather says you have a duty."

"Champendeau that old windbag," Bru laughed.

Grail lunged at Bru and struck him in the face with a quick right hand.

Dramoor quickly caught hold of both boys' tunics and was in between them before any more fighting took place. Bru pushed back heavily and the three angrily wrestled as one in the now empty hall as fires burned all around while dusk fell on Greythorn.

"Easy," he shouted. "There will be plenty of time for that at the games."

Bru stepped back and glared at both of them before he disappeared into the darkness of the silent hall.

"I don't want you to go," Grail finally said as he stood alone with Dramoor.

"Because of him."

"No, I can manage that. You are our heart and soul."

"In a few weeks that will be you."

"You have held everything together since Mother died."

"It's who I am."

Dramoor placed his arms on his brother's shoulders.

"I can never take your place. I'm not that strong."

"You are and more. Men will build armies around you, around your high ideals and courage."

"And you becoming a priest?"

"There are reasons behind my actions," said Dramoor as he started toward the stone stairs that led to the chamber upstairs. "But tonight let's celebrate and not worry about the future. Father is home."

Chapter 18
The Scorpion's Overture

Then came all of the tribes of Israel to David unto Jebus and spake saying 'Behold, we are thy bone and flesh.'

"Listen," The Scorpion said. His black sackcloth blew in the morning wind. The sun burned above the city as the troops moved in and out of the mountain pass.

"Listen," he said again.

He smiled with his fingers to his ear. He closed his eyes and rolled his head while his hands spread out and played on the breeze.

The wind beat a somber tune while a light rain brought harmony. The wild maestro moved his arms in rapture over earth and sky as the dust swirled in a disparate chorus each note one of dark battle.

The trumpets sounded and echoed off the mountains. Down came the great army, the banners of green and white blowing in the morning breeze. The horses carefully traversed the mountain trails as the men signaled with great trumpet blasts.

In front of the warriors came the priests, the head priests and their division of lower priests and their clergy.

The Chief Priest with his long flowing beard and robes came to the top of a pass and stood by as the army marched on.

"Hear, O Israel, you are approaching battle against thine enemy today. Do not be afraid nor fainthearted. Do not tremble because of Them, for R____ with you and to save you."

His rough voice echoed of the mountains and down the mountain pass.

"Our officers shall speak to those prepared to fight against your enemies, those willing of heart to strengthen them by the might of R____."

The trumpets rang off the cliffs as the priests stopped to let the warriors pass on the narrow dirt trails.

"Then you shall recount that which you spoke by the hand of Moses saying: And when there is war in your land against the adversary who attacks you then you shall sound an alarm with the trumpets that you might be remembered before your R____. And be saved from your enemies."

The priest brought his hands to his lips and raised them to the oncoming army and down the pass.

And the rains fell along the mountain pass and covered the army from harm with wet tears.

The Scorpion stood above on the cliffs waving his arms.

"Let them blast the trumpets of war, the trumpets of ambush and pursuit," he sang down the hilltop.

He yelled down the mountain, "On the trumpets of the battle formation they shall write 'The rule R____.'

On the trumpets of men of renown, they shall write 'The heads of congregation clans.'

On the trumpets of the camps they shall write 'The peace of R____ in the camps.'

On the trumpets for assembling the infantry when the gates of war open, they shall write 'A temperance of requital at the appointed time.'"

The Scorpion picked up a banner and waved it. He turned and danced high above the battlefield as the troops moved slowly into position.

He yelled into the wind, "When they draw near for battle they shall write 'The right hand of the R____, The appointed time of R____, The tumult of R____, The tumult of R____, The slain of R____.' After which will come the names of the hosts."

He bent low and whispered, "The length of the banners of the whole congregation shall be fourteen cubits long, the banner of each tribe shall be thirteen cubits, the banner of 10,000 men shall be eleven cubits, the banner of a thousand men shall be ten cubits, the banner of 100 men shall be nine cubits, the banner of 50 men shall be eight cubits."

He then stood and waved his banner as the troops continued down the steep mountain pass.

Joab stood near David under their war tent pitched high above the plains.

"Watch," he said as he pointed down into the battle.

"The army is to make a forward battle line formed by 1,000 men. There will be seven forward rows to each battle line arranged in order," he said.

"All of them shall bear shields of bronze; the length of the shield shall be two and a half cubits. In each hand shall be a lance and sword; the lance shall be seven cubits while the sword shall be a cubit and a half."

The Scorpion continued waving the banner as the army below arranged in seven battle lines one behind each other. The slingers threw seven times and returned to their position.

Then three divisions of infantry advanced and stood between the lines. The first division stood fast.

"After this, two divisions of infantry shall be marched forward toward the city."

The Scorpion stood watching the deployment of cavalry. Two rows of horsemen took a position at the right and left or on the battle line, 100 horsemen on one side and 100 horsemen on the other side.

David also stood watching as the troops moved across the plains.

"How old are these men?" he asked Joab.

"As the priest insists," he replied. "The men of the army shall be from 40 to 50 years old. The commissioner of the camps shall be from 50 to 60 years old. The officers shall be from 40 to 50. All those who are stripped and slain, plunder the spoil, cleanse the land, guard the arms and him who prepares the provisions, all of these men shall be from 25 to 30 years old."

"Ah yes, the priest and Zadok."

David turned to The Scorpion. "And what of them?"

The warrior priest closed his eyes and kept swaying to some imaginary orchestra as the instruments one by one sounded their battle call.

"When the battle lines are spread against the enemy there shall go forth from the middle into the gap between the lines seven priests of the sons of R___, dressed in fine, white linen garments, a linen tunic, linen breeches and decorated caps on each head. And these caps they shall not take into the sanctuary."

He moved to watch the troop movements below.

"The one priest shall walk before all the men of battle to encourage. In the hands of the remaining six priests shall be trumpets of assembly, the trumpets of the memorial, the trumpets of alarm, the trumpets of pursuit and the trumpets of reassembly. The priests shall go out into the gap between the battle lines and walk with the officers. Three officers shall walk before the priests; the priests shall blow rams' horns to the assembly of battle."

He began to point and move as he continued.

"And 50 infantrymen shall go out according to their order from one side and with their officers. The trumpets shall blow continuously to direct the infantry as to their position.

The priest shall blow a level note signaling for battle. And the columns shall be deployed into their formations each to his position. The priest shall blow the second note, a low legato note, the signal for advance. The priest shall continue to blow a sharp staccato note to direct battle.

Afterward, the priest shall blow the trumpets of retreat, a low-level note. And the priest shall take up position in the battle line, and all the people with rams' horns shall blow a very hard battle alarm; and as the sound of alarm and as the sound goes out their hands shall begin to bring down the slain, and all these people shall quiet the sound of alarm but the priest shall continue sounding on the trumpets the slain to direct the fighting until the enemy is defeated and turns in retreat.

When the slain has fallen the priests shall continue blowing from afar and shall not enter into the midst of the slain so as to be defiled by their unclean blood for they are holy.

They shall not allow the oil of their priestly anointment to profane with the blood of the vainglorious nations."

The Scorpion continued in his rapture waving his hands over earth and sky.

"Then the Chief Priest shall stand and with him his brother priests and all the men of the army. He shall read aloud the prayer for the appointed time of battle as is written in the book *Seth II (The Rule of His Time)*, including all the words of their thanksgiving. Then he shall form there all the battle lines as is written in the *Book of War*. Then the priests appointed for the time of vengeance by all his brothers shall walk about and encourage then for battle and he shall say in response 'Be strong and courageous as warriors. Fear not nor be discouraged and let not your heart be faint. Do not panic, neither be alarmed because of them. Do not turn your back or flee from them. They have established all their refuge in a lie; their strength is as smoke that vanishes and all their vast assembly is as chaff which blows away desolation and shall not be found.'"

* * *

The high priests of all 12 tribes had blown their trumpets and slowly appeared and stood in a line while behind them were the lower priests with banners flying in the wind.

A light rain began to fall and the sun's rays played in between brooding clouds that swept over the high plains and over the city's acropolis. The wind and rain beat the banners of war and tugged at the horses' harnesses while the clouds pulled across the darkened sky.

The sun burst forth as the troops gathered like dark fingers formed into a battle fist. The light battled with the clouds and the dust rose high into the air as the infantry came down from the mountains and moved onto the plains, each line seven men deep with banners flying.

Then came the archers who moved on both sides of the infantry, holding their line and waiting to let fly war. The slingers moved past the battle lines and moved closer to the city on the high ground facing the massive stone walls that surrounded Jebus.

The chariots danced across the plains with messages and new battle formations, turning the plains into dust that rose above the united host of Israel and Judah. The seething mass of men and weapons stood before Jebus and moved back and forth as an angry wave of war.

The rain continued to swirl while the clouds rolled over earth and sky.

David's Baptism of Fire

"Mother says we must take a swim," David said to Mybad as the men checked their weapons.

Mybad looked at the sky.

"The brooding clouds call for rain, my friend."

"No," said David as he pointed to the map. "In the water system."

"But we are fighting men not mice."

"Ah, mice and men," David laughed. "We are both scurrying around in the dark."

"We should face the enemy in the light not the dark," Mybad said.

The Scorpion came down from his perch.

"I and the scout will be your guide through the waterways," he said while keeping a careful eye on David. "There are deep things that you must keep clear of."

"Ah good, another mother," David laughed. "Mother, lead the way into the depths of the unknown."

He started the slow climb down from the mountains as the men followed him.

"Mother guide," David said as he turned back. "What wonders are waiting in the dark?"

"Things that you have no knowledge of, my David," The Scorpion said. "And things that you should not have *any* knowledge of."

"Why?" David said.

"Because you are the light," said The Scorpion as he trudged on down the rocky hillside.

David stopped and listened for a moment before using the sound of his voice as a guide into the unknown.

"Who is there?" he called out as his hands swept over the wet walls.

He walked slowly as everything became very still in the dank, rat-infested waterway. He kept his hands sliding over what was left of the smooth mud walls as he headed into the unknown while hearing the *"eeeehhhhheeeehh"* of squealing rats at his feet.

"Be not afraid," said The Scorpion as he touched his master's tunic and appeared from the shadows.

He turned toward a great fire that had quickly sprung up with its heat biting at the two men who walked toward it.

Laughter erupted near the fire as The Scorpion quickly stepped in front.

The fire burned away David's courage and as he looked further into the den he saw that the straightforward plains and hillsides of victory were lost to him as his path darkened.

The guide, the scout and his pupil continued down a crumbling, torch-lit path.

"I will show you three things that will play upon the hopes and dreams of your people as you build your future."

"But what about the battle here?" David questioned.

"You will take Jebus and build a resting place for The Ark of the Covenant," said The Scorpion as he turned and looked into the darkness. "I look deeply into the spiritual nature of things not the material world. Come," he whispered.

David was left dazed by the flames and felt his mind wander far from the battlefield.

Laughter came from where they had been and echoed off the walls for a few seconds before silence surrounded them. In the distance images quivered and disappeared. The warrior rubbed his eyes and tried to see far down the path but all was blocked.

He breathed deeply as if taking a new world into his heart and soul but this was not sufficient. He staggered slightly as he bumped into the wall and stopped for a moment to gather his strength to move forward into this new world.

"Come and behold," The Scorpion said.

David looked up while each step took all his strength.

Down the distant pathways he saw flames licking at the walls and heard the wails of men.

"Where are you taking me?" he cried out.

He clung to The Scorpion's robes as they continued onward.

"Come," came the soft reply.

"I don't trust my senses."

"Not all battles can be won by the sword," The Scorpion said.

"Do we go downward?"

David crept forward as the blind do in the shadows and stared down a steep incline of rocks and rubble. He stopped as he saw a bird approaching but rubbed his eye in disbelief. A great black albatross with a burning tail and large talons screeched as they approached.

Fire fell out of the bird's mouth while it soared above as the ceiling seemed to open in the subterranean dwelling, lighting up a burning archway. The albatross' great wingspan and the burning path made it difficult for the men to continue.

The bird flew down and stood its ground daring them to pass. The squat, powerful, two-legged guard had eyes of burning coal that seethed as it watched the unwanted guests.

The fire continued burning in the path downward and the great beast flapped its wings.

"*Caw, caw, caw!*" it bellowed at the strangers.

The entrance was a great fiery wooden arch that continued to burn and engulfed itself over and over.

David put his hands to his face guarding against the heat and the wild bird. The temperature was unbearable as were the screams heard from beyond the fiery entrance.

A horse's gallop could be heard and soon a beautiful, white stallion 12 hands high with a black mane stood at the entrance looking quietly and directly at the two intruders.

"*Purrupedd, PUR purp Edd,*" it spat.

"What are these sights that I behold?" David called out to the raging fire that sparked all around him.

"Look closely," The Scorpion urged. "Don't you see?"

The two wild animals guarded a path that was even and cleared of the rubble that fell all around the men. Torches were ablaze at regular intervals and the mist of cool air beckoned rational men down a lane of balance and harmony.

"Come away; that way leads to madness."

The Scorpion led his worried pupil straight toward the narrows of pain.

The fire burned incessantly all around but did not burn their skin. It licked and flickered on the walls of the lower aquatic system and played havoc with David's mind.

"Stop this infernal roar," David yelled into the raging fires.

A Dark Rider approached carrying a whip. The man was covered head to toe in black garments that burst into flame and subsided only to be consumed again.

The strange figure wiped the dust and dirt from his legs as his black horse rose up.

"A good day to ride," he yelled into the fire.

He laughed wildly as he pointed his whip at David and recited vengeful words:

"Ride, Dark Rider, ride

With rusty scabbard

And cold armor-plated breast

Unrequited revenge

Plunges you toward eternal unrest

For at full gallop high

Revenge never quivers

Revenge never rests."

David was about to answer but was pulled back by The Scorpion.

"We don't need to speak with these men," the prophet counseled. "Come."

He looked calmly, took his student's sleeve and guided him across a pool of boiling rocks. The stepping stones were black and hissed with steam and rage as the men trod a treacherous path toward an island of suffering.

"Hear me now," Dark Rider yelled into the blazing void.

He turned as he seemed to disappear in a ring of fire.

"The whip and saddle are all that remains…. the blood red road our only salvation and home."

He watched as David gingerly crossed the black skipping path.

"I will bring blood-soaked revenge," he yelled at the men who kept on their journey.

Dark Rider's eyes burst into tears of fire that ran down his cheeks and scalded his face until his melting visage reappeared.

"Salvation and Home," he wailed into the darkness.

The Scorpion walked in front of his prized student as a bitter moon rose in the dark sky. The cold-hearted orb pulled the tides across a river of loneliness while a blood-soaked ribbon of road led to the water and a dilapidated wharf.

The two made their way over a rope bridge that swung over hope and loss, while deep below lay bubbling watery despair.

On every rock and cranny lay wretched souls waiting to cross over. They came with arms missing and empty eyes. Their mangled torsos were mired in the slime and the mud.

David held tightly to The Scorpion's robes as the two slowly made passage through the ugly underbelly of man.

A loud outburst of bawdy laughter echoed off the cave as a wave of water pushed violently around the bend in the river.

"An old sailor, holding his tiller tightly, flew into sight around a bend in the boiling river. His upper body was bare and around his wrists and neck were strips of leather.

The old boat stayed on course while all around chaos swallowed the moment. Shrill voices rang out as the shore came alive with movement.

The Scorpion raced toward land's end and raised his hand to the tiller man.

"Safe passage," he yelled above the waves that rose over the boat and surrounded it with great swells.

The old salt looked as he threw his line to the docks and saw a Rose-colored light that blinded him momentarily. He covered his eyes and continued.

"Aye," he called above the watery din.

The stern sailor then took up his oar and began to beat back the poor souls who reached out and began to flood the boat. Without a word the ferryman smashed them back toward the dock again and again with the heavy wooden oars, wild animals unfit for civilization.

"Be prepared for two more will journey this way later," The Scorpion said while standing in the bow with his robes blowing in the headwind and gently dipping into the rough waters.

"Aye," the stern sailor replied.

They quickly made for land.

"What are the three things that you spoke of?" David asked as he jumped from a black hissing rock onto the shore of the heaving sea.

He looked behind and then around as great waves spat flames high into the thick air that hung as a black shroud covering misery and revenge.

The Scorpion stumbled and lost his balance at the last rock as his long robes dipping into the boiling sea. David quickly navigated the rocks and held onto his friend allowing the man to regain his composure.

"Steady," said David as he patted him on his large shoulders.

The men stood for a moment on the one rock and looked around at the landscape that surrounded them.

They looked deep into the cavernous void that opened before them — a boiling sun spread its evil light over jagged, rough-hewn mountain peaks that loomed in the distance while deep valley rivers hissed and cursed the walls that ran red with flames and fear. The path set before them was strewn with open black earth, ugly scars without life or humanity.

The rocks and narrow path of pain seemed molded by some evil potter who without thought or care had pinched this world out of dirty, calloused hands. They quickly touched the ugly land and looked up as castaways lost on a strange shore.

A dark subterranean river of souls hissed with anticipation of new souls to be delivered. Stalactites and stalagmites of flame swept away breathable air and smoke choked off all pathways except the narrows.

"This is the path," pointed The Scorpion as he moved deeper into the cave.

The white stallions' hooves were heard as they pushed further into the fiery realm.

"Purrrrrsbrrrwew" resounded off the walls as the great animal followed the intruders at a clip-clop pace.

"Clip-clop, clip-clop" sounded off blackened walls far down the narrow cinder path.

From time to time David would see the shadow of the beast on the cave walls like a dance in some evil carnival.

"The three things," David gasped as he made another torturous step and his very breath erupted into flame.

The Scorpion wiped the hot sweat from his brow.

"We shall come to them soon."

The shadows on the cave walls changed as the pair moved onward. The white horse ran in a forest of burning trees.

"Look!" David cried.

The great beast reared on its hind legs and continued galloping down a tree-lined path trailed with light and fire.

The men stood back as they approached a burning forest. Each tree was engulfed then reborn in an instant. Men appeared from the treetops as they jumped from one fiery branch to another trying to escape the flames.

"Like animals," David muttered as he watched the scene before him.

The silent treetop men continued their hot pursuit of the sanctuary, running with poles then flying into the air gracelessly, landing on one wooden oasis before it exploded in flames and on to the next.

The wretched, naked men held large daggers and stabbed each other over and over. The wounds burned and ran hot with flames bursting from them. The men wailed as they flew from branch to branch seeking revenge in a never-ending cycle.

A loud crash rang out through the flame forest as a man tumbled out of the tree and landed in the path of the travelers. The bare-chested man put out his hands to avoid a heavy impact. His bamboo stick crashed to the ground.

David halted on the trail. The man lay on the hot baked floor for a moment or two shaking his head and gaining his composure. His back was full of muscle and strain and each bicep was large and charcoal black.

With a quick animal movement he turned over and rose, pushing up his hands and large chest. The face appeared black and burned with singed eyelashes and short thick hair that ringed his head — a dirty crown of the damned.

The eyes slowly focused from the depths of sorrow and pain and took a burning interest in David. The man stood up slowly, wrathfulness and revenge grown to full force and height.

His eyes quickly darted between intruders before he grabbed the stick that lay steaming on the coal path. He laughed loudly and stroked his naked belly as the sound resounded off the jagged rock walls.

With great dexterity he kicked the stick in the air and then snatched it in his large, dirty, singed hands. His knuckles were red and bleeding while the hairs were long and grew back to his wrists.

His eyes remained fixed on David as he began to toss the stick back and forth from one disfigured hand to the next. The deep coal eyes cast furtive glances. He turned as if to return to the fire but then looked back and laughed as he threw the stick in David's direction.

The Scorpion stepped between the two and caught the stick in full flight. The man grunted his disapproval and disappeared. The travelers continued in silence as the fire raged all around.

"What meaning does this have for me?" the exhausted David called out.

The old man walking nimbly upon the unholy ground with his long, white robe flowing with flames looked back before continuing on his destined path.

David followed until he felt they were ascending a great hill. The narrows sloped upward and they were in a mountainous region.

Fireballs crashed around them as they wound their way up the pass. Suddenly a group of nine bare-chested men appeared running in single file down the pass.

The Scorpion threw himself against the jagged rocks and gripped the cliff as best he could to avoid being trampled. His protégé followed his actions and they held on while the group descended into the inferno.

The bare-chested men stopped at one cliff and breathed out flames, bent forward from the waist and stretched as if given new limbs then turned upwards and climbed the mountain again in a slow, painful rhythm.

They reached the high cliffs, breathed out flames and then turned back down toward the lesser rings of fire that lay far below. David looked at them and watched as the fires burned brightly over seven cliff tops below.

The runners disappeared deep into the seven rings of fire but then emerged again gaining renewed vigor with each segment of their woeful journey. The bare-chested men's breath of flames became less with each journey down and up the cliffs to the rocky and wild plateau.

The Scorpion rested on a rock and looked upward at a great cliff far off while David looked on with interest as the team of runners stretched on a smooth, black rock face.

The men breathed out their flames until nothing was left and then stretched in long slow pulls of either their arms or legs. They sat for awhile and looked longingly up toward the high cliffs before picking themselves up and returning down to the seven rings of fire below.

David once again felt an eerie familiarity with his surroundings: the barren rock face and bleak outcroppings, the stone face and rock formations were all reminiscent of battle.

He realized that the air was neither fire as it had been below nor sweet as perhaps it was in the mountain ranges above. His lungs had been purged of evil but had not been given the gift of grace.

Shadows of light fell upon the mountain from above yet a thick gray fog still hung over the cliffs. The light served only to highlight the battle between good and evil, the gray mist and the burning truth.

The nine men appeared on the rocky plains and began to stretch as before in a contest of some great importance. Each man took great care of his body and soul, warming legs and arms and visualizing his ascension within his mind.

Once this was completed in unison they all looked up again at the mountaintops that loomed over the sad scene as if a final judge sat in his throne overseeing the ritual.

A thunderclap rocked the jagged slopes as the men began to dance. Heavy clouds filled the dark sky. The dancers strutted upon a black rock stage with their hands held toward the heavens.

The group's movements and gestures, violent and angry at first, soon became full of grace as they continued whirling and whirling to an inaudible purging beat that played mightily in each man's heart and soul.

The men watched from their rocky perch but soon stood up and moved on toward a great stone staircase sculpted out of the mountainside.

David looked up and breathed heavily as the air became thin. The steps were narrow and disfigured by time, stone covenants broken by its people. The dust of the ages had turned the pristine white stone to a dark hue that hid all Fortitude, Justice, Temperance, Prudence, Hope, Faith and Love from the light of day.

Beneath wild mountain thorns that covered the painful way the tears of saints and sinners were carved into each step like so many lashes of flagellation on a sorrowful body.

A broken wooden rail lay bare to the wind. A wood of thorns covered the high terraced land which rose into the air.

The nine men who had danced below on the black cliffs moved up to greater heights. Each athlete began the work of clearing the steps of judgment and anger.

The smallest of the group, a young man with sorrowful blue eyes, climbed to the steepest part of the turn and set to rubbing off the stain from the dark steps. The mountain thorns cut his fingers and hands deeply and he bled. He picked up the tangled thorns and without thinking placed it on his head. He tried holding onto the broken staircase but that soon crashed onto the steps and blocked the path.

The other members of the group saw this and stopped what they were doing. Slowly they came to him and gently picked up the dilapidated wooden rail that fell apart with the one piece placed on top of the other.

The young man stood up as the men cleared the way. He took a few painful steps and was released from his burden.

David watched all this as the mountain trail wound upward without an end in sight and disappeared into the mist.

He saw a vision:

Rose petals blew on the wind and over the high walls of the garden one by one signal fires lit the mountain ranges below and beyond Mount Brood.

The breath of The Rose pushed the Warrior King and the Black Knight as they traveled at speed toward the Stone Pillar Pass.

"Our hopes and dreams rest on you heavy as the deep snow that lies before you," Princess Rose whispered from the garden.

The royal flag bearers and entourage were far behind gathering courage in the valleys below.

Princess Rose then took up her sword and commanded the light bearers as they waited dutifully with quivers full of light.

"Stand guard!" she whispered at the top of the last mountain post.

The war horse reared on its hind legs as two Riders crashed on into the darkness.

The mountain fires down in the valley were dwindling and giving way to darkness but rose with billows of her precious breath.

The Scorpion smiled at David as they continued up the mountain trail.

From a distance music came through the damp passage, a sweet lyrical tune that fluttered down through the passageways. They stopped their madness and listened to the sound of hopes and dreams that played around their ears dripping with milk and honey.

The Captain struggled to his feet wiping the water from his tunic.

One soldier looked at another with his staff in hand and clutched the man's shoulders.

"Your rod comforts me."

"I found it," David called as oil from a torch above anointed his head.

He turned toward Mybad, "Here is your path forward and into the city."

The Scorpion took David by the sleeve.

"Come, you must now lead," he said as the two left the waterways and headed for the high ground and Joab's tent overlooking the city.

"Hold the line!" yelled an officer as he galloped across the plains.

"Hold the line!" cried the leaders of the infantry. "Hold the line!"

The men jostled in place, iron and leather heaving and swaying.

"Wait until Jebus is burning," the old sargeant yelled to his troops.

He spat on the ground and looked up at the brooding sky his eyes blinking in the rain. He adjusted the leather belt that held his sword.

"Wait," he called down the line.

He spat again and beat his small shield with his hands.

The Warrior Priest looked down from his mountain perch and cried when he saw all the instruments of war on the plains before the city of Jebus. He wrapped his arms around his shoulders and wept with joy and then slowly waved his hands in the air as he continued his mad symphony.

The wind blew up and suddenly the sun burst forth again from behind the clouds, shining down on the battlefield of light.

"Fear not the jibes but rather their weapons," David yelled from his chariot as the main army of archers and slingers moved slowly from the plains toward the high walls of the city.

Riders approached as the chariots took their places in the fields. Messengers from both David's and Joab's positions were flying back and forth with instructions.

Across the desert plains and to the south of David, Joab had his archers ready to strike at will.

"Wait until we see the fires burning inside the walls," Joab called loudly while racing down the line on horseback. "Hold the line," he commanded far down the line.

"Jebus is burning," one soldier cried from his watch point. "Jebus is burning."

The fires and smoke from the city walls grew high and licked the dust of the plains. The rocky hills and plains trembled as the army lurched forward.

David watched as the first line of archers launched their assault, their flames flying high into the blinding sun and arcing over the city walls. The arrows went straight to his heart and the wounds were deep.

He had disguised his hopes and fears so well and yet they seemed now to be rising to the surface with every angry salvo. He stood on his chariot facing the city and watching as yet another line of archers aimed high into the air. With each arrow he became undone with his father's disdain and his mother's love, his insecurity at home, the battle with his brothers and the taunts of the townspeople; each emotion seemed to fling itself over the stone walls and then was quickly buried in the battlements as lasting reminders of his pain. These arrows fueled his inner rage and pushed him forward.

"Fly to the very heart of the city," he whispered as he motioned the charioteer to move forward.

The slingers were ordered to move closer to the great stone wall with their leaders running ahead to set up wooden siege ladders that went high into the air.

"Prepare!" the leaders yelled.

He looked up and down the line.

"Throw."

The slingers let fly their stones again and again toward the walls near the acropolis.

"Throw!" he yelled as the next line moved forward.

"Courage!" David yelled as his chariot moved forward. "Take courage."

He smiled as he saw the rocks flung over the walls and thought back to his times with Shimea.

The chariot lurched forward and he was back at the Sachne Pools again. The earth and sky stood still as he saw himself flat on his stomach slowing his breath while watching the eyes of the lion. His courage had been a deep well he had never before found but somehow he had stumbled upon it then, a well within a deep garden. He drank greedily from it for it had showed itself at a time when all around him was misery.

While drinking this potent well water he had found his bearing and his path. He now had the strength to continue alone, without guidance but with pure instinct and will. Each stone that crashed over the walls was a thunderous message of courage. The courage to fight off banishment, to lose himself in despicable acts and yet to remain true to his higher calling, the courage to lead men and the courage to be humble with those less fortunate than himself.

"Forward!" he cried as he maneuvered his chariot through the battle lines.

The cries of the infantrymen coupled with the banging of their swords against their shields rose as the men trudged toward the city. The plains became a muddy field trampled by horses and donkeys loaded with supplies. The air was thick and hot.

"What a long march," David thought as his chariot moved between the lines.

From the small town of Bethlehem, shy, afraid of his brothers and torn by his father's disdain, he felt like an outcast from his earliest days and soon it became a mantle he wore like a brand that was burned into his very being. This was all he ever knew and it shaped his world.

He had to fight for everything or take it by force or sometimes charm. He learned quickly to survive in each situation: what mask to wear and when, what to say and how to say it. He was gifted and realized at a young age that he could receive things with his natural ability to charm. He did not have to play a heavy role as a gentle way would deliver twice as much to his cause.

The infantry moved heavily over the rocky terrain as the archers threw up another volley of fire and the slingers' rocks broke against the city walls. The smoke from inside the walls grew black and thick and settled over Jebus like a pall.

At the battlements soldiers threw spears and rocks at the approaching army. Three thousand troops moved to the city as rocks and arrows braved the burning sky.

The archers held their ground and continued firing a cover of arrows while a segment of the infantry moved against the eastern walls and the acropolis and threw siege ladders against the high battlements.

"Courage," Joab shouted in the fray.

Joab brought his troops to bear on the eastern walls and let fly another round of arrows and rocks.

Above the siege ladders the Jebusites threw down boiling water and hot oil while soldiers aimed spears and arrows at the Hebrews. The screams of soldiers who fell off the siege ladders echoed into the distance.

"Move forward!" Joab yelled. He motioned with his sword for the next group of men to scale the ladders.

"Now," he called as the archers continued with volley after volley, which acted as cover for the men who once again moved up the ladders.

Blood and courage finally breached the wall while the fires inside the city caused mass hysteria. Joab's men breached the eastern walls then moved into a pincer position behind the Jebusites fighting at the acropolis.

"To the gates," one leader yelled. He took a group of men and ran down the stairs fighting hand to hand as they struggled to reach the main gate.

The Jebusite soldiers were pushed back and held little ground as more and more men poured over the acropolis walls.

"Open the gates," Joab yelled.

A group of soldiers moved toward the gates killing and slashing as they pushed through the remaining resistance and started to pull at the great chains that held the main gate closed.

"Fight, you cowards!" Bru yelled into the thick of the destroyed acropolis.

He raised his sword and struck out before his horse reared up and dashed out the gate leaving only a trail of dust as he fled.

David's troops flooded into the city pushing all in its wake far back into the recess of the narrow paths that lay far beyond the main gate.

The beautiful archways and stone carvings of the squat square buildings crumbled on the dirty streets. Stone and brick lay strewn on the narrow pathways while fire raged around the towers. The great wall that surrounded the city was destroyed in sections and crumbling in others.

A sea of lost faces wandered in and out of the burning labyrinth of broken facades and stone passageways. Jebus was in ruins.

The high priest and lower clergy, all dressed in black sackcloth, stood outside the gate in line. The rain fell lightly.

Zadok moved forward, his high priest holding The Ark of the Covenant, four priests on one side and four on the other wearing wooden yokes that held The Ark aloft.

The procession slowly walked around the city gates as the wind blew and the rain fell.

The legions of priests that entered Jebus took care not to come near or touch the dead and dying for they did not want to contaminate their purity with the blood of the enemy.

After the battle the cries of women and children filled the night air. An eerie calm took hold of the streets as rain began to fall over the dead and dying. At dusk thunder sounded and the Dung Gate of the city was thrown open to a great gust of wind.

A chariot stood silently outside. It moved slowly toward the southeast gate as Zadok with his great bulk and long, white hair came into view. He held out his hands and parted them as the chariot grew closer to Jebus.

He touched his lips to his prayer shawl and then motioned to The Ark of the Covenant, a beautiful acacia wood box with a golden cover 3.8 feet long and 2.3 feet high that laid beside him.

Lightning scorched the ground before them as it moved into the city through the Dung Gate and a thunderclap broke the calm. The Jebusite women picked up their children and scattered as Zadok pushed forward.

Fear rose in the throats of the Jebusite warriors as they clung to the thought of King David's mercy. The lightning continued and brought more fires to the burning city.

Zadok's chariot moved slowly through the streets as his gaze pierced the strongest of hearts.

"Look away," he called out as he moved through the streets. "Our King, the King of Kings, and The Ark of the Covenant bears down on your weak souls. The City of David is upon you.

Raise up, rise O God of Gods and raise Yourself in power, O King of Kings…. let all the sons of darkness scatter before you. Let the light of your majesty shine forever upon Gods and men like fire burning in the dark places of the damned. Let it burn the damned of She'ol as an eternal burning among the transgressors in all appointed times of eternity."

Zadok's chariot continued with men and children scattering before him.

"Too much blood on my hands," King David thought as his golden chariot entered the city. "Too much blood."

The king's palace was destroyed except for the lower floors. The lower level walls were broken into large chunks and birds flew in and out to drink from the large flooded fountains. The stone floors were damaged and pillars crumbled under the weight of war. A gentle wind blew through the open spaces and smoke rose into the night air.

Guards were placed on the open wing of the palace and some of David's royal guards made ready to sleep on the tile floors that surrounded his upper rooms.

The troops under Joab's command began to patrol the streets looking for insurgents and finding locations for barracks, stables and buildings to house the army.

David took over the large suite of rooms that overlooked the city of war: reed beams held a great room aloft 30 feet while windows were open to the night air; large chairs and tables carved of ivory and inlaid with teak were strewn about the magnificent rooms. There were large desert palms and exotic lamps and carvings from India and Persia.

The lamps flickered with each desert breeze much like the city had changed hands with passing strong men. The Egyptians, the Babylonians and the Romans had all been drawn to its deep mysteries.

Six royal guards stood watch over David's private quarters as barefoot servants lit more lamps and prepared for the evening. The desert palms gently rustled as the smell of incense rose throughout the rooms.

The King stood at an open window as two officials wrestled with parchment while they outlined the city's resources and labor requirements.

"Take this down now," David spoke as he lovingly held a piece of parchment in his hands. "Joab will take control of the army. How many?"

"Thirty thousand and we can muster another ten," the official bowed as he spoke.

"Put Benaiah in charge of the foreign mercenaries," David continued.

The official wrote as the king spoke.

"And what of the Three and Thirty?"

"The Gibborim will watch over the palace."

David had eyes only for the parchment in his hands yet he continued.

"We will need a Privy Councillor and someone who will monitor our manpower for building fortifications and bridges. We will need conscripts to do this work."

"Yes, my King."

Whispers came from the far corner as generals came into the rooms trailing Joab and Benaiah.

The generals were offered refreshments and lingered outside while David continued with the city officials.

The shepherd had become statesman; David took the primitive tribes of the desert and built an empire that stretched from the Nile River to the Euphrates and would last for 500 years.

"You propose an imperial cabinet like Egypt or Mesopotamia, my lord."

"Yes."

David became impatient but held back his ire.

"Study them well, also put the two priests Abiathar and Zadok in charge of the office of priests."

"Very well."

The two officials bowed and stepped back.

"Now leave me to my private correspondence."

David turned his back and walked to the open windows while holding close the parchment. He lovingly opened the long-awaited letter from his mother and let his body relax as he read the words:

"Oh, my son, my David,

How I miss you and want your warm embrace around my shoulders. I have heard from other villagers and soldiers of your great victory against the Jebusites but I have other more pressing matters that you must be made aware of because I have kept them hidden from you for so long, deep matters that cut me to my very soul for they have hurt you and kept you blind as to your circumstances.

For this I beg your forgiveness, my son.

Please understand that I did not mean you any pain, but that circumstances drove me to the actions that I took so very long ago.

I hope and pray that now is the time with you as King that you are strong enough to swallow this sad tale of stupid women.

David, my son, you have a sister who is gone from our site. She was so young as was I and with the other boys we did not have enough food or space in the family. Your father did not pay attention to this heartache but I felt it deeply in my soul as any mother would.

One day as I swaddled the infant near the orchards, I cried woefully about the baby who was so innocent yet unwanted. Oh, how my heart ached for this poor child but in my thoughts I saw that this was to be and yet that there would be something else that would come to soothe my broken spirit.

David, you were that something that healed my soul. You and you alone.

On that day, a pale knight rode into Bethlehem and stopped on his way. He felt my tears and stopped to inquire about my sorrow.

He was kind and his men were gentle as they asked me about my troubles. They gathered around me in a protective manner as if it were their sworn duty to protect the weak and timid. There in the desert sun among the orchards of figs and almonds they built a wall of compassion that no man or beast could breach and allowed me to feel this cool warmth of the heart.

Oh, how I wept. I have never before or since felt such power.... such love as these strangers offered so willingly.

I pray that you will come to know this power and give it willingly to others.

So, my dear David, after a very long time of talking and with the men on their knees in a ring around myself and the baby, the pale knight brought forward a woman who was pleasing to look at but bent over with time.

She held the baby in her arms and it looked up at her.

'She will be treasured by us,' the pale knight smiled. 'I shall call her Bethlehem and all will treasure her.'

Oh my David, I was so young .... so young."

David bent his head low as the crisp night air took hold of the city.

He held the parchment in his hands for a long time, unwilling to let it go.

"Unclean, unclean," the word rang out in the night and spread through the city like wildfire. "Unclean."

David went to the open window and looked down upon the streets. Women and men began to walk and run toward the Dung Gate.

"Unclean." The voices rose in the night. "Unclean."

A woman screamed down the narrow cobbled streets holding her baby in her arms. Children ran to the gate and started to throw sticks and rocks at the great wooden door itself.

"Unclean," they sang in unison, "Unclean."

An old man came toward the children and bid them go.

"Children," he said. "Leave. It is late."

He stretched out his arms and tried to move them away.

"Unclean," they laughed and sang as a nursery rhyme.

"Unclean, unclean, meat into a stew, all nice and lean."

One boy threw a rock at the old man and hit him in the stomach.

"Unclean, unclean, meat into a stew, all nice and lean," the boy yelled.

Two guards moved the children away and slowly the massive doors creaked open with chains that rattled in the silent streets. The guards looked at each other and refused to move further.

A covered wagon with torches on all four corners stood outside the Dung Gate. The wind blew around the canvas while all remained quiet inside.

The brave children in the city clung to each other and looked at the wagon that clung to the rocky hillside. The men and women gathered their courage as the wind blew their thoughts around.

"How sad," a woman buried her head in her husband's arms.

"Alone," one man whispered.

"Abandoned," another said.

"Unclean," another whispered. "It should not be here among us."

A messenger knocked on David's door and two guards ushered him in.

"If you please, my King," the messenger bowed.

He handed The Scorpion the parchment. He read it silently then aloud to David:

"If a leper comes…"

He turned to David.

"What is this, some mystery, some trick?"

"No." David thought for a moment.

He looked out over the city and from his vantage point saw the burning torches.

"It was a long time ago."

He took the parchment and turned to the messenger.

"I will come," he said as he gathered his cloak.

The Scorpion began to follow and motioned to the guards.

"Come," he said.

David left his Warrior Priest and guards at the Dung Gate and walked quickly across the plains while the gathering crowd stepped back and watched.

Omar and Ali stood outside the wagon and simply bowed their heads and motioned.

"Come, come," Arlemay said.

He extended a ravaged hand covered in white bandages. He arranged the white linen sheet that was draped over him and tried to sit up against his bright blue pillow. The leper spoke through a white plaster mask.

David adjusted his eyes to the darkness and sat down.

"So the desert viper has struck," Arlemay said.

David looked upon the leper's broken and torn body. Arlemay pulled down his sheet and showed his arms and the open sores on his body.

"These wounds and my torn face are nothing compared to the hurt of loss."

He slumped against the pillow.

"As a boy of nine, I was cast out into the wilderness."

He sighed and coughed.

"That was hurt and pain."

He smiled and the wagon lit up.

"This is child's play." He lifted his bandaged hand. "A small thing."

The two men laughed. He shifted his white sheet and tucked it under his chin.

"And how is our Scorpion?" Arlemay asked.

"He attends to me constantly," David said.

"As he should," Arlemay smiled. "What journeys we have had and what splendid people we have become."

"Yes," David said.

"Do you know what binds us together?" Arlemay said.

He coughed deeply and was in pain.

"Please."

He motioned to a water bag. David took the bag and lifted it to Arlemay's lips. Arlemay laughed at the water that spilled on his mask.

David carefully took part of the sheet and gently dried Arlemay's mask.

"What binds us and tear us apart," Arlemay slipped back onto the pillow. "What gives us hope and crashes us into despair."

Arlemay pointed to a basket of rolled parchment.

"Here," he said. "Take these."

David gathered them up.

"These are laws and codes of how we should live together."

Outside the wagon the wind blew across the plains.

"When the viper and the scorpion are united, it shall be well."

Arlemay fell back against the pillow, his energy spent. David looked down at the parchments in silence.

Arlemay opened his eyes once again.

"My King, I ask you one favor."

"Yes?"

"You have a warrior named Grail in your company."

"Yes."

"Would you bring him to me at daylight?"

The next day a crowd gathered again at the Dung Gate while Grail followed Omar and Ali to the wagon. The children ran and played while the men stood talking and pointing at the wagon that held the entire city captive. It became the heart and soul of a town, seen but not understood, untouched and unclean, yet riveting. Some were afraid of its presence, some were comforted by it, but all felt its power.

"What does a leper want of me?" Grail asked as he walked through the gate.

The crowd parted as he slipped through the great wooden gates and made for the wagon.

"Ah, my friend," Omar said. "Please be waiting to understand."

The Scorpion and his guards waited at the gate while the crowd of men and women looked on.

"Please."

Omar gestured to the wagon.

Grail looked behind him at the guards and crowds but soon the noise died, the scorching sun seemed to disappear and he felt himself entering the world that was so distant, just a faint memory that glimmered at the edges of his mind.

"Yes," Grail said.

There was movement in the wagon as Arlemay made ready for his guest.

"Come," Arlemay said.

He sat in his makeshift bed, his white mask on and long, flowing sheets surrounding his body. His bright pillows were behind him.

"Ahhh, it is you," Arlemay said.

He looked at the blond, strong warrior as the sun drew shadows on the wagon's canvas.

"Do I know you?"

Arlemay smiled, "You are what kept me going all these years, a bright hope."

He slumped back into his pillows.

"Not of seeing Greythorn but to feel its warmth once more."

"Greythorn?" Grail said.

"When a soft summer breeze blew and the banners were on high," Arlemay said.

He looked up at Grail.

"It was said that Greythorn gave poor men riches and rich men hope."

"That it did."

Grail sat down close to the leper, forgetting his wounds and bandages.

"And when the great fires roared in The Hall of Lower Light, they paled in comparison to your brightness."

Grail bent forward.

"How do you know this?"

His eyes glistened at the mention of his home.

"How I long to see Greythorn," Grail muttered.

Arlemay reached out his broken and ravaged hand.

"You will, you will."

"But what of you, where is your home?" Grail said.

"A simple cave," Arlemay said.

"Where?"

"The Highlands," Arlemay said.

"Where, my poor friend, where?"

Arlemay clutched at his heart and winced in pain.

"I could see the banners and hear the horsemen hunting."

Grail sat transfixed and felt the wagon spinning with the sun beating down.

"But they did not come," he said slowly. "They never came."

Grail held his head in his hands and began to weep.

"No," he said.

Arlemay slipped deeply into his pillows.

"The wicked ninth."

"No," Grail said as he slipped onto the floor and took Arlemay's bandaged stump of hand in his own.

"No, not so wicked."

He kissed Arlemay's bandages over and over. "No."

The tears streamed down Arlemay's mask as his rail-thin body shook with emotion.

"My brother."

Grail crawled in the bed and curled up around Arlemay's thin and weak body.

"How we grieved, how Father grieved when he did not find you," he sobbed. "All of Greythorn hoped for your return, your safety."

He sat up and took his brother's mask into his hands.

"On the western wall there is a lookout named after you."

He kissed the mask.

"Father would watch for hours and hours, thinking of nothing but you."

Grail sat close to his brother and wiped his tears away.

"He was found dead on the wall watching for you, hoping against hope that you would somehow return. What taught him a terrible lesson…. a tragic tale."

Grail took Arlemay's bandaged hand.

"How he changed, how he sought to find a better man inside himself from the day you were sent away. His eyes were hollow but he treated everyone with dignity and respect as if he never knew when a servant or a stranger would suddenly throw off their cloak or robe and you would appear full blown and ready to charge him with crimes of tragedy and loss."

"Shush, shush."

Arlemay held his brother with all the strength he had left.

"I am home now."

A light summer rain began to fall over the city of David, pushed further north into the Persian desert and then continued over the great desert through the camel routes along the Euphrates Valley that stood in the shadow of the Egyptian and Mesopotamian empires.

A lone Bedouin looked up from his desert camp and cried in the soft summer rain as a desert rose petal blew out onto the wind.

The rose petal followed a northern path through the war-torn towns of Gad, Issachab, Asher and Gish, the tribal sections of Israel and then further up to the Persian coastal city of Tyre before being blown out over the gray sea toward the west and the brooding Isle of Burton. Arlemay's pain was washed away in the great waters.

THE END

Chapter 19
The Stowaway

The cave dwellers at Khirbet Qumran wrote late into the afternoon with a passion that burned brighter than the scorching Judean sun.

The rocky, barren hillside lay bare to the desert winds. On the small plateau with deep ravines to the west and north, a narrow coastal path wound down toward the Dead Sea.

"The Moab priest must leave," the elder scribe said.

The scribes looked up from their work. The elder touched his prayer shawl to the carefully printed Hebrew letters written on parchment, kissed them and turned to his students.

"But he is the ninth scholar working on community laws," one student complained.

"He is not clean, not pure." The elder shook with emotion. "His whore mother was a convert."

"He is a good scholar."

"The sons of darkness may not play upon our work."

The elder stood up as a rush of wind blew into the cave.

"Cast him out as the wicked ninth."

"But what of their work, their writings?"

"Cast him out."

Months later the outcast Moab priest disembarked from a small Persian trireme, which was moored off the coast of the Isle of Burton. The ship pitched and rolled with the waves and its rigging creaked as a squall blew up. Sailors shouted orders and climbed the mast to lower the sails.

Men and chests flooded off the ship and were taken by row boats closer to the shore before wading into the cold waters near Greythorn Castle, the largest hill fort in the west.

The Moab outcast quickly dipped his robes into the frozen waters clutching a leather folder as if it were life itself.

He stumbled once, the long, flowing robe soaking wet, but he continued at a frenzied pace. Once on shore he quickly took to the fields and disappeared from the coast.

Days later he found himself deep in the mountains that surrounded Greythorn Castle. The rough seas and long voyage from the Persian city of Tyre had taken its toll on the outcast. He was dying.

In desperation the Moab found a mountain cave and clung to life while he did what his faith had commanded him to do. A fire crackled in the cave and illuminated the smooth stone walls.

"Here," he cried joyfully. "The Rose will be heard! Your laws and codes will come to life, my Rose."

The sickly priest breathed heavily, picked up a stone and began to write his last will:

1. The Rose; A Commitment

Everyone who wishes to join the community must commit himself to respect The Rose and man; to live according to the communal rule; to seek The Rose; to do what is good and upright in Her sight, in accordance with what He has commanded through Moshe (Moses) and through Her servants the prophets; to love all that He has chosen and hate all that He has rejected; to keep far from all evil and to cling to all good works; to act truthfully and righteously and justly on earth and to walk no more in the stubbornness of a guilty heart and of lustful eyes doing all manner of evil; to bring into a bond of mutual love all who have declared their willingness to carry out the statutes of The Rose; to join the formal community of The Rose; to walk blamelessly before Her in conformity with Her various Laws and dispositions; to love all the children of light, each according to....

The dying Moab let his arm fall and the stone left broken and bleeding fingers. He slumped to the dirt floor and breathed in deep gulps of cold air.

"I am yours, my Rose," he said as he struggled to grab hold of the cave wall to pull himself up.

"I am yours," he mumbled.

He fell face down on the dirt and laid still with eyes open. From underneath his dirty robes, the Moab took a water bag and drank greedily, spilling it on the earth floor. He rose by willpower alone.

The mountain wind blew up and the cave writer began again. He found new strength through his scriptures and continued into the night of the seventh day of his sermon of stone:

"The Rose's Light or Darkness; two spirits of man."

This is for the man who would bring others to the inner vision, so that he may understand and teach to all the children of light the real nature of men, touching the different varieties of their temperaments with the distinguishing traits thereof, touching their actions through their generations, and touching the reason why they are now visited with afflictions and now enjoy periods of well-being. All that is and ever was comes from The Rose of knowledge.

The Moab had written his last words and was left to die in the cave so very far from the heat and desert sun of Khirbet Qumran.

His bloodstained hand let go of the stone.